True Stories of Girl Heroines

Evelyn Everett-Green

Alpha Editions

This edition published in 2024

ISBN : 9789362090614

Design and Setting By
Alpha Editions
www.alphaedis.com
Email - info@alphaedis.com

Contents

INEZ ARROYA

"Mistress! my mistress! the Moriscos are upon us!"

Inez sprang to her feet, the rich southern blood receding for a moment from her cheek, as those words fell upon her ears—words of such fearful significance to the Christian inhabitants of the Moorish territory along the Sierra Nevada.

"Juana, what mean you? Speak, girl! What have you heard? What have you seen?"

Juana's face had been white when she came bursting in upon her young mistress; she held her hand to her side; her breath came and went in great gasps; yet already she was recovering the power of speech, and she seized Inez by the arm.

"Mistress, they are below already; they are robbing the house. Can you not hear them? When they have taken the wine and the oil they will come hither and murder us!"

Inez held her breath to listen. Yes, there were sounds from below—sounds of voices—loud, threatening voices, and the laughter of men assured of victory.

Juana, the maid, spoke in a fierce whisper. Fear was receding. The high courage which comes to weak women in the hour of extremest need possessed the hearts alike of mistress and maid.

"The master went forth not an hour ago. Five minutes since little Aluch ran up to tell me that, as the master was taking the air, there suddenly appeared a band of rebel Moriscos from Orgiba, who set upon him, and chased him, and would have killed him, but he took refuge in his father's house; and he will hide him, and get him safe away. But all Istan will join the rebels, and already they are crying that every Christian shall be slain!"

"Every Christian!" cried Inez, with a flash in her dark eyes. "And how many Christians are there in Istan? Two weak women, Juana, you and I, and my uncle, whom they have already set upon and chased to the mountains. Pray Heaven and our Lady that he may reach them safely, and send us help from Marbella, else there will be but short work with the Christian population of Istan."

There was scorn in the girl's voice, scorn in the flashing eyes. Istan was a Moorish village, where one Christian priest had been placed to work amongst the Moslems, and seek to convert them to the true faith.

Success in this missionary work had been small; but the good man had hitherto lived in peace with his alien flock. The wise and kindly traditions of Ferdinand and Isabella, and Hermando de Talavera, had for long kept under the natural hatred of Moor towards Christian in Southern Spain. But a monarch had arisen who hated the word toleration. To keep faith with the Moslem was to break it with the Almighty. The edict of 1567 was now a year or more old, and its pernicious effects were already made abundantly evident in fierce Moorish risings here, there, and everywhere.

Inez had heard stories as to the fate of Christian prisoners who had fallen into the hands of the Moors. Before she followed Juana she had caught up a shining dagger which hung against the wall; and she thrust it into her girdle as she ran down the broken steps of the tower.

"At least, they shall not take us alive!" she breathed to herself; and Juana seemed to hear, for she flashed back a glance at her young mistress, and for a moment showed the gleam of a long stiletto which she carried in the bosom of her tunic.

The priest of Istan dwelt in a strange house. It was, properly speaking, no house at all, but a Moorish fortalice, dismantled and ruinous, which he had partially repaired soon after his arrival there, and which, since the arrival of his orphan niece to live with him, he had desired to make more habitable still.

The place was, in fact, a sort of tower. The lowest floor was their storehouse for supplies of wheat, oil, and so forth; and from this level came up the sound of rough voices, as the Moors leisurely removed the spoil before proceeding upwards. There was only one door from the fortalice into the world without, and this it was impossible to reach, for the Moors were swarming in the lowest part, effectually preventing their egress. They knew perfectly that the two girls were as helplessly caught as a rat in a trap; they did not even hasten the work in which they were engaged. Inez, standing at the top of the long flight of stone steps which led downwards to the basement, heard what they were saying one to another, and into her olive cheek there crept a deep glow of red, whilst her lips set themselves, her teeth clenched, and her black eyes gleamed with a light like that of fire.

"Our Lady and the blessed saints protect us!" whispered Juana, with a furtive glance into the beautiful face of her young mistress; and Inez looked back at her without a quiver as she replied:

"The Christian's God helps those who help themselves, Juana. We are not here to wring our hands and look for a miracle to save us. We fight for our lives, and Christ and our Lady will help us. See, we are not quite defenceless, Heaven be thanked for that! Collect those stones, quickly, quietly. Keep out of sight. Do not let them observe us. Get together a number, then you shall see!"

It was as Inez had said. The repairs of the fortalice, which had been already commenced, had put the means of defence into their hands. Large quantities of great stones had been collected at first in the basement, but only the previous week had been laboriously carried up the steep, narrow stairs which led upwards to the dwelling rooms; and these large stones the two brave girls were now quietly collecting in a great heap at the top of the flight.

They were in deep shadow, and below the brown-skinned men, in their picturesque Arab dress, were far too busy examining their spoil, and making away with it, to heed the slight sounds from above. They talked together as they worked; they told of the attack they had made upon Orgiba, and of that fearful massacre of Christian men, women, and children at Uxixar. Inez held her breath to listen to the confirmation of certain vague rumours which had reached them before this, but had scarcely been believed. Peaceful Istan, with its terraced gardens overhanging the lovely gorge of the Verde, had seemed so far removed from the storm and strife; and its people were peaceable and kindly disposed, even though they were Moriscos. But these men were rebels and freebooters, with the fierce lust of blood upon them, their hands red from the butchery of innocent, helpless women and children; men who laughed aloud at tales of hideous deeds done in cold blood; men mad with hatred to the conquering race, knowing themselves doomed to final defeat, yet resolved to revenge themselves in every possible way upon those of the hated faith ere their own turn came.

Upon such a band of men did Inez look down, with the fire of courageous despair in her eyes. What could they do? what hope was there for them? two slight girls against a score of trained warriors.

The Moriscos of Istan would probably not join in the attack upon them; but they would not interfere with what their brethren of the faith might do. Help from without there would be none, unless the priest himself could find means of escape, and could get to Marbella and bring it. Inez knew that he would strain every nerve in this effort. But what chance had they of holding out for perhaps six hours or more? Could it be done? Oh, could it be done? She looked at the heap of stones. She looked at the flitting forms below in the gloom. And then she held her breath once again, listening to stories of how in other places Christians had taken refuge in towers and churches, whilst their Moorish foes piled faggots soaked in pitch, and such-like inflammable material against and around the walls, and reduced the building to one mass of flames.

If they kept the men from laying immediate hands upon them, would that fiery doom be theirs?

"Better that than to fall into their hands," said Inez, between her shut teeth; and Juana, looking at her mistress, with a world of faithful love in her eyes, exclaimed softly:

"Our Lady will surely send us help, mistress. You are too beautiful to die such a death!"

Inez put her hands upon the shoulders of the faithful girl, and said in a low voice:

"You would come with me from Granada, Juana, where you would have been safe; and there were those who warned us that we might not long be safe out here. But my duty seemed to my uncle; and you—you would not leave me. And what if I have brought you hither to your death?"

"We must all die once," answered Juana, her eyes full of love and courage; "and I would sooner die with you, mistress, than live without you. If I had stayed behind, and had heard this story of you, I should have killed myself, or died for grief and shame that I was not with you."

Then Inez put her arms about the faithful girl's neck, and kissed her thrice upon the lips.

"We will do battle for our lives, Juana; and then, if needs be, we will die together," she said.

Suddenly there was a cry from below. Some one had looked up, and had seen the two girlish figures clinging together. Perhaps the very action had been misunderstood, and instantly there was a rush towards the steep, broken, narrow steps of some dozen swarthy Moors.

Instantly the girls were at their post at the head of the flight. Inez, quiet and composed, gave the word.

"Welcome to the Moriscos!" she cried, in a clear and ringing voice, as the first great stone leapt from her hand and went bounding and crashing upon the head of the foremost Moor.

"Welcome to the Moriscos!" echoed Juana, dislodging another, which sprang from stair to stair, and then, bounding sideways, went crashing upon the bent back of a man in the basement beneath, who fell like a log from the blow, his spine fractured.

Crash, crash, crash! Down hurtled the huge stones, flinging the unprepared Moriscos from the steep stairs, where they fell in a confused mass, one upon the top of the other, pinned down by the great boulders which came rolling down upon them from above, cursing, raging, crushed and maimed, utterly taken aback by such a reception; and now only eager and anxious to get out of a place that seemed to rain nether mill-stones upon them.

The first great stone leapt from her hand and went bounding and crashing: upon the head of the foremost Moor.

Three of their number lay stretched dead upon the ground. A number more were badly hurt; and all were flying from the stairs, which threatened to become a veritable death-trap for all who tried to mount.

There was a rush for the outer door. The wounded were dragged away groaning by their comrades; those who were sound carried the dead. They turned and shook threatening fists at the two girls standing behind their heap of stones at the top of the stairs; they promised them that they were coming back. They breathed out threats which might well make the stoutest hearts quail. But Inez stood up tall and straight, with a great stone poised in her hand; and the strength and accuracy with which those formidable weapons had been launched against them before, caused the men to jostle each other through the doorway in their haste to escape from possible hurt from the same source.

Scarcely had the last man disappeared before Juana was down the stairs like a flash, had slammed-to the heavy oaken door, and had drawn the great iron bolts and the heavy iron bar across it.

"The master left it open when he went out this morning," she said to Inez, "and I never thought to shut it. Why should I? That is how they got in so easily; but they will not get in again so fast!"

This was true enough; for the door had been made to withstand attack, as, indeed, had the tower itself, and though it had fallen into a ruinous state inside, it was built in a very solid fashion, the walls being exceedingly thick, and light being admitted mainly by loopholes. The top, also, was protected by a low battlement, from which a view of the surrounding country could be obtained. This battlement had fallen a good deal into disrepair, like the tower itself, and material for repairing it had been brought in; so that not only had the girls the remainder of the stones they had already used with such effect, but there was a large quantity of such material that had been laboriously carried up to the very top only three days earlier; and some of these stones were very large and heavy, as they had been designed to form the coping of the battlement.

"See there!" cried Inez, as the two girls ran up the stairs to the top, to watch the retreat of the temporarily baffled foe. "Juana, how long, think you, would such artillery last us? We could slay a score of our foes, as the woman in the tower slew Abimelech the king. Did not mine uncle tell us that tale the other night? and how little we thought——"

Juana's eyes were shining. The thrill of victory was upon her. The peril was not over. Nay, they might have worse to encounter than they had done already. But at least they had driven forth the foe from the tower. Their citadel was their own. They had weapons of defence under their hands. If help would only come at last, they could hold out for awhile.

"See, see!" cried Inez, as she leaned over the wall to watch the baffled Moriscos wending their way downwards, sometimes turning to shake threatening fists at the tower and its defenders. "There is little Aluch hiding below in the orange grove, and making signals to us. Run, Juana, to that loophole below, and he will tell you what he has come to say!"

Juana disappeared down the stairs, and returned quickly with a face in which anxiety and satisfaction were strangely blended.

"The master has got safely off to the mountains. He will be at Marbella very soon, and then they will start out to help us; but Aluch said he heard the Moriscos vowing vengeance upon us as they went away. They will quickly be back; and he thinks if they cannot batter in the door and take us alive, that they will burn the tower down over our heads."

"They will if they can," said Inez, looking out over the fair, wild valley, with the expression of one who knows she may be looking almost her last upon a familiar scene; "but we have a welcome ready for them!"

They leaned over the battlements, those two brave-hearted girls, and they watched the little village at their feet, almost wishing that the Moriscos would show themselves; for suspense was harder to bear than action.

"Let us say our prayers," said Inez, suddenly kneeling in the hot sunshine upon the hard stone floor; and Juana instantly knelt beside her and took her rosary in her hands.

When they rose from their knees a few minutes later, suspense was at an end. The attack was approaching.

"They have weapons now!" cried Juana. "Mistress, have a care. Those bows and arrows are deadly weapons in the hands of a good marksman. And look—they are bringing faggots; and that mule has a barrel of tar upon his back! And see that great ram of wood! They will seek to batter down the door with that. If they do——"

Yes, if they did that, the girls' position would be desperate indeed. Before, the men had only been armed with daggers and scimitars, which were useless save at close quarters. Now they had the deadly bow and arrow, and if they once obtained entrance, it would be useless for the girls to repeat the defensive manœuvre of the earlier hours. They would be shot down instantly, and fall an easy prey. Inez realised that in a moment, as she watched the approach of the Moors; and scarcely had her head appeared above the battlement, before a shower of arrows fell clattering about them.

"This side!" she said to Juana, between shut teeth. "They will try the door first; we will be ready for them!"

The girls dared not show themselves openly; but the battlements were built with a view to defence, and they were able to look cautiously over without being seen. The Moors were approaching the door; they were almost directly underneath.

"Now!" cried Inez, setting her hand to a huge stone. Juana put all her strength into the task, the great coping stone was hoisted between them, and pushed bodily over.

A fearful yell and a thundering crash told that it had done its work well; a storm of furious execration went up, and in the midst of it down came another stone which dashed out the brains of a fellow in the crowd below.

Juana peered over and then drew back, a fierce triumph on her girlish face; for she had seen that there were two enemies the less.

"We have plenty of stones, the saints be praised!" she exclaimed. "They are closing in again, Mistress. Let us give them another!"

The Moors were always careless of life in battle; and again and again they advanced to fix their battering ram; whilst again and again the huge stones came thundering down, and, besides these large ones, were many smaller, which the girls aimed with such precision and coolness, that not only could the assailants not fix their ram against the door to batter it down, but the men approaching the walls with faggots and combustibles were picked off one by one, and dropped wounded or crushed beneath the hail of stones from above.

Inez looked over once again, drawing herself up to her full height, and straining her eyes towards Marbella in the hope of seeing the long-looked-for relief.

"Have a care, Mistress, have a care!" cried Juana anxiously, and sprang forward; but she was just too late. The arrow had buried itself in the shoulder of Inez; she gave a start and an exclamation of pain; but, taking hold of it firmly, she instantly plucked it out.

"Pray heaven it be not poisoned!" cried Juana, as she stanched the flow of blood with quick, skilful fingers. And Inez smiled bravely through her pain.

"Hark! They are at the door again; we must show them that the garrison is not disabled yet. That stone there, Juana; now both together! down it goes! Hark! what a yell that was. I am revenged for my sore shoulder!"

But the brave resistance of the girls seemed rather to stimulate than to baffle the assailants. The air was rent with frightful threats and curses; and Inez, looking rather white, though there was no fear in her heart, said quietly:

"There is no hope of mercy, Juana. If we are not relieved; if help comes not, we must sell our lives as dearly as we can; and plunge our daggers into our own hearts sooner than fall alive into their hands."

"We will, Mistress," said Juana firmly. "But surely our Lady will send us aid ere that!"

"Look! look! look!" cried Inez suddenly. "The banner of the cross! Oh, Juana, do my eyes deceive me? Is it a vision that I see?"

And indeed for a moment both the girls thought that it must be; for the light fell sparkling upon mailed headpieces and flashing swords; and a banner with the cross flaunting in the golden light of the southern afternoon was borne aloft, and waved as though in signal that help indeed was at hand.

"What can it be? Whence come they?" cried Inez, with breathless agitation. "That is not the road from Marbella! Our Lady herself must have sent them to our aid! Pray heaven it be not a vision!"

"See, see!" cried Juana in ungovernable excitement, running to the battlement and showing herself fearlessly. "The Moriscos—they run! They fly Mistress, we are saved! We are saved! It is our brave Spanish soldiers come to our rescue!"

Inez looked over in turn, and though the mists seemed to rise before her eyes in the revulsion of her feeling, she could see the flying figures of the Moriscos dashing down helter-skelter into the deep ravine below, to escape the Christian swords, and she saw the lifted headpiece of the officer in charge of the band, as he looked up and marked the two girls leaning over the low rampart.

The next minute Juana had dashed down and opened the door, while little Aluch, flushed with triumph, was telling Inez how this band had come in pursuit of the rebels of Orgiba; how he had met them and told them of the predicament of the Christian maidens, and had brought them by the nearest route to the rescue.

So Istan was saved—saved from Spanish vengeance through little Aluch's act, as the Christian population of three souls was saved by the heroism of the two brave girls. Inez rode into Marbella that evening beside the officer of the band, to find her uncle there, beseeching help, which the citizens could not believe was wanted in such a peaceful spot, till the young officer rode into the great square, still holding Inez by the hand, and told the tale of how she and Juana had held the tower against the rebel Moriscos.

CATHARINE THE ROSE

He held her hands and looked steadfastly into her eyes.

"You would not hold me back, Kate?"

The eyes which looked bravely at him were full of tears; but the girl shook the drops from her long lashes as she threw back her head, and spoke with unfaltering lips.

"I would hold no man back from his duty; least of all the man I love."

In a moment his arm was about her. The troth plight, spoken amid the clang of arms and the rattle of musketry, was but three days old; and the strange sweetness of it had penetrated the life of the English Captain in a fashion which he had no skill to analyse. But in these stern days was little scope for the sweetness of spoken love; and even the minutes snatched from the pressing needs of garrison life were few and far between.

But Hart had volunteered the second time for a service of extra peril, and he had come to speak a farewell to his love—a farewell which both knew might be final.

"I went and returned in safety last time, sweetheart," he said, "and wherefore not again? I shall have your prayers to Heaven on my side this time."

"You had them before," said Kate, lifting her head from his shoulder and looking straight into his eyes; and he kissed away the last of the raindrops from her lashes.

"Help we must have if Sluys is to be saved," he said. "I swim forth to-night, under cover of the darkness, with letters for England's Queen. The devil take that pestilent peace-party, who would beguile her into dallying with Spain and her tyrant King and treacherous Princes!" broke out the young Captain suddenly, in a gust of hot anger. "Can she not see that her only safety lies in joining heart and soul with the Netherlands in their struggle for life and liberty? Let Philip of Spain once get these lands beneath his iron heel, and then England will have cause to tremble for her very existence!"

"But the Queen has sent us help already," said Kate; "surely she will do more, when she knows our dire extremity!"

"Eight hundred men," answered the young officer, with a tone of scorn, "eight hundred English soldiers with eight hundred Dutch, to hold a place like Sluys! How is it possible the thing should be done? It has come to this, that if help comes not, Sluys must fall. Alexander Farnese and his Spanish host will score another triumph for tyranny and the Inquisition!"

A shudder ran through the girlish frame at the sound of that word, more hateful and terrible to the party of freedom than any other which could be spoken. Then her eyes flashed with a spark as of fire, and, flinging back her head, she cried:

"And what would the men do if they came, Harold? What work would you set them first to do?"

"There is work and to spare, both in attack and defence," answered Hart, with something of grimness in his tone. "We are in dire need of at least four redoubts between the citadel and the ramparts. The burghers have banded themselves together to build us one. We are sending every man that can be spared from garrison duty and the actual fighting to throw up the second; but how the others are to be constructed with our present force it is impossible to see. Help we must have at all cost, and I trust these dispatches which you have been so carefully sewing in my clothing, will bring it to us, ere it be too late."

He could not linger. The shadows of the coming evening were beginning to fall, although the summer day lingered long. He put his hands upon the shoulders of the girl, and looked into her face with a long wistful gaze. His own face was very thin and brown, and though he was still quite young, there were a few grey hairs to be seen about his temples. Hard living, hard fighting, days and nights of anxious toil had left their impress upon him, as upon many another compatriot at that season of bitter struggle. And the bitterness was greater rather than less for the knowledge that if England's Queen and her counsellors would but show a little more firmness of purpose and readiness of dispatch, many of the horrors of this protracted struggle might even now be saved to the courageous and devoted Dutch.

Even upon the fair young face of Catharine Rose, the perils in which she had been reared had traced their lines. That look of firm determination, of high-souled courage, of resolute devotion to duty, be the cost what it might, could not have been so clearly written there had she not lived her young life amidst scenes and tales of stress and storm.

Men and women, youths and maidens, had to face from week to week, and even from day to day, the possibility of having to yield up life and liberty, home and friends, for their fidelity to their country and their faith. Catharine's father had died a martyr at the stake. Her brother had been slain in the memorable defence of Antwerp, two years since; and the loss of her only son had broken the mother's heart, so that she faded away and died a few months later.

But these troubles and losses had broken neither the heart nor the spirit of Catharine. She had the mixed blood in her veins of an English father and a

Dutch mother; the courage and devotion of two warlike nations seemed to combine in her youthful frame.

Her quarrel with Fate was that she had been born a woman, and not a man. Her longing was to gird on sword and buckler, and go forth to fight the hated Spaniard—the tool of the bloody tyrant whose very name was not heard without curses both loud and deep.

"Oh, if I were but a man!" had for long been the cry of her heart; and if in the sweetness of feeling herself beloved by one of the heroes of Sluys she no longer breathed this aspiration, it was not because her heart was less filled with an ardent longing to do and to dare.

"Farewell, sweetheart," spoke the Captain, looking deep into her eyes, and knowing, as she too knew, that perhaps he was looking his last. But the consciousness of ever-present peril was one of the elements of daily life in the beleaguered city; and although this mission upon which Hart set forth was one of more than ordinary peril, a soldier never went forth upon his daily duty with any certainty of seeing home or friend again.

"Farewell; God be with you, and bring you safely back to us," she answered steadfastly; and their lips met once before he dropped her hands, and hurried away without trusting himself to look behind again.

Catharine looked after him from the window as he walked rapidly away in the gathering twilight. Her accustomed ears scarcely heeded the sullen booming of the great guns, or the dropping shots of muskets from the ramparts. The life of the town went on with a curious quietude in the midst of warlike strife; notwithstanding the fact that it became daily more and more evident that without substantial succour in men, and munitions, and food, Sluys could not hold out against such overmastering odds.

Suddenly the girl turned from the window, and, with fleet steps, crossed the room, descended a dim stairway, and entered the chamber beneath, where, by the light of a solitary lamp, a girl, a few years her senior, was setting out a frugal meal with the aid of a youthful servant-maid.

"Has he gone, Kate?" she asked, as she saw that Catharine was alone; "I had hoped he would have had something to eat ere he sallied forth into the night. The rations of the soldiers are meagre enough now, and he has a hard task before him. God in His mercy give him safe transit through those sullen waters, and blind the eyes of sentries and soldiers!"

"He could not stay," answered Kate, "and he said he had eaten well. May," she broke out suddenly, clasping her hands together, the colour coming and going in her cheeks, "May, I have a plan, and you must help me. I have learned what the sons and daughters of the city can do for Sluys. I am going to toil for her, and you will help me!"

"What mean you, Kate? What have you heard? What can be done for the city by weak women like ourselves?"

"I am not a weak woman!" answered Kate, throwing back her head in her favourite gesture, "I am a strong woman, and so are you, May, and so are dozens, ay, and scores of the daughters and the wives of the burghers. Listen, May. You know of the need for redoubts, and how your husband is toiling almost day and night to construct one on yonder side of the citadel. But they need more; Harold himself told me so. They need more than soldiers or burghers can build. I am going to organise a band of women and girls. You and I, May Hart, will be the leaders. I have not watched the building of forts and defences for nothing all these weeks. You and I with the women of the city, will build them a redoubt, and it shall be the work of the girls of Sluys!"

The young wife fired instantly at the suggestion. All over the city it was known of the dire want of men to construct these defensive works. Boys and men of the burgher class had gone forth willingly in defence of their town, and were working night and day at the unaccustomed toil.

But Sluys was to see another sight ere long: a great band of women, many of them mere girls, and even little children, armed with the needful tools led by Mary Hart and Catharine Rose, going forth morning by morning from their homes, delving, building, toiling through the long hot summer's day, in rivalry of the brothers and fathers on the corresponding side of the citadel; the new redoubt rising bit by bit before their strenuous efforts, the work as accurate and solid as that of the men, though every detail was the work of women and girls.

"Impossible!" had been the first cry of the burghers when they heard of the proposed scheme. Proud though they were of the spirit that inspired their women-kind, they shook their heads at the thought of their ever being able to carry out such a plan. But Catharine was a power amongst the girls of Sluys. She came of a race who had laid down their lives for the country of their adoption. Her mother had been a townswoman; and the girl had been born and bred amongst them. "Catharine the Rose" she had been called in affectionate parlance, a play upon her patronymic, and a compliment to her brilliant colouring which even the privations and anxieties of the siege had not dimmed.

Mary Hart was also a girl of Sluys, lately wedded to Roger Hart, the elder brother of the gallant English Captain, who had been sent with the small band of troops into the city a short time previously, and had already so distinguished himself by personal courage, that any specially perilous errand was readily entrusted to him.

Roger was not a soldier by profession. The Harts' father had settled in the Netherlands during a time of Tudor intolerance and persecution in England, little foreseeing how soon the land of their adoption would become the arena of a struggle to the death against a tyranny of which England in her worst and darkest hour had never dreamed. He had, however, thriven and prospered in the country he had chosen as his home, and had not been driven away by the troubles which speedily befell it. His sons, like Catharine Rose, combined in their veins the blood of England's sons and that of the Netherlands; and it was with the Harts that the girl had found a home, when her mother's death had left her alone in the world. Perhaps it was not strange when Harold Hart came to Sluys and spent his few spare hours at his brother's house, that he and the girl he had played with in childhood should draw together as they had done, animated by a common love, a common hatred, and a common steadfast resolve to do and dare all in the cause which was nearest their heart.

But how would the amazons of Sluys face the fire from the guns of the enemy when their earthworks grew to the height that would make them increasingly a target for the Spanish guns?

"Leave it to us now," said some of the burghers, who came as a deputation to the spot where the women and girls were at work. "Commence the fort if you will, brave maidens, but leave this part to men. It is too stern work for delicate girls when the storm of lead whistles about those who work."

It was to Catharine the Rose they spoke, and she turned upon them with a flash in her eyes, as she made answer:

"Think you that we have not counted the cost? Think you that we are afraid? Have we not seen? do we not know? Are we of different nature from yourselves? I answer for the maidens of Sluys. That which we have begun we will carry through. Have not you men your work cut out? Are you not toiling—ay, and dying—daily for our defence and that of our homes? Do you think we are afraid to toil, and, if need be, to die in the same cause? It was like you to offer thus to relieve us in the time of chiefest peril; but I give you the answer of the girls of Sluys—go to Captain May for the answer of the wives!"

Captain Catharine and Captain May were the titles by which the two leaders were known to their own squads; but the men called them "Catharine the Rose" and "May in the Heart"—a sort of graceful parody upon their names.

Mary Hart had the same answer to give on behalf of the wives of the burghers. And, indeed, it was abundantly evident that the men had their hands full with what they themselves had undertaken, and that unless the brave work were carried out by those who had commenced it, it must perforce be abandoned; whilst more and more needful for the safety of the city did these redoubts become.

The temper of the besiegers was known to be sorely tried, and scant was the chance that even if they heeded the sex of the workers upon the growing redoubt, they would on that account permit it to grow without opposition. Again and again in the history of those bloody wars women had fought side by side with men in the defence of their homes and liberties, and the Spanish soldier had as ruthlessly cut down the one as the other.

"Girls, are you afraid?" asked Kate, as she led forth her band upon the morrow. "You have heard the balls hissing overhead these many days; but to-day, perchance, we shall feel the sting of the hot bullet, or the splinter of some shell tearing its way into our flesh. Are you afraid to face such experience?"

"We are not afraid; where you lead us, we will go!" was the almost universal rejoinder, spoken with a quiet gravity and resolve which attested its sincerity. These girls were not undertaking the task in ignorance of its perils. They had seen enough of wounds and death. They knew what they were facing; but there were only a few waverers who, on Kate's invitation, went back; and even they could not tear themselves away from the scene of their labours; they came to look on beneath the shelter of the rampart, to give help should help be needed; and before long the stern excitement of the hour possessed them also, and scarce one but was soon working with the rest, only shrinking and perhaps uttering a little cry as some bullet might whizz close to her ear.

Under fire!—a rain of bullets falling round!—a comrade beside you sometimes falling silent and helpless, or with a cry and a struggle. It is so easy to speak of such things, but how many of us realise what they mean to those who have passed through such experience?

Catharine in the foremost post of danger worked on directing and encouraging. She had insisted that her squad of girls should take the side most exposed to the enemy's fire, leaving the less perilous place for the married women. There had been a generous rivalry for this position of peril and honour; but Catharine's word and determination had prevailed.

"You who have husbands and perhaps children to think of, and to miss you if you are taken, must give this post to us," she said; and she thought of the man she loved, of whom no tidings had yet come; who had ventured his life so many times; and in her heart she prayed that if he were taken, she might join him on the other side of the narrow stream of death, the stream which seemed so small and narrow when so many were crossing it day by day.

So the work progressed rapidly, though many a brave young life paid forfeit, and the tears would well up sometimes in Kate's eyes, as she saw a comrade carried off dead, or bent over a dying girl, to hear her last brave message for home and friends; or, when in the silence of the night, she thought upon these things, and cried in her heart, "How long, O Lord, how long?"

But there was never a quiver of fear in her face or in her heart as she stood to her post day by day; and the walls grew, and the Commandant of the garrison came and gave warm praise and thanks, and timely cautions and instructions to the heroic girls who toiled through the hot summer days without one selfish thought of fear.

Once, as he stood beside the leader of these brave young amazons, a shell came screaming through the air, and he shouted a word of command.

"Down on your faces!" he cried, and himself set the example, to show them what to do. The shell was from a new battery, and it had been directed with a view to stopping the work on this very redoubt. The girls dropped their tools and fell flat, but Catharine was a thought too late. She had been so interested in the work of that battery that she forgot for a moment the peril in which she stood. Luckily the Commandant pulled her down beside him before it was too late; but a portion of the explosive struck her, tearing a ghastly wound from wrist to elbow. The stones and rubble seemed to fly up around them; a fragment dashed itself against Catharine's head; a blood-red mist seemed to swirl before her eyes, and blank darkness swallowed her up.

When she opened her eyes next it was to find herself at home, lying upon the wide couch beneath her favourite window which looked down the street. The light showed that the evening was advancing; May was in the room setting the table for supper, and—but was not that part and parcel of the dream which still seemed to enwrap her faculties?—Harold, her bronzed-faced soldier, was seated beside her, his eyes hungrily bent upon her face.

She smiled, half afraid to move lest the dream should vanish, and the next moment he had her fingers close in his grasp.

"Kate, my Kate!" he cried; and she smiled back, and sat up.

The Commandant pulled her down beside him before it was too late.

"Harold! you have done it again! and have come back safe."

"Yes, I have come back, and to find—what? That my Kate has set an example to the women of the Netherlands, that——"

But she put her hand upon his mouth and stopped him.

"It was not I more than others; and there are some who have laid down their lives for the cause. You must not praise me; why should not women do their duty to the cause of freedom as well as men? You do not praise your men for standing to their guns."

"But we will praise you!" cried Harold hotly. "Know you not that all the city is ringing with the news that the women's redoubt is all but finished, and that in spite of the deadly fire from the new battery? And Kate, to-night the soldiers will get the guns mounted, and to-morrow Fort Venus will give her answer back. Oh, my Kate, will you be able to come and see?"

"Fort Venus?" she queried, with a smile in her eyes.

"That is what the Commandant has christened it, and the soldiers received the name with ringing cheers. The names of Catharine the Rose and May in the Heart are in all men's mouths. Surely, surely you must be there to see!"

And she was; for the wound, although severe, was not crippling, and the dauntless spirit of the girl carried her through the triumph and gladness of the next day, as it had carried her through the previous perils and hardships.

A spectator would have thought that Sluys was *en fête* that day instead of a sorely pressed beleaguered city, wanting food, help, everything. Citizens and soldiers marched in squadrons to the new fort, which had been the scene of arduous toil all the night, and from whose loopholes the mouths of guns could now be seen protruding.

And foremost in that procession, cheered to the echo by burghers and soldiers alike marched the brave women and girls, who had done such work for their country and their city, headed by Mary Hart and Kate Rose.

Then, at a given signal, "Fort Venus" opened her mouth and roared forth her message of defiance and resolve.

"Hear the voice of the women of the Netherlands!" cried Arnold de Groenevelt, the grave Commandant, as the guns belched forth fire and smoke, and the welkin rang with the shouts of the citizens and soldiers. And so true was the aim of the gunners, that the new battery was speedily silenced; and cheer after cheer went up as the destruction wrought became more and more visible; and the youths of the city bore aloft upon their shoulders through the streets to their homes, Catharine the Rose and May in the Heart, crying aloud as they took their triumphal way: "Hear the voice of Fort Venus! Hear the voice of the women of the Netherlands! Death to the tyrant! Life and immortality to the liberties of the people, and freedom of faith. The voice of the girls is the voice of the nation."

ELSJE VAN HOUWENING

For two years she had lived within the walls of a grim fortress; a prison had been her home. Thirteen massive doors, secured by iron bolts and bars and huge locks, stood between her and the outer world; and yet this maiden of nineteen summers was no prisoner; she was here in this gloomy place of her own freewill.

And for what cause was she here? Was it to guard and tend one who was very near and dear to her,—a father, a mother, a brother? No; it was none of her own kindred who were thus shut up, but her master, Hugo de Groot, or Grotius, as he is more generally known to history.

With the causes for the unjust captivity of this great and learned man, we need not deal here. They belong to the page of history, where they can be read in full. Suffice it to say, that Grotius was condemned by the States-General of the Netherlands to a life-long captivity in the great fortress of Loevenstein, under the spiteful tyranny of its governor, Lieutenant Deventer, who had an especial grudge against him, and seemed resolved to make his captivity as bitter as it was possible to do.

The one grace allowed to the unhappy prisoner was that his wife and family might share his captivity; might live within the fortress in the quarters allotted to him, although not suffering all the rigours of imprisonment. And with Madame de Groot and her family of children had come Elsje van Houwening, their young maid-servant, who had stoutly refused to leave them in their hour of trial and trouble, and had already spent two years of her young life within the walls of the prison.

The tie that binds master and servant together was stronger in those days than it is now. The race of devoted servants seems well-nigh extinct in these degenerate days; our mothers and grandmothers had experience of a fidelity which is seldom met with now. But even in their times an instance of such courage and devotion must needs be rare. Yet to Elsje it seemed perfectly natural to cleave to the family that had befriended her in a lonely childhood, and she loved her master and mistress and their children with a love which only grew stronger and stronger during the long, monotonous days of this captivity. Small wonder was it that Madame de Groot should sit for hours over their scanty fire, her children asleep, her husband poring over the books which came to him from time to time in a great chest from friends in Gorcum, talking with Elsje as though to a friend, talking over the difficulties of keeping house upon the pittance allowed them from the Government after the sequestration of their family property; the mournful future that seemed to stretch indefinitely before them, and now and again of that ever recurrent dream of hapless prisoners—the chances of escape!

And yet what was the possibility of this? How could it be even dreamed of that a closely guarded prisoner should pass through those thirteen iron-bound doors which lay between him and liberty? And if the sad-eyed wife or eager maid looked down from their windows, what did they see, save the rushing, tumultuous flow of a deep turbid river?

Nature and art had combined, as it seemed, to make this fortress impregnable alike from without and within. It stood in the very narrow and acute angle, where the strong and turbid Waal joins its rushing waters with those of the Meuse; and on the land side immensely strong walls with a double moat guarded it from attack, and held in helpless captivity all those upon whom the great doors had closed.

True Madame de Groot with her children, or Elsje with her market basket, were permitted to sally forth at will by day, or, at least, under modified restrictions; to cross by the boat to Gorcum, which lay exactly opposite on the farther bank of the Waal. They made their purchases here, and saw their friends from time to time; but how did this help the prisoner? Madame de Groot was very stout and somewhat short, whilst Grotius himself was tall and slight, possessed of singular personal beauty, and an air and bearing that would be most difficult to disguise. The idea of dressing him up in their clothes, and smuggling him out in that fashion, had been talked of a hundred times, but only in a sort of despair. Hugo himself had shaken his head over the plan. It was doomed to ignominious failure, as he saw from the first. No one was permitted to leave the prison save in broad daylight, and all had to pass innumerable guards and sentries on the way. If the prisoner were to be detected seeking to escape in such fashion, it would only lead to a more rigorous and harsh captivity, and, probably, to his entire separation from his family.

The wife had sorrowfully agreed that it was too great a risk to run; yet, nevertheless, she and Elsje were ceaselessly racking their brains to think out some plan whereby the prisoner might escape the dreadful doom of life-long captivity.

It was evening. Madame de Groot was bending over the stove, cooking her husband's frugal supper. Elsje went in search of the children, to put such of them to bed as were not already there.

Her favourite out of all the little ones was Cornelia, a lovely little girl of nine years, wonderfully like her father, and perfectly devoted to him. She and her brother Hugo were often to be found in the room in which he studied and wrote from morning to night, only varying his sedentary pursuits by the spinning of a huge top that had been made for him by friends in Gorcum, that he might not suffer too greatly from lack of accustomed exercise.

Elsje stole softly into the room, so as not to disturb her master, and glanced round the bare place again and again. Where could the children be? She had looked everywhere else in their limited quarters; there was no other room except this one that had not been searched through and through. She would not disturb her master by a question, and continued softly moving and looking about, till the sound of a suppressed child's laugh, close beside her, made her almost jump; for there was nothing to be seen, save—ah! yes; she saw it all now—there was the great empty chest that had brought the last load of books from Gorcum. She raised the lid, and a simultaneous shriek of laughter arose from two pairs of rosy child-lips. There were little Cornelia and Hugo, curled up like dormice in the chest, peeping at Elsje, with eyes brimming with laughter.

She carried them off, laughing herself, and asking them how they managed to breathe with the heavy lid closed fast down.

"Oh, there is a long crack just under the top of the lid, it doesn't show from outside; but we could see light, and your shadow came right over us, and then Hugo laughed, and you heard. We sat there a long time this afternoon and told ghost stories. It was such fun!"

Elsje put the children to bed, and went thither shortly herself, but all the night long she was dreaming, dreaming, dreaming. She saw the chest with the two children inside; and then she saw it again, and instead of two small figures there was one large one—a tall man's figure crushed together in the chest, and when he turned his face towards her it was the face of her master!

The girl was up and about with the dawn; and her mistress coming to help her, she told her in whispers of the incident of the previous night and of her dream, and the two women stood staring at each other, with white faces and glowing eyes, as the idea slowly formulated itself and took shape.

"It might be done! It might be done!" whispered Madame de Groot at last; "if he could get in, it might perchance be done. Oh! if heaven should open us such a way as that!"

That day passed like a dream to all. They waited till dark; till all the children were sound asleep, and no one from without would trouble them again, before they even dared to make the experiment. Grotius was a tall man, as has been said, though he was slender in his proportions. At another time he would have pronounced it impossible that he should so fold himself up as to get inside that chest, and let the lid be fastened down upon him. But when a man sees life-long captivity before him on the one side, and the hope of escape and freedom on the other, he can sometimes achieve the impossible. And, at last, after many efforts, the thing was done; the lid was closed, and the man found that he could breathe and endure the pressure even for a considerable period.

Day by day, or, rather, night by night, he made these trials till his limbs in some sort grew accustomed to the strange constriction, and he was able to bear the cramped posture for a more prolonged time. Madame de Groot, upon her next journey into Gorcum, spoke jestingly with a friend as to how her husband would be received were he to turn-up some day, and Madame Daatselaer answered, in the same jesting spirit, that he would have a warm and hearty welcome; for the Daatselaers were old and tried friends, though only of the rank of merchants. They owned a large warehouse of great repute, and their dwelling-house was at the rear of the shop, where ribbons and other merchandise were vended to all comers.

It was through the immediate agency of these friends that the books lent to Grotius by Professor Erpenius were consigned to him in his prison. The Professor sent them to the Daatselaers, who dispatched the chest by the boat which plied between Gorcum and the fortress opposite. It was returned in the same manner to them when the books were done with, for transmission back to the Professor. Therefore, if Grotius could conceal himself in the chest for the journey over the water, he would be consigned to the safe-keeping of friends, who might be trusted to do everything in their power to facilitate his escape to Antwerp, and so to France, where he would be safe from the malice of his enemies.

Days flew by, and the plan seemed more and more feasible, albeit fraught with no small danger of discovery. Madame de Groot's anxiety was almost greater than that of her husband, and perhaps it was her visible agitation, occasionally manifesting itself in spite of her great courage and self-control, which led the prisoner to speak as follows to Elsje, when he and she were alone one day, his wife having gone once more to Gorcum, prepared to drop a faint hint to Madame Daatselaer, without, however, really arousing her suspicions of what was in the wind; for all knew how much the success of such a scheme depended upon the maintenance of absolute secrecy.

"My good girl, is it true what thy mistress says of thee, that this whole plan is one of thine own making?"

"Not of my making, master, but rather as a thing revealed to me in a dream. I seemed to see the chest, and when it was opened there was my master within. I told the dream to my mistress, and the rest seemed to follow of itself."

"And if the plan be carried out when next that chest is returned, who will accompany it across the water?"

Elsje paused in thought. Sometimes she had gone with it on former occasions, sometimes her mistress. There had been no peril in the transit then. It had mattered nothing who went; but now things would be quite different. She looked her master questioningly in the face. He returned her glance.

"I have been thinking much on that point," he said; "it will be a memorable journey for those concerned. There be moments when I misdoubt me if my wife hath the needful firmness. It is not courage that she lacks, nor firmness of purpose; but can she pass the many barriers, the many posts of peril, the many prying eyes within and without, and so command her face that her anxiety be not seen? The sorrows and anxieties of these last years have told upon her. And if she betray too great solicitude for this chest of books, why in a moment we may be undone!"

Elsje stood looking very thoughtful. She saw at once the danger of self-betrayal; the danger that would be far more quickly noted in the prisoner's wife than in his servant. Her gaze was lifted to her master's face.

"Shall I be the one to go?" she asked.

"Wouldst thou not be afraid, my child?"

"What punishment could they give to me were the plot to be discovered?" she asked.

"Legally none," answered Grotius, whose training in the law gave him full knowledge on all such subjects; "but, my girl, I myself am guilty of no crime—yet see what has befallen me. I cannot tell what might be thy fate were this thing discovered during the perilous transit."

For a moment Elsje stood motionless, thinking deeply. Then she lifted her head, and her eyes shone brightly.

"No matter for that," she said, "whatever comes of it I will be the one to go. If they must punish another innocent person, let the victim be me rather than my dear mistress!"

Grotius took her hand, and the tears stood in his eyes. Elsje rattled on as though to hinder him from speaking the words that for the moment stuck in his throat.

"It will be better so every way," she said, "for see—the men must come in hither to get the chest, and so it must seem that you, master, are sick and in bed, else would they look to see you here at work. We must draw the curtains close; but leave your clothes visible by the bedside, and my mistress must seem to be attending upon you. So it will be best every way for me to go with the box; and the soldiers all know me, and we have our quips and jests together. I will talk to them all the while, as my mistress could scarce do without rousing suspicion, so they will not note if the weight of the chest be something greater than usual."

"Thou art a brave girl; thou hast a great heart and a ready wit," said the prisoner with emotion in his voice, "may God reward thee for thy devotion to a family in distress; for we may never be able to do so."

"I want no reward," answered Elsje stoutly, "save to know that I have helped those I love, and who once befriended me."

The next day was Sunday, and a wild March gale was raging round the castle, lashing the waves of the river into foam. The rain dashed against the windows as they sat with their books of devotion, as usual, through the earlier hours of the day. Grotius had read and offered prayer as was his wont, when suddenly little Cornelia turned her face towards the barred window, and her eyes seemed full of a strange light.

"To-morrow, Papa must be off to Gorcum, whatever the weather may be," she said; and then, slipping off her chair, took the little ones away with her for the usual midday repast.

Husband and wife looked at each other aghast. The strangeness of the coincidence seemed to them most remarkable.

"Let us take it for a direction from heaven," said Grotius. "Out of the mouth of babes and sucklings—the child knew nothing, yet something was revealed to her spirit."

Later in the day Elsje came breathless with the news that the Commandant of the fortress was just leaving it for a few days' absence. He had received his captaincy, and was to go to Heusden to receive his company. All things seemed pointing in one direction; and early on Monday morning, Madame de Groot asked leave of Madame Deventer to send back the chest of books to Gorcum.

"My husband is not well; he is wearing himself out with so much study. If the books are sent away I can persuade him to remain in bed and take some needful repose. I got him to pack them up last night; but if they stay in his sight, he will assuredly remember something more he wants to study, and nothing I can say will then persuade him to keep in bed."

Madame Deventer was a kind-hearted woman, and sorry for the prisoner's wife. She gave ready consent to the request, and said she would send some soldiers shortly to take the chest away.

The crucial moment had come. Grotius, dressed in the thinnest linen under-garments—for there was not space for much clothing—took his place in the chest. A book, padded with a cloth, served as a sort of pillow, a few books and papers were placed in such interstices as were left by the curves of his body; and his wife took a solemn farewell of him before she shut down the lid and snapped the key in the lock, giving it in deep silence to Elsje.

Outside the storm still raged and howled, but the tumult of their souls seemed greater; yet Elsje stood with a careless smile on her face as the soldiers entered the room, and Madame de Groot bent over the fire, stirring something in a saucepan, and telling her husband that she would soon have his soup ready, and she hoped he would enjoy it more than his breakfast. The curtains of the alcove bed were drawn, and the ordinary clothes of the prisoner lay upon a chair near it.

"My word, but it is a heavy boxful this time!" exclaimed the men, as they laid hold of the chest.

"To be sure," cried Elsje; "what would you have? They are Arminian books, and those are mighty solid, I can tell you. You had best have a care how you treat them when you get to the water. Arminian books have sunk many a good bark ere now, before it has got into harbour!"

The men laughed at the innuendo of the girl's words. It was in truth their adherence to the Arminian side of the great Arminian and Calvinist controversy which had shipwrecked the lives of Grotius and so many others. Elsje chattered gaily to them as they dragged and lifted the heavy chest down the stairs and through the thirteen ponderous doors. She kept them laughing by her droll remarks, and the little anecdotes she retailed for them whenever a halt was called. At last it stood without the last of the doors, and the soldiers paused and wiped their brows.

"Is the chest to be examined before it goes on board?"

Elsje's heart thumped against her ribs. This was the crucial moment. At first when the box had gone in and out its contents had been carefully examined; but as nothing save the books had ever been found there the practice had been given up latterly. But there was never any actual certainty.

Elsje dangled the key from her girdle, and swung it carelessly round and round.

"It always used to be done," she said, "but methinks my lord Commandant love not the smell of Arminian books; perchance it smacks too much of brimstone to please him! For of late he has not troubled. But I care not, only pray you make haste. I have marketing to do in Gorcum, and what if all the best things are sold ere I get there, and my poor master lying sick?"

"Is the chest to be examined before it goes on board?"

"Ask the will of madame," said somebody; and the messenger went and returned, whilst Elsje stood almost sick with apprehension, though she never ceased laughing and talking the while.

"Madame says it may pass," came the answer back, "since her lord troubles not now, she will not delay the transit."

"Perhaps she fears lest some little Arminian imp should spring out upon her!" quoth Elsje merrily; and away they went with their load towards the boat.

It was indeed a rough passage that lay before them; and the girl's heart was in her mouth many times ere she got her precious chest safe on board, and securely lashed to keep it from slipping overboard. They laughed at her solicitude; but she always had a ready retort; and a young officer of the garrison, crossing at the same time, was so taken by her rosy face and bright eyes that he sat himself down upon the chest and drummed upon it with his feet, as he chatted with the little servant girl.

"Why do you wave your kerchief?" he asked, as the boat began her rough voyage across the tumbling waters.

"To tell yon children at that window that I am safe afloat. They feared the boat might not go in such a storm. And, fair sir, be pleased to leave kicking of that box, and come away to this better seat; for there is some precious porcelain inside, and if it be broken, I shall get the blame, for I packed it."

But Elsje's signal was for the straining eyes of her mistress far more than for those of the children. All was well thus far, and the worst of the peril was over; but—but there was still the landing on the other side.

"Take my box first," she pleaded, as they approached the wharf.

"That lumbersome thing?—that can wait till the last," answered the skipper, rather surlily; "'tis as heavy as if it held a man."

"I have heard tell how a criminal was once carried from prison in a box," remarked a soldier's wife laughingly, "and, methinks, if one has so escaped another might. Let us peep inside, maiden!"

Elsje laughed, bending to tie her shoe-string.

"What, and let the Professor's books be all scattered this way and that, and perhaps fall into the water! He would never send my master another chest; and, methinks, without books he would die."

"I'll get a gimlet and bore a hole in the Arminian!" laughed the soldier, whose wife had first spoken.

"Ay do!" cried Elsje; "get a gimlet long enough to reach the top of the castle. I will stand by and watch you as you bore!"

"Out of the way there!" cried the skipper and his son, as the boat swung towards the wharf; and in a moment all was bustle and confusion. The soldier helped his wife ashore, the young officer made a bow to Elsje and sprung over the side; there was hurry and bustle, and a welcome confusion; and the girl stood beside her precious chest, and at last, by the promise of an exorbitant fee, got the skipper and his son to transport the chest at once to the Daatselaers' house, on a barrow.

She walked a little ahead in her excitement; but was recalled by a surly question from the old man.

"Do you hear that, girl—do you hear what my son says? You have got something alive in that box!"

"Ah, to be sure, to be sure," she cried, laughing, "it is the Arminian books; they are often like that, because they say the devil helped to write them. Why, when I was a little girl I knew an old woman who lived all by herself in a wood; and she had a big book, and they said the devil had given it to her; and if she wanted a ride, she just got astride of it and it flew with her wherever she wanted to go! That's my mistress says about some of these big books. There's magic in them, and she wants to be rid of them."

The men looked awed; but superstition was rife in those days, and their one aim now was to be rid of the uncanny load. It was wheeled, and then lifted into the back room of the house, and Elsje paid and dismissed the bearers with perfect calmness.

The next minute she had glided into the shop where Madame Daatselaer was serving customers, and whispered something in her ear.

Leaving everything, but with a face as white as paper, the worthy woman hastened after Elsje, who rapped on the lid, but got no reply; for a moment her fortitude gave way, and she cried aloud in her anguish:

"My master!—my poor master—he is dead—stifled!"

"Ah!" cried Madame Daatselaer in bewildered dismay, "better a live husband in a prison than a dead one at liberty; my poor friend, my poor friend!"

But a sharp rap on the trunk from the inside reassured them.

"I am not dead," gasped Grotius, "but I was not sure of your voices. Open and let me have some air!"

Elsje unlocked the chest, whilst her friend locked the door of the room, and Grotius raised himself slowly as from a coffin.

"Praised be God for this deliverance!" he cried, as Elsje brought a cloak in which to wrap him, for he was cramped and numbed by cold, and the constraint of his posture. "God be praised for His mercy; and how can I thank you enough, good friend, for receiving me thus into your house!"

"If only it bring not my husband to prison in your place," cried Madame Daatselaer, whose face was deadly pale.

"Nay, nay, sooner than that I will return to my prison in yon chest as I came forth!" answered Grotius.

But Madame Daatselaer rallied her courage and spoke quickly.

"Nay, nay, that shall never be since thou art here. But thou art no common person, and all the world talks of thee, and will soon be talking of thy escape. But before that we will have you safe from pursuit. My husband will see to that. And now I must hide you in the attics till dark, when we can make farther plans."

Elsje's work was done. Her master took her hands in his, and kissed her on the brow.

"Farewell, my brave maiden. May God reward you and keep you always safe from harm. There will be many heartfelt prayers offered that no ill shall befall you through your devotion to me and mine. And now go—tell the story to my dear wife; and so soon as I be safe in France she and the children shall join me, and in our home there will always be a place for thee; if thou dost not find another and a better home for thyself."

Elsje's tears fell as she said farewell to her master; but her heart was full of joy as she returned to the castle with the story for her mistress. And soon they knew that Grotius had effected his escape to France, and that all peril was at an end.

The Commandant, it is true, raged at the women when he found how his prisoner had escaped him; but nothing was done to them, and they were shortly released.

They joined their lord and master in his new home, and from thence one day, not so long after, Elsje van Houwening was married to a faithful servant of the family, who had also shared their captivity in the fortress of Loevenstein; and had been so well taught by his master the rudiments of law and of Latin, that he rose in time to be a thriving advocate.

But of nothing was he ever so proud as of the bravery and address of his wife in her girlhood, when she had been the instrument by which the celebrated escape of Grotius had been effected from the grim fortress of Loevenstein.

GRIZEL COCHRANE

Father and daughter stood facing each other in the gloomy prison of the Tolbooth: the girl's face was tense with emotion, and the man's eyes seemed to devour her with their gaze; for Sir John Cochrane believed that he was looking his last upon his favourite child.

He was not a man of great parts, nor one who can be regarded as in any sort a hero. He was more rash than brave, and his ill-judged support of the claims of the luckless Duke of Monmouth had brought him to his present doleful position—that of a prisoner in the hands of a deeply offended and implacable monarch, expecting each day to hear that his death-warrant had arrived from London.

Sir John had been one of the leaders of the insurrection in Scotland, which had been even more of a fiasco than the one conducted by Lord Grey in the West of England, where a temporary success at the outset had cheered and encouraged the adherents of the champion of Protestantism.

King James II., savage of temper and bitterly angry with all those concerned in this rebellion, had sent the terrible Jeffreys to the Western Assizes, which henceforth were to be known as the Bloody Assizes; and here, in Edinburgh, lay another illustrious victim, awaiting the king's warrant, which would doom him to the scaffold.

Whatever might have been his faults and errors in his public life, Sir John was a tender and loving husband and father. His wife, a delicate invalid, shattered by grief and anxiety, was unable to leave her room; but Grizel had come. Grizel had paid visits before this to her captive father, and each one was more sorrowful than the last, since the end must now be drawing very near.

"Methinks, my child," said the father hoarsely, "that this will be our last meeting on earth. They told me to-day that the death-warrant would, in all likelihood, be here in three days' time from this."

A quiver passed over Grizel's face; yet her voice was calm.

"Can our grandfather do nothing?" she asked.

Now Sir John's father was Lord Dundonald, a man of wealth and influence, and the question was a natural one to put.

"He is doing his utmost," answered Sir John, "I have had tidings of that. He has got the King's Confessor on his side, and they hope to gain the ear of His Majesty. But I fear me it will be all too late. If the warrant could be delayed, pardon might perchance reach in time; but as things now stand I fear to cherish hope. Let the will of God be done, my child. We must believe that He knows best."

A sudden light had flashed into Grizel's eyes, it illumined her whole face.

"Thou dost speak truth, my father," she said. "God, indeed, does know best; and let His will be done. But is it His will that one should perish whom even an earthly sovereign has pardoned, and who has never offended against Him?"

Sir John looked at her with a questioning gaze.

"God's ways, my daughter, are not as our ways, and His thoughts are past finding out. Let us brace our spirits for what may lie before us, and resign ourselves to that which He shall send. Kiss me once again, and bid me good-bye. It will not be for ever. This life is but a span, and we shall meet on the shores of eternity."

She flung her arms about his neck, and pressed her lips to his.

"Farewell, sweet father, farewell," she cried, with a little catch in her voice. "Farewell, but not good-bye. Something within me tells me that we shall meet again—in this life."

He looked into her strangely shining eyes, noted the resolute expression of her beautiful mouth, and asked almost anxiously:

"What dost thou mean, my child? What hast thou in that busy head of thine? Thou must run no risk for me; for thou art the stay and prop at home. Thou must be son, daughter, and husband—all to thy poor mother—when I am taken."

Steps were heard approaching. Grizel drew herself away, and looked once more into her father's face:

"Son and daughter—that will I be in all sooth, dear sir; but husband!—nay that will not be needed, methinks——"

"Grizel, what dost thou mean? What——"

The key was turning in the lock. She put her hands upon her father's shoulders and kissed him once again.

"Fear nothing," she said, "I am a Cochrane." And with those words on her lips she turned and left him, following her grim guide, the gaoler, till she stood outside in the street once more.

The same expression of high courage and resolve was on her face, as she pursued her way through the darkening streets, followed by the man-servant who had been awaiting her. But she did not go straight home. She turned aside up a narrow thoroughfare, and entered a house in it, with the familiarity of one who is known there intimately; and her servant had to wait long before his youthful mistress reappeared.

She went home, and went straight to her mother, who was weeping and praying in her upper chamber; there, kneeling beside the bed, Grizel told of the interview with her father, and then said in a low, earnest tone:

"Mother mine, give me thy blessing, for I must needs start forth this very night to save my father."

"Thou, child? What canst thou do?"

"Mother, I have a plan. I will not tell it thee, for it were better none should know. But pray for me whilst I am gone, that God will bless and watch over me. Methinks it was He who put the thought into my heart, and that He will speed me on my way and give me success in the carrying out of it."

"Thou wilt not run into danger, my child?" said the mother, who had come to lean upon Grizel, since her husband's captivity, almost as she would have done upon a son.

"I will not seek danger; I will avoid it where possible. But thou would'st not have me flinch, mother, when my father's life is at stake?"

"And thou must go to-night? But not alone?"

"I will take old Donald with me! And we must have the two best horses in the stable. But fear not, mother mine! In three or four days I will be back; and I trow that I shall have such news to tell, as will make thy heart sing aloud for joy."

That night, just before the gates of the city were shut, the guard saw two men riding forth together, the elder of whom he recognised as the old servant of the Cochranes. The younger of the pair, who looked like a youth, had his hat drawn somewhat close over his face. Donald gave the man a ready "Good-night," and paused a moment or two to gossip with him over the latest news from England.

"They say the next mail-bags will bring poor Sir John's death-warrant," remarked the soldier; "they must be in sore grief yonder, doubtless."

"How long does a letter take passing betwixt London and Edinburgh?" asked Donald.

"A matter of eight days each way," answered the man; and, after a few more words, Donald rode on, and joined his companion speedily.

"Eight days?" spoke a soft voice, not much like a youth's, as Donald told the news; "then, should anything go wrong with the warrant, it would be full sixteen days ere another could be got from London. Sure that would give the time—the time so sorely needed. Sixteen days!" and the words ended in a deep-drawn breath.

The old servant looked with loving eyes at the youth—who, of course, was none other than Grizel habited in the attire of a lad—a plain and inconspicuous riding suit, which she had borrowed from the brother of a dear friend, and which a little skill had altered to fit her slim figure well. Her floating locks aroused no suspicion as to her sex, in days when huge wigs adorned (or disfigured) the heads of men, and where those who could not afford these costly luxuries, and yet desired to keep in the fashion, let their own hair grow, and kept it curled and powdered. There was nothing specially womanish in the aspect of Grizel's abundant, curly hair flowing over her shoulders. She looked exactly like a smooth-faced boy, and bore herself with a bold and boyish air so soon as they were beyond the radius of the locality where her face might be known. By the time that the pair rode into the city of Berwick-upon-Tweed Grizel had come to feel so well at home in her part that she feared neither to converse with those about her, nor to show herself abroad in the unfamiliar habiliments of the other sex.

"Donald," she said, that night before they sought their beds, "we are in time. The mail has not yet passed through. To-morrow, bide thou here, whilst I ride to Belford, where I hear the messenger with the mails always pauses for a few hours' sleep. If he come hither with his mail-bags undisturbed, use thou thy wits, and seek to accomplish that in which I shall then have failed; but if he should bring news that he has been robbed, then set spurs to thy horse, and meet me at the house that I did point out to you as we rode into the town; and bring without fail the bag containing mine own attire and saddle: for then I must no longer travel as I do now."

Donald was loth to let his young mistress ride forth unattended; but Grizel would not have it otherwise. She believed that she would accomplish the thing better alone; and by leaving Donald in the place through which the messenger must pass, she felt that she gave herself another chance, should her first scheme miscarry.

The landlady of the little wayside inn at Belford smiled upon the bright-faced youth who reined up at her door and asked for a meal for himself and his horse.

"Step softly, if you will, fair sir," she said, pausing as she opened the door of the one room the inn boasted for the accommodation of travellers, "for the bearer of His Majesty's mail-bags stops here each time he passes, and has a spell of sleep ere he rides on to Berwick. He is sleeping soundly now, and I would not willingly have him disturbed. 'Tis a weary ride from London."

Grizel's heart beat thick and fast as she stepped softly within the room, golden possibilities presenting themselves to her imagination of getting at the bags and destroying certain of its contents, whilst the messenger slept the sleep of exhausted nature close beside her. But alas for her hopes! when she saw the sleeper, stretched snoring upon the alcove bed let into the wall, she noted that he had placed his bags for his pillow, and that each bag was securely sealed. This being so, she could neither possess herself of them without too great risk, nor undo and purloin papers without instant detection.

Food was brought to her, and she forced herself to eat, for she knew well that she might need all her strength and powers of endurance that day. And whilst she dined, and the man slumbered, her quick wits were working at full speed.

Outside, the voices of the landlady and the ostler told her that she would not be disturbed by a visitor just now. The pistols of the messenger lay upon the table almost within reach of her hand. With a quick, stealthy gesture she drew them towards her, and quickly removed the charges; putting the weapons back accurately in their place when she had done.

Then, rising from the table, she went out, paid her reckoning, mounted her horse, and rode leisurely away.

"Your guest sleeps sound," had been her parting remark to the woman.

"Ay, that he do, poor fellow, and I'm grateful that you've not wakened him, sir; but I must go and do so soon, since he must be on the road again in half an hour's time."

"Then I shall not have long to wait to know my fate," said Grizel, between her shut teeth, as she set her horse at a gentle trot. "If he looks to his pistols when he gets up and loads again, the chances are that I shall have an ounce or two of cold lead in my brain ere an hour be past. If not, well then I may have my father's death-warrant safe in mine own hands in that time! Is that hope not enough for me gladly to take all the chance of what may else betide!"

The light sprang into Grizel's eyes—the light of a deep devotion. She looked round at the fair world of nature with the unconsciously wistful gravity of one who knows he may be looking his last; of one who feels possible death within measurable distance. Yet there was not a sign of flinching in that fair face. The soldier spirit, and the spirit of devoted love were burning upon the altar of her heart. There was no room for thoughts of self there.

The beat of horse-hoofs behind her told that the moment had come. The man with the mail-bags strapped to his saddle was advancing rapidly towards her. Grizel reined back her horse into the shadow of the trees, and drew out a pistol from her belt. Her heart beat fast and furiously.

Next moment the man had ridden up.

"Stand and deliver!" shouted Grizel, in the most masculine voice she was capable of assuming; then as the man reined up and regarded the slight, boyish-looking youth with glances of inquiry and surprise, she added in a quieter tone: "Sir, I desire to obtain possession of certain papers in those bags of yours; wherefore deliver them up peaceably to me, and your life will be safe. Otherwise——" and here Grizel rode full up to the messenger with her pistol pointed at his head.

In a moment the fellow had whipped out his own weapon; and was holding it close against her cheek.

"Lay so much as a finger on His Majesty's mails, and I blow out your brains," he cried; "I am not one to shed blood needlessly, and thou art a mere boy; but not a finger shalt thou lay upon my bags."

"Nevertheless, it is those bags I mean to have," said Grizel, and put out a hand to take them.

Click! went the trigger, there was a flash in the pan—nothing more. Grizel's heart leapt up within her. He was at her mercy now. She would gain her end! With an exclamation of astonished dismay the man pulled out the second pistol. Grizel watched him with a smile. The weapon played him the same trick. He flung it from him with an oath, and threw himself off his horse to grapple with his slim antagonist, notwithstanding that the lad held a pistol in his hand.

Now was quick-witted Grizel's opportunity. She seized the reins of the horse, dashed spurs into her own, and set off at full gallop with the mail-bags, ere the astonished man well knew what had happened. She had travelled a quarter of a mile before she paused to look over her shoulder, and saw the breathless messenger tearing along, panting and blowing. Grizel calmly dismounted, and tied the horses to a tree hard by. Then, pistol in hand, she advanced, and signalled the man to stop, which he did.

"Good friend," she said, "I do not desire to kill thee, so come no nigher. Nor do I want any but a few of the papers in yon bags. Wherefore, go back, I pray you, to the inn for one brief hour; and then, when you return, you shall find your horse and your bags all safe in this spot; and you may take the news to Berwick as fast as you will!"

A strange bewilderment had taken possession of the man, or else there was something very compelling in the presence and pistol of Grizel, for he turned back slowly and walked away, whilst the girl went back to her precious bags.

These were soon opened and the mere private letters tossed aside. Here was a likely looking bundle of great parchments with the seals upon them, which told that they had come from high places. With a beating heart Grizel tore open this bundle and looked at its contents. Her head seemed to swim and her cheek grew white as her eyes read the fatal words that doomed her father to death. There were other parchments, too, with lighter sentences of fine or imprisonment for others—some of them friends—who had taken part in the recent insurrection. All these she took with her, carefully hiding them upon her person; tied up the bags, replaced them upon the tethered horse, and, mounting her own, set spurs to him, and never drew rein till she was safe within the walls of Berwick, and within the friendly shelter of a kinsman's house.

With a beating heart Grizel tore open this bundle and looked at its contents.

Here, with bated breath, she told her tale, and showed the priceless papers. Here Donald found her, bringing tidings that the whole town was ringing with the news of how His Majesty's mails had been robbed by a daring young highwayman. Here, by a blazing fire, Grizel destroyed, one by one, the fatal documents that else would have desolated so many homes; and whilst soldiers were going forth to scour the country round for the youth who had done that daring deed, and who was regarded as a member of some regular gang, Grizel, in her own attire, was quietly riding away towards Edinburgh from her kinsman's house, with the old serving-man in attendance at her side.

It was dusk one evening when Grizel found her way to her mother's room, and, kneeling down beside the bed, broke quite unexpectedly into convulsive weeping. Nature was taking her revenge at last; but Lady Cochrane sat up, and, folding her arms about her daughter, cried in a strangled voice:

"The will of God be done, my child. No one can achieve the impossible!"

Grizel could not speak; she tried many times, but always broke down, and suddenly there were sounds in the house of confusion and excitement, the door was burst open, and two of the younger girls broke in.

"Mother, mother, all Edinburgh is ringing with the news! A young highway robber has stopped the messenger who was bringing our father's death-warrant, and it has been stolen, and other expected papers too. And there can be nothing done to him till the news has gone to London, and the messenger has returned with a new warrant. And that will mean time!—time!—time! And if our grandfather's letter be true: why time is all we need!"

The mother's face had turned from red to white, and from white to red. Grizel's was hidden in the bed-clothes. Her sisters thought her overcome by the news they had brought.

"Ask me nothing, mother, yet," gasped Grizel, when they were alone together, "I will tell all when my father is pardoned!"

Great was the stir and excitement that prevailed when the story of the robbery became known. Lady Cochrane herself was so far uplifted by hope as to be able to leave her bed, and drive to the Tolbooth to visit her husband; and thus it came about that she had the joy of being with him when the Earl of Dundonald, who had travelled with the greatest possible speed from London, in terror and almost despair of being in time, was ushered into his son's prison, and fell upon his neck crying:

"Ah, John, John, thou hast been a sad fool, my boy; but the King's Majesty has been pleased to grant thee a pardon, thou art a free man from this hour!"

Then husband and wife fell into each other's arms and wept aloud, whilst the old Earl, after storming up and down, and rating his son for his folly, broke down and wept too; and who so proud and happy as Lady Cochrane as she led her husband home at last, and set him in his own accustomed chair before the fireside!

That night Lord Dundonald had to tell all his tale of how the pardon had been procured; bought practically for many thousand pounds, through the influence of a priest. But little cared the family for aught save the one great fact, they had their loved one home again. His life was safe. He was theirs indeed!

But Sir John missed Grizel from the group. She had slipped away whilst her grandfather's tale was drawing to a close. Why did she not return?

It was old Donald who entered the room after a while and said: "May it please you, master, the young man who stopped the messenger, and robbed the King's mails, craves leave of speech with you, if you will give him a brief audience."

Sir John uttered an eager exclamation of astonishment and pleasure. His wife caught her breath, and her hands began to tremble.

"Let him come in! Oh, bring him here!" was the general cry, and Lord Dundonald added: "Doubtless he comes for his reward, and right willingly will I give it him; for had it not been for that daring deed of his, my labour and my gold would alike have been thrown away. I could never have arrived in time. Thy head would have fallen, John, or ever I had reached Edinburgh. It was with more of despair than of hope that I rode those weary miles. Though something within me always bid me not give up."

It was a large room in which they sat, and the farther end was in deep shadow. All turned with breathless expectancy as Donald come in, bringing with him a slenderly made youth, who wore his hat so deeply drawn over his face that nothing of the features could be seen. Perhaps it was from a lack of knowledge of good manners on his part that he did not remove it upon entering; or perhaps he was too shy to lift his eyes, and observe the presence of ladies. Shyness does occasionally go hand in hand with considerable personal courage.

"This is the youth who robbed the King's mails," said old Donald, in a voice not quite his own.

"My deliverer!" exclaimed Sir John, rising, "and so young and slight, and of such tender years too! How can I ever thank you enough! Pray you, dear sir, come somewhat forward, and let us see the face of one to whom we all owe this great and unspeakable happiness."

Slowly the stranger advanced, at first with drooping head; then suddenly he flung away his downcast air, put up his hand, and snatched off his hat!

There was a cry from all present! The mother clasped her hands together and whispered:

"I knew it! I knew it!"

The Earl stared as though he could not believe the sight of his eyes. The sisters shrieked and broke into incoherent questioning; but Sir John opened his arms uttering no word, and Grizel went straight into them, and hid her face on his breast.

EVA VON GROSS

She lay face downwards upon her pallet bed, in the dim, narrow cell that she had been striving to regard as a home of sanctity and peace. She had torn from her head the stiff, white covering that it had worn for hard upon a year now, and which now seemed ready to stifle her. The long heavy robe of the nun which she wore fell about her in a mass of gloomy drapery. Everything was gloomy here. The narrow walls seemed to hem her in; the loophole window to admit an insufficiency both of air and light. It was all like the narrow, narrow, pent-up life of the cloister to which she had been doomed, and which had by this time become as a very dungeon to her.

"How can I bear it? How can I bear it?" she moaned; "I am so young, so very young. I have not taken the full vows yet. Oh, why would they not let me forth? Why may I not be free? I cannot bear the thought of the long, long years that lie before me—fifty—sixty, perhaps; who can say? The Reverend Mother is over seventy; and one sister lived to be nigh upon ninety. Oh, how did she bear it? How did she bear it?"

The young head sank down upon the hard pillow; a moaning came from the lips that should have been smiling and happy with the dawn of tender womanhood. But on that fair young face there was a look as of fixed despair.

Clasped in her hand was a letter, which seemed the immediate cause of her grief, as in a sense it was; for it was the stern reply sent to her by her parents in response to her passionate appeal to be taken away from the convent, and permitted to live the life of happy girlhood in her father's house, where, as she strove to point out, her place had been set.

"It is some subtle device of the enemy that is tempting thee away from the higher life," her father had written; "thy choice was made. It would be sacrilege that would imperil thy soul's salvation to seek to retrace thy steps."

"I did not choose! I did not choose!" cried Eva, as if in passionate remonstrance with the unseen father; "I was weak from sickness; thou and the priest did persuade me. It all sounded so peaceful, so beautiful, so holy. But I have tried it; and it is not peace, it is not joy. The Church is composed of all holy men and women, and we who are baptised into it become its members, knit into its life. I ask no more. Are these nuns better than other women? No—I say NO! I have watched. I have listened. I have felt. It is not a holy life; it is no holier than what we see led by the saints in the world outside cloister walls. There are saintly nuns, I deny it not; as there are saintly wives and mothers, and saintly maidens and virgins without the cloister wall. It is not the dress, the vow, the life, that makes the saint. It is something far,

far higher. And the Spirit divides His gifts as He will. He is not bound by gates and bars and high imprisoning walls!"

Again the passionate sobs broke forth; and there was a sound as of anger and fierce resolve in that weeping, rather than of mere helpless despair. Eva suddenly sat up, a bright light shining in her eyes, her mouth taking an expression of almost grim determination.

"They cannot force me to ratify my vows at the close of my novitiate! What would happen if I refused? What are the tales that are whispered within these walls of nuns who have been found unfaithful—as they are pleased to term it?"

The girl was silent. There was a tense look upon her face. She was pondering deeply. In her dark eyes there showed from time to time a gleam as of fire. It was plain that within the spirit of this novice of the convent there dwelt a daring and a courage that is not vouchsafed to all.

And whence had come to Eva and to some other of her sister nuns this sudden disgust of convent life?—this sudden conviction that it was not in accordance with the dictates of nature, nor with the scheme of salvation as set down in Holy Writ? How came that convent-bred girl to have glimmerings of a higher calling as a member of the Church, than as just a so-called cloister bride, brought, as it was then believed, in some way nearer perfection by having abandoned the place in the world in which she had been set.

That question is easily answered. Not very long before there had broken from the bonds of monastic life a young monk, Martin Luther by name, who had since then been taking the world by storm, preaching and teaching doctrines of liberty and enlightenment which had made the ears of his listeners tingle. This bold young teacher was related to some friends of two sisters, nuns in the Convent at Nimptsch, where Eva was undergoing her training, and in some way or other many of his writings had been introduced and circulated within the convent walls, with the effect that nine of its inmates, including the young Eva, had become so keenly dissatisfied with the life of seclusion to which they were vowed, that they were making every effort in their power to gain permission to rejoin their own families, and to be taken home by their parents.

But however much men's minds might be working with a sense of impending change—a suspicion that the things in which they had hitherto put their trust were about to fail them, and crumble into dust;—in spite of all the upheaval that was beginning in the Church and in the world, men's minds were not yet prepared for the revolt of nuns from their cloistered homes. The breaking of the solemn vows they had taken still seemed a thing impossible to condone or to permit. Not one of the fathers appealed to had consented to the earnest petition addressed to him. Not one had admitted the arguments by which the cloistered captives had sought to win upon the hearts of those in authority over them. Eva's heart had sunk within her these past days, as the stern replies came back; but she had ever buoyed herself up with the hope that in her case mercy would be shown. She was so young. Her full vows had not been taken. She had pleaded so earnestly. It seemed impossible that her father should not be moved to compassion. And yet his answer was now in her hands, and it was a stern, uncompromising refusal to consider her petition for a moment.

"It was just a temptation of the devil," he concluded.

A step was heard in the corridor without, and Eva quickly resumed her discarded headgear. Order and discipline were strong elements in her present life. What would the Reverend Mother or one of the senior sisters think, if they found her in such dishevelment? But the door had barely opened before she uttered a little cry of joyous relief.

"Oh, Katharine! is it indeed thou?"

It was one of the marks of those who longed to renounce the convent rule, that they had discarded, amongst themselves, their convent names. Katharine von Bora[A] was known as Sister Therese, as Eva was known as Sister Angela to their sister—nuns; but with the longing after home ties had come the longing after home titles. It gave Eva a thrill of joy each time she heard her once familiar name pass the lips of those about her.

[A] Afterwards the wife of Martin Luther.

"My little one, I saw by thy face in the chapel just now, that thou art in trouble. Is it that thou hast had thine answer too?"

Eva held out the crumpled sheet, and the elder nun's eyes quickly ran over the written words. She sighed as she read.

"It is no more than I feared; although so much less than I hoped. The walls and bars of the convent are strong indeed."

"Katharine—ah, sweet Katharine!—do not tell me that thou hast yielded up hope! I would dare so much! I would do so much! If a monk has escaped—like that brave Martin Luther—and nought is done to him, why may not we?"

The elder woman looked searchingly into the eager, quivering face, and caught the light of courage and purpose in the soft, dark eyes. Her own kindled beneath the glance.

"Little one, art thou brave enough, and discreet enough to be entrusted with a secret?" asked Katharine, "or wouldst thou rather remain in ignorance until the final moment? There is safety sometimes in ignorance; and thou art little more than a child."

The colour was coming and going in Eva's face; the look of purpose in her eyes deepened each moment.

"Tell me," she whispered, her eyes beginning to shine, "is it that there is hope for us? Can it be that help can reach us, even within these grim, strong walls?"

Katharine glanced round her to be certain that the door of the cell was fast shut. She even moved to it, and looked down the bare corridor, as if to assure herself that there was no spy within hearing. Who could tell, in such a community as that, whether it would not seem the bounden duty of any passing nun to play the eavesdropper, should she harbour for a moment a suspicion that all was not well with her fellow sisters? Who could tell whether or not the Reverend Mother had got wind of the discontent of some of her nuns? Probably she knew somewhat about it, since the appeal of certain of their number to their friends had been made. Might she not have set traps and devices in order to discover whether or not the answers they had received would be sufficient to quiet their discontent, and induce them to settle contentedly in their cloistered home? Would she not be intensely alert to discover if any other phase of revolt were passing in the minds of the imprisoned nuns?

"Thou art brave enough to know the truth and not to betray it?"

"I will die sooner!" cried Eva. "Ah, sweet Katharine, tell me! Is there indeed some hope for us?"

"I trust so. I believe so. We have done what we can. We have made appeal to Martin Luther himself!"

Eva's hands were clasped closely together. Her breath came and went in an ecstasy of excitement and hopeful expectation. The elder woman spoke on in a carefully lowered voice.

"It hath been done through Margaret and Katharine von Zeschau. Thou knowest that their relatives are friends of this Luther's, and that although their parents are still beneath the thrall of the old beliefs, others of their house are beginning to break through the toils. They have the letter, and will place it safely in the hands for whom it is meant. Word came through a safe channel to-day, that we might be assured of this; Martin Luther will never turn a deaf ear to such an appeal. He will rest not until he has answered us, and won for us our liberty!"

A look of ecstasy transfigured Eva's face. She threw her arms about Katharine's neck; her voice quivered as she cried:

"Oh, Katharine!—to be free—to be free! To drink in the pure air of heaven! To see one's life opening before one amid the sweet surroundings of home! To have brothers, sisters, a father and mother once more! But——" and here she paused, and a look of anxiety crossed her face. "But what if our parents refuse to receive us when we are free?"

Katharine's calm face expressed full comprehension. She drew Eva towards her, and they sat close together on the narrow pallet bed. The elder nun supported the quivering frame of her girl companion, as she sought to make her understand the situation.

"There are many things to think of, little one," she said; "and thou must not embark upon such an enterprise not knowing all its risks. First there is the peril to ourselves should this thing get wind before we are safe without the walls."

Eva shivered a little, and clung more closely to Katharine.

"What would they do to us?" she asked in a whisper.

"Nay, I know not. There are many frightful tales of the punishment inflicted upon nuns who have been 'unfaithful to their vows,'" answered Katharine steadily; "thou dost know the bricked-up niche in the crypt beneath the chapel, where they say such an one was walled-up to perish by hunger and thirst."

"Katharine," said Eva suddenly, "is it right to be unfaithful to our vows? We are not doing that which is abhorrent?"

"I think not—and truly believe not," answered Katharine, her eyes glowing and dilating; "and I have spent many a night in prayer and fasting, asking to be led and guided. These vows were forced upon us ere we understood their meaning. They wrapped up the real truth in such a way that we were much deceived. There is a terrible side to convent life which is never breathed beyond the walls. There is a wide-spreading corruption going on that shows to me the system is not Heavenly. God will understand that, in the spirit, our vows to be His for ever will be kept, as far as poor frail flesh can keep them, albeit the letter be broken. I fear not to cast myself upon His mercy in this thing. I know that were I to remain here they could not be kept as truly as they shall and can be without!"

Eva felt a shiver run through Katharine's frame. She only partly understood; but she knew enough to cause her to spring to her feet and cry, although in the instinctively hushed tones that soon become natural to the convent-bred girl:

"Then take me, take me too! I will do anything, I will dare anything, to escape from these terrible walls! I would even face that terrible fate; for is it not a living death to be for ever here without the prospect of release?"

After that the days seemed to go by strangely in the convent. It was Lent; the celebration of the Lord's Passion was drawing very near. The nuns were engrossed in their appointed hours and religious exercises; they grew thin and pale from vigil and fasting; but there was another reason why some of them looked white and careworn. The looked-for answer to their appeal had not reached them yet. Could it be that the thing was too hard for this bold advocate of liberty to attempt?

Good Friday had come. The long exhausting services had been gone through with rigorous exactitude; and the Reverend Mother had now retired to her own room, the nuns being bidden each to her cell, to spend the interval in meditation. Eva felt a light touch upon her arm as she was leaving the chapel. Katharine's voice in her ear spoke in the softest whisper:

"Come to my room."

A sudden hope flooded Eva's heart. She dared not lift up her eyes lest they should betray her. She continued her soft walk with drooping head and hushed footfall; but there was a clangour in her temples of the young blood coursing there, and she was asking herself a thousand eager questions as she slipped like a ghost past her own door, and to the apartment of Katharine von Bora, where, to her amazement, there were gathered together the whole party of those nuns who desired escape, a look of strained expectancy upon all faces.

When Eva entered, Katharine closed and locked the door, and flung the key through the open window into the courtyard below. There was something in her aspect so resolute and tense, that Eva's heart leapt up within her, and she cried:

"Katharine—tell me—ah, tell me!"

"They have promised to come for us to-night," answered the other Katharine. "We are to wait here for the signal. When it comes we are to drop noiselessly into the court below, and they will have means to convey us over the wall and away! It seemed a good day; all the world resting and exhausted after the day's exercises. Suspicion dulled, we trust. We may hear the signal at any moment now. Pray heaven it comes speedily!"

They were all trembling with excitement and a nervous terror that was inevitable in their reduced condition. Katharine von Bora looked round upon the ring of white faces, and said:

"If we have been betrayed;—if the thing is known—and who can be certain that it is not? Spies abound within cloister walls, as women have found to their cost ere now;—if it be known we shall be captured, and our punishment will not be light. If any is afraid, there is yet time to turn back. Let none who is faint-hearted seek the perils of flight!"

Her eyes dwelt chiefly upon the tender flower-like face of Eva. Her love for the youthful novice was deep and tender. She longed for her to escape from the terrible bondage of the convent; but what if they should be discovered and brought back? She could bear the thought for herself; but for Eva——

But there was no fear in Eva's face as she read the thought in the eyes of her friend. The pulsations of her heart seemed to become quiet and regular; her gaze was steady and fearless. She was the youngest and tenderest of all that band; but there was no tremor in her tones as she said:

"Heaven will help us, I am sure of it. Have we not been asking it? But even if not, let me go with you. Far better is death itself, than a living death within these pitiless walls."

"The signal! the signal!" cried a strangled voice from the window; and Magdalene von Staupitz, who had been leaning out with straining ears, held up her hand to enforce instant silence.

They all heard it then; the rumble of wheels, and the careless whistling by the driver of a familiar tune, agreed upon as the signal of approaching help.

The room in which they were assembled was quite dark, save for the dying twilight of the April evening. The bars of the casement had been carefully filed through before, and could be removed noiselessly now with a single wrench. The courtyard was not far below; and the sisters helped each other to drop silently down into it, having selected this particular window on the north side of the convent, as being most remote from danger of observation.

Eva was the last to descend; she was so light and bird-like in her movements, that having helped to lower the others, she found no trouble in hanging by her hands from the sill, and dropping lightly into the arms of her sister nuns, as she fancied. To her astonishment, and for a moment to her terror, she found herself confronted by a goodly youth of fine proportions, but, of course, a perfect stranger to her, who set her gently on her feet with the reassuring words:

"Your pardon, sweet maid; but time presses, and your companions are being hurried over the wall to the waggon. They tell me you are the last. So let us lose not another moment."

He took her hand and led her across the courtyard, the beating of her heart sounding in her ears like the clangour of an alarm-bell in the tower overhead. Suppose this was a trap? Were they walking blindfold to their destruction? For a moment her feet faltered; but a strong hand upheld her, and a voice spoke in her ear with masculine reassurance:

"Fear not, sweet lady. Having so far succeeded, we will not give you up without such a struggle as shall set all Germany in a blaze!" He looked at the fair face beneath the nun's coif, and added with sudden fire and chivalry: "I would lay down my life to save you from all hurt!"

Eva felt herself quivering and tingling all over. The blood was racing through her veins as it never seemed to do within those stagnating cells. The next instant she found herself being helped up a ladder to the top of the wall, and immediately a pair of strong arms lifted her, and she was placed beneath the friendly covering of a waggon, where she felt, rather than saw, that her friends were all packed together.

"Ladies," spoke the voice of the elder man, "we must ask you, for awhile at least, to consent to somewhat cramped quarters. There are a dozen big barrels in the waggon. Each is roomy enough to hold a human being. The only safe way in which we can convey you through the country we have to traverse is by concealing you in these barrels. I trust you will not find the captivity a very oppressive one."

Instantly there was willing bustle and confusion, as the nuns joyfully concealed themselves within the great casks, which were sufficiently roomy to permit of their squatting down upon the thick layer of straw considerably provided, whilst the air-holes previously bored gave them ample breathing space when the tops were fastened down.

Eva was helped into her cask by the youth who had caught her on her descent from the window, and whom she heard the elder man address sometimes as "Leonard." He picked up a rug from his own seat upon the box, and tucked it about her to make her nest softer; and when she looked up with a grateful smile, and asked:

"Whither are we going, fair sir?" he answered eagerly:

"We take you first to Dr. Martin Luther, who has arranged all this. But afterwards you will be housed and sheltered by some of the good citizens of Wittemberg, till it be seen whether or not your parents will receive you back. But even if not, methinks there will be other happy homes speedily open to you. My mother is even now hoping to house and shelter some of you. Wilt thou be willing to trust thyself to my mother's gentle care?" And as he spoke young Leonard leaned a little nearer, and just touched Eva's hand with his.

She felt a strange thrill run through her frame. She was half-terrified, half-delighted. It was like a strange dream, this tent-like waggon, with its heavy cover, and the gleam of the lantern that lighted up the rows of casks with their living occupants, and shone upon the flushed and eager face of the handsome youth, and the grave bearded countenance of his father. It recalled to her a thousand blissful dreams of childhood, when she had revelled in the romances and stories of knights errant and bold heroes. As the light was shut out from her eyes, and she felt the heavy waggon begin to move on, she realised that the first and worst of the peril was past. They had escaped! They were outside the convent walls! They had broken the chain which bound them!

Peril might still menace them for awhile; but at least they had achieved something. Eva had a feeling, which she was almost afraid to analyse too closely, that "Leonard" would fight a very grim and determined battle before he would let her be carried back to the gates of the cloister.

Many were the halts and interruptions of the journey; and many times did Eva's heart seem almost to stop beating, as a voice would ask close in their ears, as it seemed:

"What have you here in this waggon?"

"Barrels of herrings," was the reply, made in a grumbling tone from the driver; "barrels of herrings, and a very slack market for them since Easter is so nigh. I should have had them before; but there was delay, and now nobody wants our wares."

Eva had fallen asleep, and her sleep was so sound that she was startled at last on waking suddenly, to find the sunlight illuminating the bright world. The head had been taken from her cask, and the tall, handsome youth was looking eagerly down upon her, saying with a smile and a blush:

"Mistress Eva, you are safe now. Dr. Martin Luther wishes to welcome you with the rest. And when you have refreshed yourself, and changed your attire, my father and I are to have the honour of welcoming you and Mistress Katharine von Bora under our humble roof, there to await the result of such representations as will be made by you to your parents."

Eva never forgot that memorable breakfast taken in presence of the great man, whose name was becoming a household word throughout the length and breadth of the land.

She remembered less clearly the drive to Torgau with Councillor Koppe and his son Leonard. It was like a dream to sit in a coach, attired in the ordinary garb of a citizen maiden, and to be in conversation with a handsome youth like Leonard, whose devotion never allowed her a moment's anxiety or a single ungratified wish.

But the motherly kindness of Frau Koppe was worth all the rest to Eva, when that worthy matron opened her arms and folded her in a loving embrace. And when it came out at last that her offended parents declined to receive her home, Eva could meet the disappointment bravely; for had she not found a second home and second mother in Torgau; and what was to hinder her speedy marriage with Leonard, when both knew their own hearts so well?

EMMA FITZ-OSBORN

"The King forbids the marriage!"

Raoul de Gael sprang from his seat beside his betrothed, and stared with incredulous astonishment into the face of the bearer of this piece of strange tidings.

The beautiful Emma lifted her head and gazed wonderingly into the dark, stern face of her brother.

"The King forbids the marriage!" repeated Roger Fitz-Osborn, a dark flush gathering upon his cheek, as his anger slowly kindled and rose; "he has sent a special courier across the sea with his Royal mandate, but no word of reason to explain his tyranny. Are we to be the slaves and chattels of the man we have made?"

"The King forbids the marriage?" repeated Emma, in her clear, ringing tones; "and by what right does the King forbid it? Does he not owe to our father the crown that he wears so proudly upon his head? And are we to become the slaves of the man in whose cause our father spent his blood and money, and at last his life itself? Oh, shame!—shame!—shame!"

A thunder-cloud rested on the brow of the bridegroom-elect; that swarthy Breton face was capable of expressing the extreme of haughty passion and resentment. He paced the long apartment to and fro like a wild beast in its cage. Then he went up to Emma and took her hand in his.

"Dost thou fear the anger of this King, who, but a few short years ago, was but the Duke of Normandy? whose title to the broad realm of England would never have been won but for the aid of thy noble father, and of men like ourselves, who have fought and conquered by his side? Dost thou fear his Royal displeasure?"

Emma threw back her head, and looked into her lover's eyes. The blood of a soldier race ran in her veins.

"I fear nothing," she answered, with simple sincerity.

"Spoken like a Fitz-Osborn!" cried her brother, whose pride and self-esteem had been stung to the quick by the haughty mandate from the Conqueror, and who had himself favoured the marriage of his beautiful sister to his brother-in-arms and chiefest friend, and had completed every arrangement for the ceremony, which was to take place almost immediately.

Roger Fitz-Osborn was Earl of Hereford by right of sword, as Raoul de Gael was Earl of Norfolk. Both had distinguished themselves by their bravery in the war which had made William of Normandy King of England, and had received these earldoms in recognition of their services. William the Conqueror was at this time in his own native land, having left the Primate Lanfranc in temporary charge of England. During this breathing space the warriors had had time to think of other matters than the excitement of arms. Raoul had paid a visit to Roger in his new and stately castle, and the beauty and grace of Emma had so completely won his heart that they had become affianced in a few weeks' time, and he was already urging on an immediate marriage.

Such a marriage was entirely to the mind of the brother, and as for Emma, her heart had been won by the attractions and manly beauty of Raoul, whose fierce temperament seemed to find its complement in her lofty courage.

Such a thing as any opposition upon the King's part never once entered the minds of any of the parties concerned. Nor has it ever been made clear why the Conqueror raised this objection, and by his haughty mandate alienated the allegiance of some of his most faithful followers.

Had there been time for the journey to and fro, perhaps the brother might have crossed the sea and returned with the Royal assent, and the subsequent tragedy might have been averted; as it was, the mandate only reached them a few days before the wedding was to be celebrated. They were already assembled at Norwich Castle, where (in spite of its being the bridegroom's home) the ceremony was to take place, guests were even now flocking in to witness the marriage and attend the subsequent feast. To be forced to give out that the bridal could not take place owing to the prohibition of the King was a thing abhorrent to the proud spirits of Roger and Raoul, whilst the equally high spirit and courage of Emma revolted against the imperious intermeddling of the King, who but a short while since had been nothing but a noble himself, and whose recent sudden rise in power was greatly owing to the support of the very families whose happiness he now sought to mar.

It wanted but a little to arouse in many hearts a sense of revolt and anger against the absent William. No man can rise so suddenly to such power without raising up a host of enemies amongst those who begin to feel the iron hand of monarchy, where once was only the clasp of a friend. The genius of the Conqueror had won him a kingdom, supported by the loyal assistance of the Norman and Breton nobles; but he had not always been careful to conciliate his friends, even though he had not been backward in bestowing upon them broad lands and new titles. Sometimes the very wealth and power thus placed within their reach became, in some sort, a snare to them. Dreams of ambition are ever quick to rise when angry men get together, and are heated with wine; and during the days which intervened between the arrival of the King's message and that fixed for the marriage ceremony, there were fierce and eager discussions between hot-headed nobles, young and old; and a wave of rebellious hatred seemed to be sweeping them along as they discussed the tyranny of the newly made monarch, and spoke together in angry, threatening tones, or in still more dangerous whispers of the possibility of bringing about a better state of affairs in the country, and one more distinctly advantageous to themselves. If William had so easily conquered the kingdom and established his own power, perchance that power might again be easily displaced.

The spirit of anger and discontent is easily aroused, and Raoul and Roger resolved to defy the King; yet, half afraid of the consequences of their defiance, knowing well the implacable nature of the man with whom they had to deal, they were eager to win to their way of thinking all those nobles who were assembling to do honour to bride and bridegroom; and certainly it seemed as though the spirit of disaffection were not hard to wake.

"If Waltheof would but join us we might rouse all England against the Conqueror!" whispered Raoul into the ear of his betrothed upon the night before their nuptials, as he spoke his fond farewell; and Emma's eyes glowed, for she knew Earl Waltheof well as a great and warlike man, whose popularity with his own countrymen would render him an invaluable ally, supposing that this sudden wave of rebellious impulse were to break forth into actual insurrection. Girl though she was, she had lived in an atmosphere of strife, and the sound of battle or the clash of arms had no terrors for her. Anger was in her heart against the King, and she cared little if her brother and her future lord chose to take up arms against him. Sooner than submit to his tyrannous decree, she would fight with her own hands, and shed the last drop of her blood. For what was life without Raoul?

Very lovely was the face of the young bride beneath its drooping veil, as, in the midst of a stately gathering, she plighted her troth to the man of her choice.

The deed was done. The King's mandate had been defied. A subject was in open revolt. The realisation of this came home to all those present as the fatal words were spoken. William was not a man either to forget or to forgive. The gauntlet had been thrown down—what next?

The wedding guests sat at the long tables in the great banqueting hall. Bride and bridegroom, together with all the nobles and men of high degree, sat at the table on the raised daïs, the others of lesser degree at the tables in the body of the hall. Normans and Bretons were there, together with a sprinkling of English, Earl Waltheof, who had married the Conqueror's niece, the afterwards infamous Judith, being one of them. But his wife was not with him, else perchance even the boldest had not dared to speak so openly.

It was as if (after the wine cups had gone round many times, and men's hearts were inflamed by good cheer and by the whispers that had been circulating with the cups) some sudden impulse came upon them, for a murmur arose, and the murmur waxed louder and more fierce, and suddenly a cry seemed to shake the rafters of the hall:

"Down with the Usurper! Who is he that he should reign over us? What is he better than others? Down with him! Let us divide the realm, and choose Kings of our own!"

Then came isolated voices crying fierce questions:

"Did he not poison Conon, our brave Count of Brittany?"

"What has he done for us, who shed our blood for him?"

"Has he fulfilled the promise he made?"

"He gave us barren lands for our wounds, and what does he do when we have made them of some value? Does he not take them from us by force, to give them to some new favourite?"

"Down with him!—Down with him!—Shall we call such a man our King?"

The deed was done! The die was cast. The banner of revolt was raised. The assembled company knew that already they had gone too far to draw back. The King would hear of this thing, and would never forgive. Action must now follow hard upon words. The Conqueror was absent; much might be done ere the news of insurrection reached him. Not one of those precious days must be lost.

With the first light of the new day the bride stood watching the departure of her brother and her lord. Roger was to travel night and day with all speed to Hereford and beat up his followers and the hardy Welsh on his borders, with whom he had maintained friendly relations. Raoul was to collect forces nearer at hand in his own earldom; but he must needs go in person, and to his girl-wife he left the care of the grim castle which had been the scene of yesterday's wedding and feast, and which was garrisoned with black-browed Bretons, devoted to the service of their master, and ready to lay down their lives for his beautiful bride.

Did her heart fail her as she saw the departure of her husband, her brother, and their noble guests, together with the armed followers which they had brought? Did she feel fear in the knowledge that she and they were now accounted rebels, and that any day might bring an armed force before the walls of Norwich?

No; there was no spark of fear in her heart, though there was for one moment a glint of tears upon her long lashes as she saw her lord and master ride away, and knew that peril threatened him and his comrades in arms, so soon as it should become known that they were in revolt.

She set herself, as a true soldier's daughter and bride, to see to the defences of the castle. The Breton garrison were true as steel. They had no love for Norman or English; but they loved their lord, and for his sake, as well as her own, they loved his sweet young bride; the sight of her courage and devotion kindled new ardour in their breasts day by day, and they toiled with all the energy in their power to strengthen the stone walls, to obtain supplies of food and such munitions of war as were needed in those days, and to prepare themselves for whatever might betide.

Rumours were flying hither and thither, rumours of strife and of disaster. It was said that Roger of Hereford was cut off from returning, and was penned in behind the broad waters of the Severn; and again there was a whisper nearer at home that Odo, the warlike Bishop of Bayeux, was in the vicinity with a force of finely equipped men. On hearing this Emma's cheek grew pale; not with fear for herself, but lest some hurt should befall her lord, whom she had as yet scarcely learned to speak of as "husband."

The watchman upon the tower had blown a warning blast. Something was in sight; the horn sounded forth again and yet again.

There was hurrying within the walls of the castle, archers hastening to their loopholes, and men at arms buckling on their helmets and breastplates, and seizing their good broad-swords in readiness for the word of command.

Emma, breathless and dishevelled, raced to the tower herself, and, as she looked, she beheld a scattered band of fugitives, flying, as it were, towards the castle; and so forlorn and woe-begone was the aspect they bore that her heart seemed to die within her.

"Bretons, to the rescue of your brethren!" she suddenly cried aloud, and the cry was taken up and passed from mouth to mouth. Wide swung the great gates, down sank the drawbridge; the soldiers streamed forth to meet the flying Bretons and Saxons, who came in crowds for the protection of those strong walls, bringing with them the gloomy tale of death and disaster.

Late in the day, conducting a ghastly company of maimed and mutilated men, who had been bold stalwart soldiers a few days before, rode Raoul into the courtyard, the blackness of night upon his brow; and Emma rushed forth to clasp her husband to her heart, scarce knowing yet what was the meaning of the things she saw and heard.

"It means ruin to our hopes of life and liberty, if we cannot yet change defeat into victory," said the young Earl, as he let his bride divest him of his heavy armour, whilst he told the tale of his overthrow at the hands of Bishop Odo.

"Many died of their wounds; but some few I rescued, and have brought them hither to thee, my sweet bride. But for myself I may not linger. Our only hope now lies in getting help from beyond the sea. I must take ship with all speed to mine own domains in Brittany, and there, when this tale is told, methinks they will rise to a man in the defence of their brethren, in answer to my call, in the hope of vengeance and plunder! I will return with an army at my back, and William, the so-called Conqueror, shall yet learn to quake at the names of Raoul de Gael and Roger Fitz-Osborn!"

"And my brother?—what of him?" asked Emma, "will he go with thee? And wilt thou take me too?"

"Nay, my life, I must leave thee here to hold this fortress for me. Roger is penned in the west; albeit he will break loose I doubt not ere long, and march day and night to thine assistance. But our Breton garrison must needs serve under one they can trust and love. Sweet, my bride, hast thou the courage for the task? Though thou art so young in years, thou hast the heart of a soldier. Wilt thou hold the castle here against proud William's forces, till I or Roger come to thine aid?"

She looked him full in the face.

"Thou dost think that they will follow and lay siege?"

"They are so close behind me, that with the first dawn of the morning I must be gone, else I shall be too late to escape them!" answered Raoul; and his eyes rested with anxious questioning upon Emma's face. "Our poor Bretons are treated with savage ferocity by the English," he added. "If I lead them forth hence, and they fall into the Bishop's hands—well, thou hast seen with thine own eyes how their brethren have fared."

The fire flamed in Emma's eyes; she threw back her head with her own queenly gesture.

"Go, then, my husband, and I will guard thy castle for thee. I will keep safe those thou dost leave with me. Go! fly over the water, and return with the friends of the cause. Thou shalt find thy castle here, safeguarded as though thou thyself wert at the head of thy soldiers. The pitiless Bishop shall not lay hands on one of our Breton boys!"

So the brave young bride was left for the second time alone in the grim castle, to hold it for her lord till he should arrive with succour. But this time she was quickly ringed round with foemen, who, in the King's name, bade her surrender; and when she fearlessly refused, they laid close siege to the castle, vowing to serve every Breton they should henceforward take as those hapless creatures had been served, some of whom she was tending now with her own hands within the walls of the grim old keep.

Emma had grown up inured to perils, to hardships, to the sights and sounds of warfare, and warfare is always cruel. But her soul revolted against needless cruelties; and the sufferings of the poor maimed followers of her husband, who had been rescued and brought back by him, nerved her to every effort to keep from a like fate those who served her faithfully here, and looked to her to save them from it.

Parted from her husband upon their very wedding day, wife only in name as yet, the brave daughter of William Fitz-Osborn played the hero's part during those three long months of siege. Every day she made the circuit of the fortifications, careless of the flights of arrows that often made such exposure of her person a perilous matter; she spoke words of encouragement to the archers and watchmen; she devised ingenious methods of frustrating the various attempts made by the wily and determined foe for cutting off supplies, and for forcing an entrance into the castle.

When it was known that a woman was in command, many devices were practised for intimidating her and her soldiers; but all in vain; and free promises of pardon for herself if she would but betray her trust were answered with indignation and scorn.

The hard part of it to the brave young chatelaine was the uncertainty of what was passing elsewhere. Penned within the four walls of her eastern fortress, she knew nothing as to the fate of her brother in the west, nor how the rebellion against the Conqueror was spreading in the ranks of the disaffected Norman barons and the dispossessed Saxons. It had seemed to her, upon their wedding feast, as though all the realm was weary of the rule of "the Norman." Yet if that were so, if the revolt were ready to break forth all over the kingdom, why did none come to her aid? Surely her brother and others must know of the peril in which she stood. Why did not some of them seek to raise the siege? Why did not Raoul himself return with his Breton reinforcements?

As the long summer days went by, one after another, and weeks dragged on to months, brave Emma's cheek grew pale, and her eyes took a wistful yearning gaze, as of one whose heart is sick with hope deferred. But her vigilance was never for a moment relaxed. Her courage never faltered. Day by day she was to be seen upon the ramparts, speaking brave words to the weary soldiers, hurling lightning glances of defiance at the lines of the besiegers, and gazing with eager, expectant eyes in the direction of the sea, asking of the birds of the air whether they had seen the white sails of the coming vessels that should bring relief to her.

At last the voice of rumour reached even this beleaguered castle. First it was an isolated whisper, then other whispers followed. Bit by bit the story of woe was pieced together, and a fugitive from the west, who had been sent with dispatches for the Lady Emma, contrived to gain entrance, and to tell all the tale.

It was said that the treacherous Judith, wife of Earl Waltheof, had learned the secret from her husband and had instantly betrayed it. The rebellion had been quelled almost ere it broke out. In the west the son of Fitz-Osborn had been taken captive, and was awaiting his doom on the return of the King. Others had been taken or slain; Norwich alone was holding out. Raoul had sent word that to return from Brittany was now impossible. It would be but to fall into the hands of an implacable foe. His word to his bride was to secure such terms as she could for herself and her garrison, and to make her way across the sea with all speed to join her husband there.

With whitening cheek and sinking heart Emma heard and read all this evil news. Her brother a captive, her husband an exile, their friends scattered and dispersed. Surrender inevitable! But what was she to surrender? This very messenger brought horrid tales of mutilation and cruelties of all sorts inflicted on hapless prisoners by their bloodthirsty conquerors. Was she to give up to such a fate the brave men who had learned to look to her and trust in her? For the castle she cared little. Where her husband was, there was her home. But her soldiers and servants, were they to be given up? Never! Never! Never!

"I will go forth and die at their head, fighting to the last, sooner than that!" she cried.

The Bishop had many times sought to open negotiations with the brave Emma, but hitherto fruitlessly. Now, with her own hand, she penned him a missive, offering to surrender to him the castle and its munitions of war, but only on the condition that every living creature within its walls went forth unharmed, and that they should be permitted to take ship unmolested for the shores of Brittany.

"Else will I never give up whilst one stone remains upon another. You shall see how long the daughter of William Fitz-Osborn can bid defiance to the man whom her father made England's King."

Was it chivalry, was it admiration for the spirit of the brave woman, or was it the policy of a soldier wearied by a long three months' siege of a fortress that seemed no nearer falling now than it had done upon the first day?

Whatever was the motive for the concession, the answer that came back was courteously, even generously worded. The brave young wife rode forth at the head of her whole garrison, and the Norman soldiers who had fought against the rebels in other places raised a shout of admiration as she appeared. She sat her horse like an Amazon, and returned the salutation with a dignity worthy of her name and race.

Saluting and being saluted by the Bishop, and lustily cheered by the soldiers, she passed through the town on her way to the coast, where vessels were awaiting her, while her men marched boldly behind her, singing the songs of their native land to which they were about to return, and chanting aloud the praise of the beautiful Emma to whose courage and resolution they owed their lives.

She and her band of devoted Bretons were thus permitted to march to the coast with all the honours of war, and to take ship for her husband's domains in Brittany without receiving insult or violence of any kind.

How high her heart was beating as she sighted the shore, and knew that her lord was awaiting her there, in that home which she had never yet seen! True, she was sad for her brother, and for the cause which had been lost in England; but after all, was not her husband safe, and waiting for her to rejoin him? and might not the tide turn some day, and they return to England in triumph, to help to overthrow the rule of Norman William, against whom they had sought to incite this rebellion?

These were fond hopes not destined to be realised. The courage and state-craft of William the Conqueror carried him safely through all the plots which assailed him during his stormy reign. Raoul de Gael knew where he was safe, and abandoned his claims upon English soil.

"I did well indeed to entrust my castle to the keeping of my bride!" cried the proud husband, when he held her in his arms once more; and the answer that went up from a thousand throats was a shout of admiration and praise in honour of their lord's fair young wife, the brave Emma Fitz-Osborn.

ELIZABETH STUART

A princess, yet a captive in the hands of her father's foes; those foes who were already whispering their fell intention of putting him to death!

This was the situation of the youthful Elizabeth, the second daughter of the ill-fated monarch, Charles I. Her mother and her eldest brother were beyond the seas, having made good their escape from Cromwell and his Roundheads; but she, with her two brothers, James, Duke of York, and Henry, Duke of Gloucester, were captives in the power of the Parliament, and though treated with courtesy and a certain kindliness, they were permitted no liberty to come and go, or even to write to their friends. Every action was carefully observed, and their persons were so closely guarded that there was little hope of evading the many watchful eyes that were ever bent upon them.

"If I could but reach my brother and our mother!" was the exclamation ever on the lips of James, when he and his sister were alone together. It seemed to the high-spirited boy that once free from these encircling walls and the vigilance of his warders, once across the sea to join the others of his name and race, he must surely achieve some great thing for the deliverance of his father; his restless mind was ever pondering this theme. The thought of making good his escape was never absent from his mind night nor day.

Perhaps he plotted almost too much for his own success; for a day came when he was summoned to an interview with certain of the Parliamentary authorities, and he returned to his sister's apartments with flushed face and flashing eyes. Elizabeth saw that he had been deeply angered by what had passed, and she quickly got rid of her attendant, that she and her brother might speak in peace together. This liberty was the only one accorded to the Royal captives. Their rooms were guarded; they never went abroad unwatched and unattended; but within the precincts of the palace they had some privacy permitted to them, and they could speak together without being overheard, though never without a fear of possible eavesdroppers.

"Sister, I have been grossly insulted!" cried James, with flashing eyes; "they have intercepted my letter to our sister of Orange; they said they had discovered treasonable matter in it."

"Treasonable matter!" echoed Elizabeth, her breath coming and going. "They dare to talk of treason!—They!"

"Ay; that was the very word—treasonable matter! They saw, or thought they saw it, in my desire to quit the country—to escape to Holland——"

"But the letter was in cypher," interrupted Elizabeth. "How could they read it when they had it?"

A dark frown clouded the brow of James.

"That I did not condescend to inquire; but I heard some talk between those knaves themselves. I gathered that they had got the letter, and had then sent for the Earl of Northumberland, and had shown him how we had evaded his vigilance; had warned him, that if he could not find the key of the cypher in which it had been written, he should be committed to the Tower. Did I not tell you the other day that I was certain my effects had been ransacked? I did not miss the cypher key. I know it so well that I scarce ever have to look at it now. Doubtless they found and took it away; but I did not observe it."

"And they were angry with you, James?"

"Angry? Ay, that they were. They dared to threaten me with the Tower, too, if they found me plotting escape again!"

Elizabeth clasped her hands closely together, her face worked with the emotion she strove to master. She came and stood beside James, and laid her soft cheek against his.

"Jamie, Jamie," she cried piteously, "if they were to take you from me, I think that I should die!"

He put his arm about her, and they stood together, looking out of the window, thinking and pondering deeply.

"But, sister, you would have to learn to live without me if I were to escape this thraldom, and win my liberty. Could you bear to let me go for that?"

A little tremor ran through the girl's slight frame. She was very frail and delicate, this gentle, young Elizabeth; little fit to bear the buffets of outrageous fortune, to stand alone in her strange captivity; cut off from father, mother, friends, and kindred, and beset with so many cruel anxieties and fears on behalf of those she loved best. Her greatest solace in these sorrowful days was the companionship of her brother James, who, being a year or more her senior, and endowed with robust health, seemed like a tower of strength to the frail girl, hardly more than a child in years, though misfortune had given a strange maturity to her mind and disposition. It could not but be a dismal thought to lose the constant companionship of this brother, to send him forth into the perils of the great world without, where so many foes awaited him. She might well have sought to keep him beside her, fearing the perils of any project of escape; but despite her natural fears and shrinkings, and the delicacy of her frame, the spirit of kings and warriors was within her, and that spirit rose to meet the sacrifice which might be required of her.

"I would bear to let you go for that, Jamie," she answered. "But it would break my heart were you taken from me to be immured within the walls of the Tower."

"It may come to that one of these days," said James, "if I be not able to effect my escape. I cannot show the patience that you are able to command; and I am not a child like Harry, there, of whose words and acts no special note is taken. And did not our father bid me use every effort to regain my liberty, and reach the side of our mother and brother? It may be that already they are planning how to invade these shores, summon all loyal hearts to join them, and set my father on the throne once more! Oh! if such a thing were to happen, I must be there to help."

His eyes kindled, his frame seemed to expand and grow tense; and an answering thrill ran through that of the young Princess.

"Ah, Jamie, Jamie, if only it might be!" she cried.

"And why not, sister, why not? Other captives have escaped from far stricter bondage than any we suffer from. What one has done another may do. Why not?"

"But they were men, and we are so young. We are scarce more than children, albeit often I feel so old—so old!"

"You are old enough to have the ready wit of a woman!" cried James; yet even in his stress of feeling and excitement he kept his voice pitched in a low key. "I have thought and thought and planned, but everything falls to the ground; or we are betrayed into the hands of our enemies, and threatened with stricter captivity than this. Elizabeth, put your wits to work! Can you think of nothing? In bygone days it has been the women sometimes who have done the thinking, whilst the men have done the acting. Why should it not be so now?"

The boy's dark, strenuous face looked earnestly into the fair spiritual one of his sister, and into the cheeks of the young Elizabeth a faint colour stole.

"Oh, Jamie, I will try: I will try!" she answered. "But even could I think of some stratagem or plan by which you could gain the freedom of the world without, who is there outside that would dare to help you away across the sea, whom we could dare to trust with such a secret?"

"There is Colonel Bamfield," answered James promptly. "He is the man whom I would trust for that."

"Colonel Bamfield?" echoed Elizabeth doubtfully. "He who turned traitor to our father's cause when all was lost? Would you trust such an one as he?"

"He is not a traitor at heart," whispered James eagerly. "He is the staunchest friend we have. He has but feigned adherence to the Parliamentary cause that he may the better serve us. I have had speech with him, sometimes, for a few minutes. I trow he is to be trusted. And as our enemies know that none is so bitter as a renegade, they think he is our deadly foe. They do not suspect him as they would suspect others. He plays his part right cunningly. He rails upon the King and his brood most lustily; but all the while he is on the watch to serve us. I know, could I once escape from these walls, that he would make all the rest easy."

There were footsteps without, and brother and sister started apart, as the attendants entered the room on some pretext. They were well used to this sort of thing. They were seldom left long alone together. The little Duke of Gloucester, who had been playing quietly in a corner whilst his brother and sister were talking, now came running up, and begged for a game of hide and seek.

This was one of the favourite sports of the Royal children; but to-night Elizabeth excused herself on the plea of fatigue, and the two young Dukes played alone, running hither and thither, and forgetting their troubles for awhile, in the interest of the game.

Elizabeth sat alone with her face hidden in her hands, thinking, thinking, thinking, till it seemed as though her brain would scarcely stand the strain of the mental conflict going on within her. She was roused from her reverie at last by little Henry, who came and pulled impatiently at her dress.

"Come and help me to find Jamie," he begged. "He has hidden so well we can none of us find him. You come and try!"

Elizabeth rose quickly to her feet; she suddenly felt as though some inspiration had darted into her heart. At the moment she did not pause to examine it. She felt that when night came, and she was alone in the darkness, she must take out this thing that had forced itself with lightning rapidity into her being, and examine it at leisure. Might it be that already the clue was in her hands?

The Royal children were, at this time, under the care of Algernon Percy, the Earl of Northumberland, and his Countess, and it was the desire of both to make the captivity of the Princess and her brothers as little irksome and trying as possible. At the same time, since they were held responsible for their safe-keeping by the Parliament, they dared not but use every precaution; and it was no easy matter for any of the children to escape the vigilance of their guardians.

A short time before this they had been at Sion House, and when there had paid several visits to Hampton Court, to see their father who was in confinement there. Once, not long since, they had spent two nights with him in that Palace, to their great and mutual happiness.

Now they had been removed to the Palace of St. James's, then on the outskirts rather than actually in London itself, and surrounded by pleasant gardens, in which the Royal children took exercise in fine weather. They were very kindly treated by the Earl and Countess, and all the servants of the household were instructed to show due and befitting respect to the children of the King. So, in one sense of the word, their life was not an unhappy one; but the shadow lying over their father's fate, and the knowledge of their own inability to go to him or to go anywhere, save at the will of their captors, made life somewhat bitter to all, and roused a fierce sense of revolt in the heart of young James.

It was during the children's sports that they were permitted most liberty; and certainly James had found a clever place of concealment this evening, for neither brother nor sister nor attendants could find him; and it was only when Elizabeth called his name aloud from the different corridors, and the great bell for supper clanged, that the boy made his appearance, dusty and half covered with cobwebs, and laughingly told Harry that he had found a fine hiding-place up near the roof, and would show it him another day.

The spring days were beginning to lengthen out now. A little while ago it had been dark when they rose from supper, now it was growing lighter every day. There was that promise of spring in the air that makes glad the hearts of all young things. But it is hard to be a captive, penned within walls and gates, when nature itself seems calling aloud upon men to rejoice and to come forth into the gay free world without.

"If it goes on much longer, Elizabeth, methinks I shall go mad!" spoke James one day, when he and she were alone together.

Then it was that, with bated breath and beating heart, Elizabeth whispered into her brother's ear the thoughts and plans which had given her so many sleepless nights of anxiety.

"Jamie, have you ever noticed when we have passed Benyion's cottage, the great key that hangs beside the door? That is the key of the outer garden leading down to the river. I have seen him use it many times as we have walked in the gardens."

"Yes, I have seen him unlock that gate too. What of it?"

"Jamie, if you had that key some evening at dusk, and if we had hidden out yonder in our hollow tree some of my clothes, made to fit you, so that none could suspect you were a boy, could you so arrange that Colonel Bamfield should be awaiting you at the river side with a wherry to take you to some vessel bound for Holland? I have still left a little of the gold that our father entrusted to me. And I am told that seafaring folk will brave much for gold. Colonel Bamfield could arrange all that."

"But how, how could I gain that key and use it at such an hour?" questioned James, in an eager whisper. "How could such a thing be? Are we not followed and watched everywhere?"

"Yet have you not eluded all watchful eyes times without number in your games with Harry? Have we not often searched the house for an hour, and then have had to call you to come to us? If you can elude watchful eyes in play, why not in earnest some day, whilst they think the play is going on, and will make no marvel of missing you for an hour or more? The days are getting long. Let us have our game after supper instead of before. Let us so play night by night for a week or more, that they will not dream we have any motive in the change. Let our friend the Colonel, if he is to be trusted, make his plans. Then, upon a certain night, when all is in readiness, and the boat is lying waiting for you, we will play our hide-and-seek with a difference, and whilst brother and servants are seeking for James within the house, and even the gardens—he will be far down the river, making for the vessel that is to carry him hence."

"But the key, Elizabeth, the key!" cried James, in great excitement; "how can I gain possession of that?"

"Listen, Jamie," answered Elizabeth, "I have thought of that. You must begin to pretend to have exhausted the hiding-places of our portion of the house, and you must ask to-day that the house steward will let you conceal yourself in his pantry. Then the next day get leave of the cook to hide somewhere in the kitchen. Another day be bolder still, and get into the hay-loft, where the coachman will be proud and merry to hide you. And then when the day comes that you ask the gardener for the key of his cottage, to hide you there awhile, neither he nor any other who hears will think it aught but a merry jest. Then as Harry will every day be an hour and more in hunting you, that should be time enough for you to change your attire and slip away through the gate; and if Colonel Bamfield only do his part, you should be out of reach ere the pursuit has fairly begun."

James suddenly flung his arms about his sister's neck.

"Oh! Elizabeth, Elizabeth! and you have thought of all that?"

"I think of nothing else whilst we are playing hide-and-seek night by night."

"And suppose they find out that you were privy to the scheme all the while, what will they do to you, Elizabeth!"

She looked into his eyes, a brave smile on her pale face.

"Think not of that, Jamie; in sooth I care little what they do to me. If you only get safe away let them take me to the Tower, or whither they will. Little Harry is too young to care greatly, so long as we are together; and I do not think they will take him from me, even though they do more straitly confine us."

"But you—what would you do in that grim place?" asked James, with something of a shudder.

"I think all places are alike to me now," answered Elizabeth, with her strangely spiritual smile, pathetic on the face of one so young; "God will take care of us there as well as here. Do not fear for me, Jamie. We must strive to do what our father wished. I shall be happy indeed in knowing that you are safe and free. For my part, I am content in feeling myself near to him, and in knowing that if he is a prisoner—so am I."

Who would have thought, to watch the merry games of the Royal children during the bright spring evenings that followed, what tumultuous thoughts were surging within them, and what a daring plan had been hatched in the brain of that delicate young girl, who so patiently hunted the house, evening by evening, with her little brother, in search of that clever hider, James.

The servants were by this time devoted to the children, who treated them with that invariable high-bred courtesy that never failed the hapless Stuarts, whatever else they might lack or fail in. Coachman, steward, cook, pantler— all were ready to assist the young Duke to some new hiding-place, night by night. They enjoyed the game almost as much as the children themselves. Indeed, they seemed to take a pride in lengthening out the search, though in the end some whispered hint would be given to the little brother if his energies showed signs of flagging, and he would start forth hot upon the scent that would eventually lead him to the hiding-place, if James did not spring out upon him first.

The Earl and Countess were well used to the shouts and cries of little Harry as he ran hither and thither through the house. The Earl generally visited his young charges early in the evening, often just after supper, and then he left them to their games till about nine o'clock, when he attended first the younger Prince, and then the elder to their rooms, and paid them the compliment of superintending in person their toilet for the night.

At last came the long-awaited Friday, the twenty-first day of April. The twilight lingered long now, and the game of hide-and-seek was regularly played after supper, lasting generally till the bedtime of the Duke of Gloucester.

He stopped short on seeing the Countess.

The Countess of Northumberland visited Elizabeth and her brothers this evening, and sat awhile with the Princess after supper. Little Harry was playing in a corner of the room; but the Countess looked rather anxiously into Elizabeth's face, and remarked how white it was.

"But I am not sick, I thank you, Madam," said the girl gently. "Belike it is but the first of the springtide heat. I pray you not to send the doctor. He does but give me physic which I know not how to swallow. I shall be better anon—in a few days, I trust."

At that moment James came running into the room, as though to speak to his sister. He stopped short on seeing the Countess; but then, coming forward, joined in the conversation, and chatted merrily enough. None noted the quick glances that passed between brother and sister, nor the strange wistfulness that brooded in Elizabeth's eyes.

Suddenly James started up, as though just bethinking him.

"Why, Harry, we must have our game; shall I hide again? Then give me five minutes' grace, and come after me!" He looked at Elizabeth, and said, "Wilt thou go with him? Or art thou tired to-night, sister?"

"In sooth, I think she is aweary," said the Countess; and James put his hands on Elizabeth's shoulders, boy fashion, and snatched a kiss from her lips.

"Then go to bed, sweetheart, and one of the servants shall attend Harry," he said; "but he will not be content without his game of play."

The boy was gone, and Elizabeth was thankful that little Harry now claimed the attention of the Countess; for she felt as though every drop of blood had ebbed from her face. What would be the next thing that she heard of her brother?

She could not be persuaded to remain in her room. She roamed all over the house with Harry, whilst the Countess went back to her husband. Harry's bedtime came at last; it was dark outside, save for the light of the moon; the Earl came out, and asked where the boy was, and learned that he was still seeking his brother.

"Then I must needs help find him too," said the good-natured nobleman, taking Harry's hand, and as the child seemed somewhat weary of the search, he looked inquiringly at the servants.

Then one came forward, and whispered that the Duke was hiding in the gardener's cottage, of which he had begged the key; and thither they all proceeded, Elizabeth commanding herself to laugh and chat with Harry, and wonder where next Jamie would hide, and how many more strange places were still left for him to find.

Harry ran gaily into the cottage, when somebody had forced open the locked door for him, at a sign from the Earl, whose face had suddenly clouded over. But ransack as they might, not a trace of the fugitive could be found.

With a stifled exclamation of dismay the Earl dashed down to the water-gate, which he found open. Then the truth flashed across him, and he bit his lips in perplexed confusion.

"Conduct the Princess and the Duke to the house," he said, "we must make further inquiries into this matter!"

Then Elizabeth knew at least that James had escaped from the Palace, though she could not know for many days whether he would succeed in making good his escape to Holland.

She sought the privacy of her own rooms, and, falling upon her knees, gave thanks to God for His great goodness in watching over them thus far.

Every day she expected to hear that some severe punishment was to be inflicted upon her—perhaps even death itself, so little did she understand the laws of the land—for the part she had taken in her brother's escape. But strange to say her own complicity in the plot was never suspected at that time. Her very calmness and courage, which enabled her first to plan the clever scheme and then to go through her own part so tranquilly, averted all suspicion from her.

Even the Earl, when all the facts of the case were known, was exonerated from blame. He had before told the Parliament that he declined absolute responsibility with regard to the Royal children, unless he made actual prisoners of them—a thing he was not prepared to do; and although there was some angry discussion in the House, and several stringent measures were recommended by certain extreme men, yet in the end humane counsels prevailed, and the Princess Elizabeth, together with her little brother, were permitted to remain beneath the kindly care of the Earl and Countess of Northumberland.

James escaped after a few perils, and got safe over to Holland; but the hasty kiss he snatched from his brave young sister upon that April evening was the last he ever gave or took from her.

The girl Elizabeth never recovered the shock of her father's death two years later, and though she lingered for more than a year, winning the hearts of all about her by her sweetness of disposition and the wonderful courage and fortitude she exhibited in the midst of so many trials and sufferings, she passed peacefully away to a world where pain and partings are no more, and where the sorrowful and weary are at rest.

Little Harry was with her to the last, receiving at her hands such few poor possessions as remained to her. A while later, by an unwonted freak of generosity on Cromwell's part, the boy was permitted to join his mother in France.

CHARLOTTE HONEYMAN

"Pirates! Oh, Charlotte, how romantic! How do you know? Are you sure? Oh, how I should love to see a real live pirate!"

Charlotte smiled a little grimly.

"I'm not quite so sure of that, Adela; I rather think if you were to encounter him you would wish he were anything but a live pirate—you would much prefer him dead!"

"What a horrid idea, Charlotte!" and Adela shivered slightly. "But do go on! Tell me some more! I thought there were no pirates left now. Smugglers one knows abound; but pirates!"

"I truly hope that there are not many such wretches in the world as the man Gow seems by all accounts to be," said Charlotte, who, as the daughter of the High-Sheriff of the island and county of Orkney spoke with a certain amount of authority. "If half the tales they tell of him are true, such a monster in human shape has seldom walked the earth. He and his mate Williams have been a pair; but he found his subordinate one too many for him, made him a prisoner, and handed him over to some English man-of-war, under charge of various crimes, and the wretch has probably been hanged ere this. But Gow yet goes scot-free!"

"And is his vessel in one of our bays?" asked Adela, in a tremor of excitement.

"If the man's story be true, who came and asked speech of father last night. He told a wonderful and a terrible tale. Father has gone off to-day to make some particular inquiries into the business. He seems to think very gravely of it."

"And where is this terrible pirate vessel now?"

"We do not know exactly. The seaman who came to seek for a magistrate does not know the coast, and could not describe the place accurately. It is not very near to our homes, thank heaven! We do not want pirates for our neighbours!"

"Oh, but pirates only rob at sea, not upon land," exclaimed Adela; "we need not be afraid. I should love to see what a pirate ship looked like! Does it carry a black flag? And do the men wear crimson sashes round their waists, and black crape masks upon their faces?"

Charlotte laughed a little. From her position as the daughter of the Sheriff she knew a little more of the grim realities of crime than did the younger and romantic Adela, whose pretty head was stuffed with a good deal of nonsense. Sheriff Honeyman was very fond of his "little child," as he still called

Charlotte, notwithstanding the fact that she had blossomed out into maidenhood of late years, and had left her childhood behind. She was always ready for a clamber along the cliffs with him, or a ride across the bare country on her sure-footed little pony. He talked to her with unusual freedom for those days of his own affairs, and was often amused by her shrewd comments and questions, as well as by her little airs of worldly wisdom and fragments of meditative speculation.

He noted in her with approval, too, an intrepid spirit, and a readiness of resource in moments of emergency, which she had inherited from him. He was sometimes caught in storms when his daughter was with him, both on land and on the sea, and he always admired her fearless spirit on these occasions, as well as her presence of mind and quickness to think and act.

Charlotte had no sister, and her brothers were all away either at school or college; but she was not lonely, for she had always plenty to occupy and amuse her, and for companionship there was ever Adela to be depended on; for Adela was an only child, and was devoted to Charlotte, who seemed to her to be like brother and sister in one.

Adela was the daughter of Mr. Fea, a wealthy gentleman (as wealth was accounted in those days and in those parts) of the island. He owned considerable tracts of land there, and he and Mr. Honeyman were intimate friends as well as near neighbours. In his youth he had been a poor man, but of late years things had greatly prospered with him, and he was accounted only second to Mr. Honeyman in importance in that district. As the two girls were walking up and down, and talking eagerly together over this matter, Mr. Fea himself appeared coming towards them.

Adela at once darted off, all eagerness to tell the news.

"Oh, papa, papa, what do you think! Charlotte says that there is a pirate vessel sheltering in one of the bays of our islands, and that we may all be murdered in our beds any day!"

Adela's face was quite glowing and beaming with excitement, and her father could not forbear a laugh, in which Charlotte joined.

"Well, my dear, that thought seems to give you wonderful pleasure! As the old proverb says, 'there is no accounting for taste!'" Then, turning to Charlotte, he asked: "But what is the sober sense of all this, my dear? What news has come to your father about pirates?"

"It is this, sir," answered Charlotte, turning to him quickly: "a poor seaman came early this morning and asked speech of my father, and when he was admitted he told a most terrible tale. Do you remember there living once in these parts a man of the name of Gow, who afterwards took to a seafaring life?"

"Gow? To be sure I remember him," answered Mr. Fea at once. "He and I were once at the same school—a hot-tempered, rather dangerous lad, of whom nobody spoke well. We were none of us sorry when he shipped himself off to sea. I have never heard of him since."

"Well, the man who came to speak to papa told him that Gow had been mate in a vessel called the *George Galley*, where he was a seaman. They had a very good captain and officers; but Gow got up a mutiny on board, shot the captain and some of the officers, got the well-disposed sailors shut up helpless, took possession of the vessel, and changed its name to the *Revenge*. Since then he has been scouring the seas, making the seamen who did not join in the mutiny do the work of the vessel under threat of cruel punishment or death, taking prizes, robbing and sinking small vessels of many nations in the most reckless way, and now, by stress of weather and through lack of water, they have put in here, where they hope the news of their many misdeeds will not be known. They know themselves to be in sore peril, for they have committed such depredations on the high seas that their doings have become notorious, and they are being watched for in many ports and on many oceans. But here Gow thinks he may be safe for awhile, and, perhaps, even yet he may elude justice, for he seems one of those men who carry charmed lives."

"Pooh-pooh, my dear; I don't believe in that sort of charmed life. Those fellows always come to the gallows at last. But how did this man dare to come with such a story? Gow will cut his throat if ever it comes to his ears."

"Yes; but he is not going back to the vessel. He escaped from her to give notice to the authorities, and papa took him away with him, and has promised him protection and help, though he will be wanted to give evidence when Gow is brought to trial, as we hope to bring him. Papa has gone off to take counsel with some others, and will not be back till to-morrow; but the man said there was no fear that the *Revenge* would leave her moorings in that time. Gow was resolved to come ashore and enjoy himself, and there were several more sailors who hoped to escape from the ship, and to find their way to the mainland, there to give notice of the pirate vessel."

Mr. Fea was keenly interested in this story. He was a law-abiding citizen, with a horror of bloodshed and violence, and he made up his mind that he would do everything in his power to assist in the capture of the pirate ship. It irked him to think that an Orkney man should have sunk to the level of Gow, and the very fact of having known him in his early days made him the more anxious to bring him to justice. It was a horrible thing that such men were still ranging the seas, plundering and murdering; and that honest seamen were forced to serve in such vessels on pain of instant death!

"I will see your father as soon as he returns," said Mr. Fea, "and we will talk together as to the best method of making the capture. A pirate sloop is not an easy prey to tackle; but we must see what can be done by strategy or by force."

Adela's eyes sparkled with excitement.

"Oh, papa, will there be a battle? Shall we be able to see it? Will there be danger and fighting, and all that sort of thing?"

"I hope not, my dear; at least, not too much. There is always a little risk in these affairs; but I hope most sincerely we may get off without bloodshed. I should think that Gow was already sufficiently notorious, without wishing to draw down upon himself the further ire of the representatives of the law. Perhaps if he finds himself overmatched, he may yield without much of a struggle."

Mr. Fea was not in any way alarmed for his own or his neighbours' houses, even though there was a pirate schooner lying hidden in one of the many indentations of their coast. It seemed to him, from Charlotte's story, that Gow had run in here in the hopes of lying safe and quiet for a short spell, and that his aim and object would be to avoid stirring up any sort of inquiry about himself and his vessel. He appeared to desire to enjoy himself on shore for awhile, and he certainly would not be able to do that if he incriminated himself by any acts of violence there. So again telling Charlotte that he would be over the next day to see her father, and would meantime think of some plan as to what might be done to entrap the pirate and his crew, and gain possession of the vessel, he took his daughter with him, as he turned to go to his house, and Charlotte sped over the few dividing fields, and reached her own home just as the dusk was beginning to fall.

She and her mother took their supper comfortably together. Mrs. Honeyman was an elderly lady, of considerable spirit and strength; but she was very hard of hearing, though a little sensitive about this failing, so that she was content often not to understand exactly what was passing, rather than ask for an explanation.

Charlotte did not mention the pirates to her; for she thought if she shouted out the story, that some servant would be certain to hear, and take alarm, and there might be a sort of panic in the house. The butler knew, as Mr. Honeyman had given him a few extra instructions about locking up the plate at night; but he did not wish his household needlessly alarmed; the more so as he was not able to be himself at home till the next day.

After supper, it came into Charlotte's head that, in her father's study there was generally on this day a considerable amount of gold, ready for the payment of the weekly wage to labourers and people of the place on the morrow. It occurred to her that she would do well to take her father's cash-box up to her own room that night. Ordinarily, there was so little fear of robbery here, that many people forgot to lock their doors at night; but perhaps, with a crew from a pirate vessel lurking somewhere near, it would be better to be on the safe side.

So after supper she went away quietly, took the heavy cash-box out of the drawer, and carried it up to her room. She had in her keeping, in an old-fashioned bureau, a good many family heirlooms in the shape of jewels, some of them of great value; and beside these there were some precious family documents greatly prized by her parents.

Charlotte could scarcely have told why it was that she took these out of their hiding-place, folded them carefully up, and strapped them to the cash-box, which she wrapped in a cloak and placed the bundle in her wardrobe, where a dark driving-cloak and hood hung from a peg. She was conscious of feeling a little restless and excited, though hardly uneasy.

"It is Adela's nonsense about being murdered in our beds, and all that," she said to herself; "I will go down and get a book, and not trouble myself about those stories any more."

Everything was very quiet as Charlotte and her mother sat beside the cheerful log fire with their books. The house was rather a rambling building, having only one upper storey of rooms, and covering a good deal of ground. The sounds from one part of the house did not easily penetrate to another; and Charlotte had not heard anything to awaken any uneasiness, when suddenly, hasty steps sounded outside the door, which opened to admit of Peter, the butler, who had such a white, scared face, that, instinctively, Charlotte jumped up and placed herself so that her mother might not see the man's expression of terror.

As a matter of fact, Mrs. Honeyman, being engrossed in her book, did not heed her daughter's movement, and, of course, had not heard the approach of the servant.

"The pirates! the pirates!" cried Peter, in strangled tones. "My mistress—my dear young mistress! Fly for your lives! They will murder every one who tries to thwart them!"

"How many are there?" asked Charlotte breathlessly.

"Ten; nine are to go through the house and take everything. The tenth guards the door. They say they will not hurt anybody who offers no resistance; but they will shoot the first one of us who tries to save his master's property!"

Charlotte's eyes flashed. Her spirit was rising within her; but she was no reckless fool to adventure herself and others in a futile struggle.

"The men are armed, of course?"

"To the teeth, with knives and pistols and cutlasses."

"Then, Peter, we cannot tackle them ourselves. We must get your mistress away at once. She must not even know what is happening in the house, else I am not certain she would not face the whole pirate crew herself, and defy and resist them. She must not run that risk. Be ready to follow up what I shall say. I do not like to deceive; but we must stoop to subterfuge for once."

Then, turning back into the room, she shouted to her mother—but rather slurring over her words, and making many breaks.

"Mamma—mamma, you are wanted. Something terrible has happened. Mrs. Fea—you must go there instantly. Please do not lose a moment. It may be life or death. Peter will take you. Your cloak and over-shoes are yonder in the lobby. That is the nearest way; and I will follow you quickly and see what is the matter."

Now Mrs. Honeyman was the most notable nurse in all the island, and in all cases of sudden emergency she was always sent for, and delighted to go and show her kindliness and skill. She was on her feet in a moment now, and hurried with Charlotte into a little lobby on the other side of the room, where her walking things for the garden always hung, and where a side-door led straight out into the garden on that side of the house nearest to the Feas'. Peter caught up a cap and gave his arm to his mistress, but bent an imploring glance upon Charlotte.

"Missy, Missy, you must come too. I cannot leave you."

"I will be after you directly. I have but to run up these stairs here to my own room for something. Don't lose a moment. I shall overtake you. But I have something I must secure first. Lose not a moment in acquainting Mr. Fea with what has happened."

Mrs. Honeyman, was by this time unlocking the door, and Peter had no choice but to follow his mistress. Charlotte, drawing a long breath of relief in the consciousness that her mother was now safe, darted up the little stairway to her own room, and already fancied that she heard strange steps and voices in the house.

Her heart beat to suffocation in the thought that at any moment the other door might be dashed open, and some ruffian suddenly come in and snatch away her precious treasure. What a mercy it was that she had thought of secreting it like this! Here it was under her hand. She was already wrapped in her cloak; her precious package was in her arms, she was about to run down the little stairs again, when, to her horror, she heard rough voices in the parlour below, and the sound of oaths as the men called one to another in their hasty search.

"'Tisn't here! There's nothing here worth laying hands on. They must have hid it somewhere. Let's be off upstairs. Here's another staircase. Let's see where that leads to!"

Charlotte darted back into her room again, and drew the little bolt across it. But that would only give her a moment's respite, she knew. One or two heavy blows would bring the door crashing inwards; and what then? She could not fly out by the other one, down the main staircase, without encountering the man on guard at the hall-door. The sight of her precious package would be certain to attract their instant attention, and they had threatened with death all who strove to resist their project of robbery.

But if she were to give up the valuables? Then she might well escape. They had no personal quarrel with her; and nobody had told her to constitute herself the guard of the family property. For one brief instant, Charlotte hesitated; then, with a snort of contempt at her own cowardly thought, she dashed open the window, threw her precious package down into the garden beneath, and herself vaulted lightly after it.

She had performed this feat occasionally before, in the days of her tom-boy pranks with her brothers, but she had not often practised such a leap of late, and the darkness made it more difficult. She was conscious of a sharp thrill of pain in her foot as she reached the ground, but, striving not to think of this, she caught up her bundle and fled; a light instantly flashing from the window of the room she had quitted, showed her that she had only just made her spring in time.

With a heart that thumped so loud in her ears as to deaden all other sound, Charlotte sped onwards as fast as the injured foot would allow over the rough ground that separated her home from that of her friends. But, in a few moments, she was certain that she was pursued. She heard angry, threatening voices in the garden behind her. Glancing back she saw flashing lights, and through the still night air came the sound of curses, which bespoke very real disappointment. Evidently, the men had heard of the cash-box to be found in Mr. Honeyman's house, and were enraged that it was not forthcoming.

"Somebody has taken it and made off!" cried a stentorian voice. "After him, men!—scatter, and scour the place. He can't have got far! Blow out his brains if he resists. That money I will have. I don't come all this way on a fool's errand!"

Suddenly, close above her, the steps came to a dead stop.

Charlotte heard, and instantly was aware of flying footsteps in many directions, some coming her way. What could she do? Try as she would her progress was not rapid. The distance to the Feas' house, so short on ordinary days, now seemed endless. There were no trees to give cover. That windswept island was bare of any save stunted bushes, and even of these there were none to serve her purpose. If the moon should shine out she would instantly be seen. She was not certain that some of those fierce shouts did not mean that she had been seen already.

Breathless and terrified, but still clutching her treasure tightly, Charlotte made for a great hole in the bank that she had known from childhood. Into this friendly, yawning chasm she crept, pushing her bundle before her, and here she crouched in darkness, covered by the folds of her sombre cloak, expecting almost moment by moment to feel a rough hand pulling her forth, or the threat of a bullet through her brain if she did not instantly give up her treasure.

Footsteps came nearer and nearer. She shrank closer and closer into her hole. She felt her flesh creep as the ground shook beneath the heavy tread; it was all she could do to keep from uttering a cry. The horror of that approaching discovery was so very real to her.

Suddenly, close above her, the steps came to a dead stop. She had been discovered! She knew she had! Her senses almost forsook her. It was a moment that she never forgot. Then a voice spoke, a rough, raucous voice:

"You'd best come back. It's no good staying here. They're coming out from that other house with lights and servants. They've got wind of something up, and the sooner we get off with what we've found the better."

A sudden rebound of feeling made Charlotte almost cry aloud. And as she strained her ears to hear, the heavy tread of feet shook the ground once more, now in full retreat. A few minutes later, limping in her gait, her face as white as death, her dress covered with sand, her hands still grasping the bundle that held the treasure, Charlotte almost fell into Mr. Fea's fatherly arms, and told him all her tale.

"I don't know what Mr. Honeyman will say when he hears how near his little girl went to losing her life for the sake of some valuables," he said, as he led her into the house; "but one thing I know: he will be mighty proud of having such a heroine for a daughter."

"If he doesn't think I was only a little goose," panted Charlotte, beginning to look like herself. "But, oh, I am glad those wretches have not got the things! And are you sure they have hurt nobody?"

That was the end of Charlotte's personal exploit with the pirates; but there were many exciting days to follow, for in trying to get their vessel away quickly, they put out on a stormy night, and were driven ashore in the bay called Calf Sound, not far from the houses of Mr. Honeyman and Mr. Fea. There, after much effort and some little stratagem, the crew was finally captured, and Gow met his richly deserved fate and perished on the gallows.

MARY BRIDGES

"Eleanor! Sister! There be days when I know not how to bear it. I feel that I shall do something desperate."

"Nay, hush, Mary! hush! why shouldst thou speak so wildly? We must be patient! Things will not always be so black!"

"Patience, patience! I am sick to death of the word! We have borne with these odious men about the house, till sometimes I feel that I can bear it no longer. And now that our father hath gone, and Robert with him, I feel that the house is scarce a safe place for our mother or ourselves."

"Come, come, Mary, thou dost go something too far!"

"I trow not. Those bloody, hateful men of Kirke's, what do they care how they frighten or annoy those who are forced for a time to shelter them? The maid servants dare never be alone for an instant. They never know but that one of those half-tipsy fellows will not come lurching in upon them. And listen, 'twas only just now that I met one of them, smelling so vilely of beer and spirits that it made me sick to go near him, wandering up the stairs into our part of the house; and when I bid him begone to his own quarters, what thinkest thou the wretch did?"

"He did not hurt thee?" quoth Eleanor, with sudden solicitude.

The eyes of the younger girl flashed fire.

"Had he laid a finger upon me, methinks I would have slain him as he stood!" she cried.

"Oh, hush, Mary! hush! hush!" pleaded Eleanor. "It is not good in these times to speak such rash words."

"A pretty pass things have come to if sisters may not speak freely together in their own home!" flashed out Mary, whose quick temper was easily aroused, and whose pent up indignation of weeks was coming upon her like a flood. "No, the creature did not dare lay hands upon me. I gave him a look—that was enough; but he vowed with many a vile oath that he would kiss me ere he did my bidding. If I had shown one mite of fear, Eleanor, I verily believe that he would have been as good as his word."

The fair Eleanor shivered with a sense of keen disgust. She had not her sister's courage and readiness and masterful looks and ways. Suppose she had met one of these men upon the stairs, and he had spoken thus to her, would she have been able to escape the hated salute? It turned her sick to think of it—albeit in those days kisses were given and received much more commonly than has since become the fashion between men and women, youths and maidens. Mary read her sister's thoughts, and cried out:

"Yes, yes, that is how I feel! Suppose it had been thou! Suppose insult were offered to thee,—or to our mother,—who is there to defend you? Oh, why was I not born a boy that I could set these surly knaves in their place? Robert should not have gone and left us, when our father was called hence too. It is not right or fitting; and with all these fearful things going on around us. It is enough to make one turn against the King, when he makes use of such vile instruments!"

"Oh, hush, Mary! hush! have a care! It is not safe to talk in that reckless fashion. Who knows but that there may be some meddling spy prowling about? And they say men and women are sent to prison and to death for such small offences now."

"Ah, yes, it is the cruelty, the horrid cruelty we see perpetrated on every hand that makes me so desperate. Think of that man Kirke, feasting and laughing on the balcony overlooking the place where his victims were being hanged and dismembered! think of it, Eleanor! and calling for music for them to 'dance to' when their poor bodies twitched and swayed on the gibbets; eating and drinking and making merry when human lives were passing from the world in all that agony and shame!"

"Thou shouldst not listen to such stories, Mary, it does no good; and it does but make life seem unbearable sometimes."

"And then, after Sedgemoor!" cried Mary, without heeding; "I heard another thing of him there. Did they tell it thee too, Eleanor? There was a man about to die—without trial—without condemnation—just strung up as so many were on the trees by the moor's edge, at the bidding of that man of blood! He was one of many; and the bystanders said that he was the fleetest runner of any on the country side, and could run with a galloping horse. Colonel Kirke asked him if that were true; and he said he had done it. Kirke asked if he would like to do it again to save his life; and he caught eagerly at the proffered hope. He ran with the horse, he kept up the whole course, he returned breathless, exhausted, but full of hope of the promise of life, and what does that monster of cruelty and injustice do?—just has him swung up with the rest, ere the poor wretch can find breath to plead for the promised pardon! Oh, it makes my blood boil—it makes my blood boil! I have been loyal to the King's cause all this while; but how can we help loathing and despising a monarch who will use such tools as that?"

"Perhaps he does not know," faltered Eleanor.

"Not know!" echoed Mary, in scorn. "It is because he knows all too well their temper that he sends them here! Hast heard what men are whispering now?—that soon there will be an assize in the west to try all those who have been concerned in this rebellion; and they say that His Majesty will choose for the judge the most cruel, the most notoriously evil, the most passionate and ungoverned of all the judges on the bench, and that his name is Jeffreys. And people say if once he come hither, no man in Taunton, nor in the west country will ever forget his coming. We shall have such a deluge of blood as has never run in England before."

"Oh, Mary, what fearful tales thou dost get hold of!"

"They are fearful; but they are true. That is what makes them so terrible," answered Mary. "Oh, how I hate and detest cruelty and lust of blood! Art thou not glad, Eleanor, that even Kirke himself could not cozen or threaten any Taunton man into acting as executioner to those poor wretches taken on the field of Sedgemoor? They had to send to Exeter or elsewhere to get a man to do that bloody work. Fancy cutting the poor wretches down ere they were quite dead, and cutting out their hearts, and flinging them on the fire, whilst the Colonel made merry at his window, and the music drowned the curses of the crowd and the cries of the victims or their friends! Methinks we have gone back to the days of the Druids and their human sacrifices. Oh, how can the King permit it? It is enough to drive the whole nation to hate him!"

"And yet we do not want a usurper to rule over us, even if the lawful King be such an one as His Majesty is now. Thou art not foolish enough to wish that the Duke of Monmouth had been victorious, Mary?"

"N-no, I suppose not! I love not usurpers; and our father hath always averred that it is an open question whether the Duke is the son of the late King Charles. No man seems able to say for certain what is his parentage, albeit he was treated like a son; and there be those who swear that the King did marry his mother in secret, and that he is rightful heir to the crown."

"Mary, Mary, thou dost not believe all those foolish stories that thou hast heard passing about? Men are always ready to believe that which they desire to believe. But the Duke of Monmouth, if the late King's son at all, has no claim upon the crown. Had it been otherwise he would have been acknowledged as heir; for every man likes his son to reign in his place. Our father thinks that the Duke is the son of one of the Sydneys; he says he is so strangely like him; and the King never called him son, though he was so fond of him, except when he presumed too far."

"Oh, I know, I know," answered Mary restlessly, "I have heard it all argued a thousand times over. No, I do not want the Duke of Monmouth or any other pretender; but I long for a King who can show mercy and kindness and generosity; not a man full of the most bitter and vindictive spite, who chooses as his tools and instruments those to whom cruelty is a delight!"

It was no wonder that Mary Bridges' soul was stirred within her at this time. She was the second daughter of Sir Ralph Bridges, of Bishop's Hull, near Taunton, and when she was a young girl of some fourteen summers, the whole district was stirred into violent excitement and violent emotion by the sharp outbreak of rebellion under the Duke of Monmouth.

The unpopularity of James II. was on the increase in those places where the Protestant faith had its strongholds. It was openly asserted that the King was a professed Romanist now, and that, in time, the whole constitution of the country would be undermined by him, and that persecutions of a terrible kind would break out under his rule.

The Duke of Monmouth came as the champion of the Protestant faith; and hundreds who would not, in calmer moments, have admitted his claim, or have thought it right for a moment to support one whose birth was so very doubtful, were carried away by religious enthusiasm, and let themselves be easily persuaded that this young man was the champion of the faith; and that, be he who he might, he was a heaven-sent messenger for the truth.

Far-seeing men, however, and men who knew something of the true character and the past history of the Duke, were not so easily carried away by the enthusiasm of the moment. Even had his claim been sounder, he was not the man to push the enterprise to a successful issue. His first burst of success, which had raised the hopes of his followers, and had occasioned a certain alarm and uneasiness in the minds of his opposers, had quickly been followed by a succession of reverses, and on the field of Sedgemoor the hopes of the Duke and his adherents met with a final overthrow.

Sir Ralph Bridges had been one of those who had watched the course of the rebellion with keen interest, and had thrown his influence upon the side of law and order. He had upheld the lawful King throughout, and had done good service in keeping order in his own immediate neighbourhood. But now that the revolt was at an end, and that the proportions to which it had swelled had not been very great, it seemed to Sir Ralph and to others as though clemency and consideration might be meted out to the victims of the ill-timed movement; and he had been greatly scandalised and shocked by the fury shown by Colonel Kirke and his men—his "Lambs" as they had been named in fierce derision—for the heartless brutality of their conduct.

It was, in fact, this indignation on the part of Sir Ralph which had caused him to leave his home somewhat suddenly, and before the withdrawal of the King's soldiers, billeted upon his house, in order that he might post to town with all possible speed, and join with other influential persons interested in the matter in seeking to win over the King, through his ministers and advisers, to a milder and less vindictive policy in dealing with the many persons now under arrest for having been concerned in the rebellion. He had gone with some reluctance; but it was told him by Kirke himself that the soldiers would very shortly be removed from his house, and he had taken his son with him as a precautionary measure; for he was a hot-headed youth, rather of Mary's disposition, and the father was afraid that the lad would get into trouble if he were not there to look after him; his disgust against the atrocities of "Kirke's Lambs" being almost as great as was Mary's. It was from her brother she had learned most of the more ghastly tales of which her mind was full. Eleanor and her mother shrank from hearing such terrible things; but Mary seemed consumed by that fearful curiosity that longs, and yet hates, to know.

The very next day, to the immense relief of Lady Bridges, who, though ever a dignified and self-contained woman, was one of a nervous temperament, the order came from Colonel Kirke that the soldiers were to depart from Bishop's Hull. Great was the satisfaction of the household and its mistress; but equal was the disgust of the men. They had had a fat time of plenty in this house where everything they demanded was accorded by its mistress, who, since the departure of her lord, had found it easier to give than withhold, although Mary's heart often burned with anger at hearing the insolent demands of the brutal fellows, who seemed to her to drink and carouse from morning till night. They had been away during the time of the battle; but they were soon back again, more swaggering, more insolent, more insupportable than ever; and, in the absence of Sir Ralph, there seemed no end to their exactions.

The order which came was that they were to depart upon the morrow; and it was fervently hoped that they would take themselves off at break of day; but this was an idea which never seemed to enter their heads. They called for more wine and beer than ever; sat drinking and dicing in the buttery hall, as though that was their only occupation in life; and when asked when they were going to take themselves off, replied only with curses and foul abuse.

So insolent and intolerable did they become at last, that even Lady Bridges' wrath was stirred within her. She and her daughters and household had been dining as usual in the upper hall; and when the noise from below at last became overpowering, she bid her house-steward go and send the men away, saying that they should have nothing more from her larder or brew-house, that their Colonel had recalled them, and they had no longer any right to be there.

Mary clasped her hands together in delight at hearing this message. The tables in the hall were now cleared. The servants had dispersed save a few who were setting the place in order, Lady Bridges and her daughters were standing upon the daïs where was the upper table, when suddenly several drunken soldiers came lurching towards them in a state of such anger and intoxication as made them fearful and repulsive objects.

They were swearing and cursing after the foul fashion of the day; and though sober enough to see the ladies and make straight towards them, they were not sober enough to choose their words, and continued to pour out vile and insulting threats and abuse.

Lady Bridges, trembling in every limb, sank down in her chair, giving hasty and terrified glances round her to see if help were near, and yet mortally afraid of doing anything that could be construed by spiteful misrepresentation into a charge of treason. The King's soldiers were the King's servants. And who knew what power they might not have?

Eleanor cowered behind her mother as the soldiers lurched up the hall, making gross demands of their hostess, and speaking in violent and insulting language to all three ladies. The frightened servants crowded together in the background waited for their lady's orders ere interfering; and she, fearing to speak the word, only sat there rigid and trembling, whilst ever nearer and nearer came the threatening soldiers with their evil faces and foul words.

Mary's eyes were blazing. Her whole frame was shaken with a passion of fury. If they dared to come up the steps and lay hands upon her mother,—dared to touch one of them,—she drew in her breath, she clenched her hands till the nails dug into the palms. Her eyes were upon the foremost man. They had begun to sparkle strangely. Just as he staggered up the first step she darted forward, stooped quickly, and drew from its sheath the shining sword he carried. Then, backing a few steps in front of her mother and sister, she cried in a voice shaken with passion:

"Dare to come one step nearer, dare to lay hands upon any of us, and thou shalt see what a maid of Taunton will do!"

What happened in those next few seconds it were hard to say. The girl stood rigidly before her mother and sister with the keen blade in her slim hands, pointing it immovable at the drunken soldier still advancing in menacing fashion. He did not believe in the girl's threat, or in the strength of those little white hands. He laughed to see her pointing the sword at him, and words even grosser than anything that had passed before were hurled at her as he came on with drunken violence and brutality. Was it the impetus of that lurch forward, or did Mary herself lunge her weapon at him? Those who looked on could never rightly determine. Mary herself never could answer the question. But the sword pointed straight at the man's heart was so firmly held by those girlish hands, that, as he precipitated himself upon her to break down her guard, the shining blade ran clean through his body, and he fell pierced to the heart, a dead corpse at Mary's feet.

Eleanor shrieked, and covered her face with her hands. Lady Bridges fell back white, and gasping:

"Mary! Mary! What hast thou done? Unhappy child! God be merciful to thee and to us!"

Mary stood very straight and upright. There was no colour in her face; yet there was no faltering in her eyes. Soldiers and servants alike stood still and motionless, too much startled and awed by what had occurred to move or speak; all eyes being fixed upon the motionless figure of Mary.

"Take that thing away!" she said at last, pointing with a fierce repulsion to the dead soldier at her feet. "Take him and begone every one of you! Is it for girls to teach you the lesson how to be men and not brutes?"

In absolute silence, and with something like fear in their faces, the other soldiers, thoroughly sobered, came and carried off the corpse of their companion, and withdrew from the house. Only one significant word was spoken by the chief of the band ere he finally withdrew.

"Colonel Kirke will have to hear of this, mistress," he said, addressing Mary with more of respect in his glance than there had ever been before. She was standing in precisely the same spot and in the same attitude, and she merely bent her head very slightly as she heard the words.

"Tell him everything!" she exclaimed suddenly, as the man turned to go. "Do you think I am afraid?"

He gave her a look of admiration, bowed, and retired. It was then and only then that her mother and sister broke into lamentation and tears; and Lady Bridges, holding her to her breast, sobbed in the bitterness of a mother's anguish.

"Oh, Mary! Mary! What hast thou done? And what can they do to thee? Oh, that man of iron! that cruel, cruel Kirke! And is it before him thou must go?"

Mary kissed her mother, and freed herself gently from her embrace; her nerves were still strung tensely up. She felt no qualm of fear.

"Mother," she said, "there was no one else to defend you and Eleanor. None else would have dared to lift a hand against a soldier of the King's. Was I to stand by and see and hear such things? God in heaven alone knows whether it was my act or his that did him to death. But even if I did strike him to the heart, is not he a man of blood? And is it not written that they who take the sword shall perish by the sword?"

"Oh, my child, my child," wept the mother, "God in His mercy grant that such a fate be not thine own!"

It was two days later when Mary Bridges stood pale and dauntless before that terrible soldier, Colonel Kirke. Her offence was judged to be a military one, and she was arraigned before him by court-martial. Lady Bridges, her self-command and dignity recovered, stood close beside her daughter; and behind them clustered a number of servants, all ready to swear upon their Bible oath that Mistress Mary had never lunged at the soldier by so much as a hair's breadth, but that the man had run upon the weapon with which she was defending her mother and sister.

But their testimony was not destined to be asked or given. Colonel Kirke was a man of few words, and of rapid decision. It was seldom that any case coming before him was granted any space for discussion and hair-splitting.

His own soldiers told the tale fairly enough, admitting the insult, the drunken violence of their dead comrade, and the fact that they had no real right to be in Lady Bridges' house or presence at all. They described the death in detail; and Mary stood silent listening to all that passed; but speaking never a word, nor giving one sign of wavering or of fear.

The Colonel's sombre glance rested again and again upon her face; and, when the accusation was brought to an end, he asked her to state her defence.

"I did it," she answered, speaking fearlessly, "I am going to tell you what your 'Lambs' are like, and you can kill me afterwards in any way you choose. I am not afraid. Your men are cowards and drunkards. I grant they can fight; but they are cowards in their cups. They insult women and girls; they make themselves feared and hated and detested wherever they go. Men speak of them with execration, and they will go down to posterity hated and loathed. Mother, don't try and stop me! I will speak now that I have the chance. Colonel Kirke, have you a mother? Were you ever asked to stand by and hear her grossly threatened and insulted? If you had been there, what would you have done? I am not a man, I am only a weak girl, but I was not going to endure that. I would have killed every man who had sought to attack her. Whether I killed him by an open pass at him, or whether he ran upon his own sword, I do not know—I do not care. I stood there to save my mother and my sister from outrage. You can condemn me to death for it, if you will. I am not afraid!"

There was deathly silence in the hall for a few seconds after those words were spoken. Then Colonel Kirke's voice rang out firm and clear:

"Bring me the sword with which this deed was done!"

The sword was brought. The Colonel took it in his hands and looked upon it. There was the stain of blood upon the shining blade.

Lady Bridges gasped when she saw him turn towards Mary. Was he about to slay her child before her very eyes?

Straight and tall towered the terrible Colonel before Mary; he then did a very strange thing—a thing so strange that those who witnessed it drew their breath in silent amaze. He slightly bent the knee, and placed the naked sword very gently in Mary's hands.

"Mistress Mary Bridges," he said, in that voice which had caused so many to tremble, and which had of late given so many fearful orders of merciless savagery, "this sword is yours. Take it; and take with it the full acquittal of this court. The act that you have performed is no crime; it is an honour to the strong young hands that performed it, and the noble young heart that nerved those hands to the deed. Take this sword, and keep it; let it be in your family a treasured heirloom. Let it be handed down to other Mary Bridges yet to come, and with it the tale of how, in the past, a girl, a daughter, a tender maiden, was found strong enough to rally to the defence of her mother, whilst craven hirelings shrank and feared, and coward soldiers looked on and raised no hand to check the violence of a comrade!"

His fierce eyes swept round the hall, and many shrank before the glance; then it softened once more, and he looked straight at Lady Bridges.

"Madam, I bid you farewell. Take home your daughter, and be proud of her. Guard her well; and when the time does come, find her a mate worthy of herself. Mistress Mary Bridges, I kiss your hand. Fare you well, and may you be known to posterity when this tale is told, as 'Mary Bridges of the Sword.'"

THERESA DUROC

The city was ringed about with walls of fire. By night it presented a terrible aspect to those who could gain a safe vantage ground out of range of the batteries, and watch for awhile the fearful glare from them, as the fiery missiles were sent hurtling forth, charged with their errand of death and destruction. And even if the batteries were silent there was generally some terrible glow of fire in the sky, for almost every day a conflagration broke out in some portion of the city, and the terrified inhabitants never knew from day to day whose turn might not come next.

Theresa lived with her widowed mother in one of those large houses common in all great cities, where the poor were herded together at close quarters, and in days like these had to suffer many privations, as well as all the nameless terrors which beset men's hearts at such a time. Some of their neighbours had fled before the encompassing army shut in the city; but Theresa and her mother remained. For they knew not where else to go. And if Pierre, away fighting for his country, should be recalled by the exigencies of war, and the siege should suddenly be raised by help from without, where would the poor boy find them, if not in the old home?

"The good God will care for us and protect us, if we trust ourselves to Him," the Widow Duroc had said; and, whilst others collected their few possessions and quitted the city, she and her daughter remained in the almost deserted house.

It was necessary for them to remain, if possible, as it was in the city that Theresa's work lay. She went daily to one of the shops where fine starching and ironing was done, and, with the money she earned in this way, she had kept the little home comfortable for some time. Her mother was a cripple, and could only do a little needlework when she was able to procure it. Sometimes Theresa was enabled to bring her home some from the shop, but for the rest they were dependent upon the earnings of the girl. If they were to seek to fly the city they had nowhere to go, and would lose their only means of support. It seemed better to remain and risk the peril within the walls than fly they knew not where.

And now they were fast shut in, and had grown so well used to the booming of the guns or the sharp scream of the shell hurtling through the air, that they spoke and moved in the midst of the tumult as quietly as they had done before it began. Indeed, sometimes, when for a night, or for part of a day, the batteries became suddenly silent, the stillness would seem almost more awful than the roar that had gone before. It would cause them to awake from sleep with a start, or to stop suddenly in what they were saying or doing, and always the question arose in the heart, or to the lips:

"What is it that has happened? Has the city fallen?"

The tall house in which they lived was far more silent and empty now than it had been before the siege began. The authorities had encouraged all those who were able, to depart before escape should be impossible. They foresaw that food was likely to become scarce, and the fewer useless mouths there were to fill the better for all. But those who had sons, or husbands, or brothers in the army were suffered to remain, as were all who could not leave without suffering heavily; and it was known to Theresa, from what she heard spoken about her, that should famine threaten, and the city be put upon rations, she and her mother would be entitled to receive a share, as being among those whose bread-winner was with the army.

But at first there seemed little fear of this, and Theresa's work went on as before. The tall house where they lived was not in range of any of the batteries, and though their hearts were often torn by fear for others, and by sorrow for their beautiful buildings being so sorely shattered and ruined, they themselves did not suffer, and they grew accustomed to the conditions which had seemed at first so strange and terrible.

But day after day passed by, and the days lengthened into weeks, and still the hoped-for relief did not come; those within the beleaguered city only heard whispers from the world without, and knew not what was passing there.

"If only our Pierre could get a letter to us!" the widow would say, again and again; "then we should know how it was faring with him and with the army."

Theresa going daily to her work heard all the flying rumours which reached the city; but she did not speak of them always to her mother, for she knew not how much or how little to believe, and she feared either to buoy her up by false hopes, or to crush her with needless fears.

Gay Paris is slow to believe in disaster, or to credit that the arms of France can meet with any severe reverse. Each generation is as full of hopeful confidence as the one that has gone before, as full of enthusiasm and patriotic fervour, as little disposed to believe in misfortune.

"The victorious army will march to our relief!" was the cry that was always finding expression. "A little more patience—only a little more!—and these accursed foes will be flying before our brave *garçons* of soldiers like chaff before the wind."

And nobody believed this more implicitly than Theresa for a long, long time. The soldiers would come, and Pierre with them. They would see them marching in, in all the bravery of their gay trappings. Oh, what a day that would be! How the bells would ring, and the guns salute, and the people go mad with joy! She lived through the experience a hundred times a day as she stood at her ironing-table and worked at her piles of snowy linen. But the sullen boom of the guns was still the accompaniment of all her musings. And every week as it passed brought home to her heart the conviction that things were not going well: that the lines of the enemy were being drawn ever closer and closer: that there could not be good news from the outer world, else surely it would be noised abroad with acclamation.

But soon a trouble was to fall upon her for which she was quite unprepared. Fires had become sadly common in the city. A glare in the sky was such an ordinary sight that it scarcely aroused any interest or speculation, save in the immediate neighbourhood where it occurred. Soldiers and citizens were always on the alert to put it out wherever a conflagration occurred, and often the flames were speedily extinguished. Nevertheless, the number of burnt and uninhabitable houses was becoming daily larger, and persons were removing their goods and furniture from those streets where the danger threatened into safer localities; so that the house where the Durocs lived had already been invaded by various newcomers, seeking an asylum from the storm of shot and shell.

Theresa, however, knew little or nothing of their new neighbours. She was busy with her work by day, and her mother did not get about easily enough to learn much of those who had arrived in this sudden fashion. They were of the class that, in the English phrase, preferred to "keep themselves to themselves."

One morning Theresa started forth to her work as usual, and, after taking the accustomed turnings, found herself in the familiar street. But once there she stopped short and rubbed her eyes. For what did she see? The whole side of the street, where her workshop had stood, lay a mass of smoking ruins; and the people from the opposite houses were hurrying away, carrying their goods and chattels with them.

The terrible news was passing from mouth to mouth. A new battery had been opened. A new portion of the city was in peril. People small and great were hastening away before another fusillade should shatter the remaining part of the quarter. Theresa stood gazing in great dismay at what she saw. Where was her occupation now? Where was her kindly employer whom she had served so long?

Even as she asked herself the question a woman from an adjacent house, well known to Theresa, came hurrying out, the tears raining down her face.

"Alas! alas! little one, she is dead—God rest her soul!—buried beneath the fall of the house in the dead of night! Ah, those accursed Germans! What have they not to answer for? Our good neighbour Clisson!—so kindly, so merry, so ready to lend a helping hand. And thou, my poor child—what wilt thou do? Everything swept away in one night! And who knows whose turn may come next?"

Theresa was indeed dismayed for herself as well as for others. The terrible fate of her kind mistress cut her to the heart; but when that shock had passed by, there came the other thought suggested by the kindly neighbour. What was to become of her and her mother, now their only means of support was taken from her?

"Thou wilt have to apply for rations as others do," said her friend, with a look into the troubled face. "Courage, little one! These black days cannot last for ever! We shall soon see those *canaille* of Prussians flying helter-skelter before our brave *garçons*. The good God will hear our prayers and will send us succour. It will only be for a time, and then our beautiful city will be gayer and more beautiful than ever!"

But Theresa had heard words like these too often to put the old faith in them. Her heart was heavy as lead within her. She was revolving many plans by which she might still earn something and support her mother. But the price of food was rising so fearfully that already she scarcely knew how to keep the wolf from the door; she knew, too, that her mother desired, if possible, not to be forced to send for the doled-out rations from the great Government building; and no one could more desire to be spared the task of fetching it daily than Theresa herself.

She had heard what that meant from others. The long, long, weary wait in the daily increasing crowd; the hustling and the jostling before one could get a place in the *queue*; the bitter cold often to be faced when the wind blew down upon the crowd; the peril, sometimes, of having the hardly earned food snatched away in some back street by a hungry ragamuffin before ever it had reached its destination.

All this Theresa knew that she would have to face if they lost all other means of support. And, moreover, for her was another great danger: to reach the quarter of the city where the food was doled out, she would be forced to cross a wide boulevard that was swept from end to end by the guns of a battery, and each time that she went she would have to take her life in her hands, as it were.

"But mother must never know that," she said to herself, as she thought of these things. "She is fearful enough as it is of having me go about the streets. She must never know that, else she would not enjoy a moment's peace. Perhaps the good God will save me from it. Perhaps I shall get work elsewhere. And if I must go—for mother's sake—I must pray to Him to keep me safe, as so many are kept who have to go day by day."

Theresa's search after regular employment was not successful. There was so little doing in the city now, and, with food at famine prices, all were saving their money, as far as possible, for the bare necessaries of life. For a few weeks the girl was able to earn just sufficient to enable them to keep body and soul together, by jobbing about here and there, turning her hand to any sort of work so long as she might earn a trifle by it.

But the day came at last when she could no longer find any one to employ her. Every one told the same tale—it took all they knew to keep the wolf from the door. Money was scarce; food was scarcer. Larger crowds were daily going to the places where the rations were doled out. Theresa made up her mind as she lay in bed one night, that she must go there, too, on the morrow.

For several days this conviction had been growing upon her; and her nights had been restless and broken, partly through anxiety and trouble of mind, partly because she was really in need of more food, having pinched herself to supply her mother, professing that she got enough to eat at the houses where she worked—a profession that was by no means the literal truth.

"Yes, I will go to-morrow," said Theresa to herself. "It is foolish to be afraid. Others do it, and so must I; and mother must never, never know how I dread the thought. I will ask the good God to make me brave."

And having thus made up her mind, Theresa turned over and slept more soundly and peacefully than she had done for many nights before, rising with a cheerful courage on the morrow.

"Alas, my child!—but if it must be, it must. I would that I could go, for thou art over-young to bear so much fatigue."

"Nay, mother; it is right for the young to spare the old, and the strong the weak. I shall be long gone, I fear. There are so many now to serve; but be not afraid; it will be no more than a day's work, and I will bring thee the food in the evening."

So, with a smile on her face and a brave and cheerful aspect, she took her basket and set off, first to get her order and then the much-needed food.

There was a deal of jostling and pushing and hustling before Theresa could present her claim; but when she showed how her brother was fighting in the army, and her father was dead, it was instantly allowed.

"How many are you?" asked the official, in his quick, peremptory tones, for everything was hurried through as quickly as possible. Without a thought, Theresa answered:

"Three."

A ticket was thrust into her hands, and she was passed out to make way for others, and only when she was in the street once more, hastening along towards the other great building, did she realise that she should have said, "Two"; for, though they always thought and spoke of Pierre as one of them, he was not entitled to the rations within the city.

The girl paused and hesitated; but she saw that it would be impossible to go back. She looked down at the paper in her hand, and a rather longing gleam came into her eyes.

"I am so hungry; I could well eat two portions," she said; but almost at once she shook her head with resolute gesture, and spoke out half aloud: "But no—that would be wrong; that would be like stealing. I know what we will do. We will set aside Pierre's portion each day, and we will give it to some poor hungry creature who may not be able to get to the depôt. There must surely be many such in the city. I will find out one such, and she or he shall be fed every day, for the order cannot be changed now. I think that is what the good God would like me to do. Perhaps it was His will that I made that mistake, His eye looks down and sees all."

Full of this thought, Theresa hastened on through the streets and quickly reached that dangerous spot which she had so feared to pass. But to-day the great guns were silent; there was no peril to be feared; and, with a happy smile upon her face, she ran across, thinking within her heart that it seemed almost as though an angel were watching over her and making her task easy.

Another piece of good fortune befell her, in that a second place had been recently opened for the distribution of rations, in order to meet the increasing demand. Theresa heard of this from a woman hurrying away with her basket, and, instead of pushing into the larger crowd, she joined the smaller one, and being served far more quickly than she had thought possible, hurried home with a very light heart.

"It was not half so bad as I thought and feared," cried Theresa, putting down her basket, and sinking into a chair. "Oh, yes, to be sure, I am tired; but then what of that? We have food to eat, and a certainty of more when that is done. And now, my mother, I must tell thee of my plan. I think thou wilt be pleased that I should carry it out. The good God has taken such care for us, that I think He would have us take thought for others."

So Theresa, rising and opening her basket, carefully divided the food into three portions, and, notwithstanding the fact that she could well have consumed the double portion, after her long fasting and wearying day, she set it smilingly aside, and told her mother how it was "Pierre's dole," and must not be eaten by them, but given to some one in greater need.

There is sometimes more heroism in an act of such self-sacrifice than in one of those deeds at which all the world exclaims; but Theresa had no thought of being brave as she laid her plan before her mother, nor did the widow praise her daughter. She took the girl's view that the ration was not theirs, and must be passed on to somebody else.

"And, indeed, my child, we shall not have far to go, for, in truth, I have begun to fear that those two old ladies up above us in the attic must be well-nigh starving by this."

"What old ladies?" asked Theresa eagerly, as she set to work with keen-set appetite upon her own portion.

"Ah, thou hast not seen them, like enough. I hear that the mistress is called Madame de Berquin, and that she is of very good family; but she has been ruined by this cruel siege, her house shattered, supplies cut off, and she knows not where to turn. She and her old servant sought refuge here a few weeks back, and I think they had money then, for the servant went forth daily and came back with a basket. I would see her pass and give her a good day, and she stopped once or twice just to take breath and speak a few words, which is how I came to know that little about them; but I have not seen her these last days, and I cannot well get up the stairs. So thou shalt go, and take with thee some of this hot coffee and the food. It may be they are in sore need. My heart has been sad for them before, but what could I do?"

Theresa almost forgot her own hunger in her eagerness to pay this visit; and, taking in the can some of the fragrant coffee, steaming hot, she put the rest of the food in the basket and ran lightly upstairs with her load.

At the door she knocked; the old servant opened it a little way and looked suspiciously forth. All at once it seemed to Theresa that it might not be quite easy to get old Madame de Berquin to accept the food of which she stood in such sore need.

"What do you want?" asked old Jeanne suspiciously.

"I have brought Madame de Berquin's rations," answered Theresa, with a sudden inspiration. "You know the city is on rations now, and, as we live in the same house, I thought I might fetch Madame's with ours. It is not very much, I fear, but——"

The old woman opened the door wider and beckoned Theresa in. Something in the white, drawn face of the servant went to the girl's heart! her aspect, and that of the attic itself, bespoke the direst poverty. Madame de Berquin lay upon the bed; she looked almost like a corpse to the girl; her eyes dilated with fear.

"She is not dead, but she would soon have died," said the old woman. "I was praying it might be soon for both of us. She will not let me fetch the rations; she will not have her name set down for a dole. How did you get it from her?" and despite the almost wolfish hunger in her eyes, old Jeanne seemed disposed to push the food away.

"I did not give your name; I did not know it," answered Theresa simply. "I just got some with ours. They are in a great hurry at the office. They do not ask many questions."

"Then may the saints and the good God reward you!" cried the old woman, with a sob in her voice; "for verily I thought to see my dear mistress perish of want before my eyes!"

Now, however, with Theresa's assistance, she raised the prostrate figure, and Madame de Berquin revived as the hot, fragrant coffee passed her lips. They gave her morsels of bread soaked in it. They fed her gradually, as an infant is fed, until the light began to come back into her eyes and the grey pallor of her cheeks to change to something more lifelike.

"I shall come again to-morrow and bring some more," whispered Theresa, as she slipped away at last; and the look which the old woman gave her was reward enough.

But all days were not such good ones for Theresa as this one had been. Sometimes she was in terrible fear as she went her way, for the bullets seemed to be whizzing in the air about her, and the sounds of fearful explosions all round made her doubt whether she should escape with her life. And the long, long waiting in the biting cold, and the perils she encountered from daring little gamins or ill-conditioned men, made her daily journey a growing terror to her. But the thought of the crippled mother and those two patient old women upstairs, all dependent upon her for the food which kept life in them, nerved her to conquer her fears and to persevere, in spite of all the dangers she had to face.

Then came the day when her bravery met with an unexpected reward. She was waiting to cross that terrible boulevard. She had been waiting long, and still she dared not face the peril. She heard the bullets biting the stones, and a shell had exploded in the centre of the road just as she came up. She began to fear that she was losing her nerve, that she was growing less brave rather than more, when suddenly she was held riveted to the spot by the sight of a boy, about seven or eight years old, dressed as a gentleman's child, who came running along gaily, rather as though he had escaped from restraint, and dashed into the middle of the broad roadway. Then suddenly he threw up his hands, gave a quick cry, and fell forward.

Theresa forgot everything in the sight of the child's peril.

Theresa forgot everything in the sight of the child's peril. Dashing forward, she caught him up in her arms, dropping basket and can and everything, and staggered across the road with him, just as a pale-faced gentleman, in semi-military dress, came rushing up in a terrible state of anxiety and excitement.

"Etienne, Etienne, what hast thou done?"

The little boy had given forth one lusty yell at the sight of blood on his tunic, but a hasty survey satisfied the father that it was a scratch rather than a wound the child had received, and the colour began to come back to his face.

"My brave girl," he said, turning to Theresa, "how can I thank you for this great service? Do you know that scarcely had you snatched up the boy and got him away than the ground where he was lying was torn up by some fragments of a shell? Had he lain there a few seconds longer he must have perished!"

"Ah, how glad I am I was there just then," said Theresa simply.

"Were you not frightened, my child? Did you not know the peril of passing that street?"

"Oh, yes; I know. I am rather frightened, but I have to go by every day to get food. I must be going now, or I shall lose my turn."

"Nay, nay; come back with me, and my wife shall fill the basket to-day," answered the gentleman, with a kindly authority that the girl could not resist; and, as she walked beside him, Etienne, proud of his adventure and his little hurt, hanging to his father's hand, Theresa found herself closely questioned as to herself and her circumstances, and heard a wondering exclamation pass the gentleman's lips as she spoke the name of Madame de Berquin.

That day saw the end of Theresa's troubles about food; for, from thenceforward till the close of the siege, General Varade, whose little son she had saved, made the care of her and her mother and of Madame de Berquin his especial task. He knew something of the history and family of the latter, came to see her, and would have moved her into better quarters had she wished it; but she had grown so fond of Theresa and her mother that until better days should come she preferred to remain where she was.

"It is to thy bravery, my child, that we owe all this," she once remarked; and Theresa, looking quite astonished, answered:

"Oh, Madame, I was never brave. I was always scolding myself for being such a coward!"

But others when they heard these words smiled.

JANE LANE

Those were anxious days for the adherents of the Stuarts. The late King had perished upon the scaffold, and his family were in exile in foreign lands. The iron rule of Cromwell had England in its grip. But anxious eyes were fixed upon that gallant attempt of the King's son—King Charles II., as the loyalists already called him—to win back for himself the kingdom his father had lost, and overset the military thraldom beneath which the people now groaned.

It was a time of intense suspense and heartbreaking anxiety. It seemed impossible that the young King, crowned in Scotland, and on his way to the south, could overthrow those redoubtable troops commanded by their redoubtable General, the great Oliver Cromwell himself. And yet hope which springs eternal in the human breast filled the hearts of the cavaliers with bright anticipations of coming triumph; anticipations that were changed to dire fears and forebodings when the news of the result of the Battle of Worcester became known.

At Bentley Hall, in Staffordshire, the loyal family of the Lanes were following the fortunes of their Prince with the keenest solicitude; and yet, as family life goes on its way in spite of wars and rumours of wars, so it befell that Jane, the beautiful unwedded daughter of the house, was making preparation for a journey to Abbotsleigh, the home of her married sister, where she had been rather urgently summoned, as Mrs. Norton was ill, and desired much the companionship of her favourite sister.

As Abbotsleigh was in Gloucestershire, and as the journey would involve the passage through the Parliamentary lines and through the disturbed portion of the country, a pass had been obtained for Jane and her party from the Parliamentary General.

Colonel Lane had gone himself to see to this matter, and Jane was awaiting his return in some anxiety. He had not been with the King's forces on the field of Worcester, though he was very loyal in his disposition towards him, and was privately working in the royalists' cause. But it was possible, as his sister knew, that he might be suspected, and have some difficulty in gaining what he was seeking to obtain; and she awaited his return with great impatience and some nervous trepidation.

The sound of horses' feet in the courtyard below brought a flood of colour to her cheek. She ran to a window, and sought to peer out into the autumnal evening's gloom, but though she could see little, she heard the tones of her brother's voice, and at once she rushed to the room of her mother to announce to her the welcome tidings that the traveller had returned.

Soon word reached the ladies upstairs that the Colonel had not come alone. Lord Wilmot had accompanied him, and would remain a few hours, till his horse was rested, and the ladies made preparation for meeting him at supper in an hour's time. Lord Wilmot was only slightly known to them; but they received him courteously, and learned from him a good many details of the disastrous fight at Worcester, and the hopelessness of any farther resistance to the Parliamentary leaders.

"But His Majesty is safe, I trust?" questioned the old lady anxiously. Lord Wilmot made guarded reply:

"His Majesty is with friends, who are forwarding him to the coast where he must take ship for France once more."

"Pray heaven he fall not into the hands of his foes!" cried Mrs. Lane earnestly; and the two men breathed a fervent "Amen."

Jane heard that her pass had been obtained, and that was a relief to her, since she greatly desired to be with her sister. But she observed that her brother and their guest were somewhat absorbed and anxious in manner, and she was not surprised, when they rose from table, that her brother made her a sign that he had somewhat to say to her.

Their father was at this time not very well, and Mrs. Lane excused herself to her guest, saying that she must go to her husband. They did not seek to detain her; but the Colonel beckoned to Jane to follow them into a small parlour, where they would be safe from prying eyes or listening ears; and after he had kicked the logs into a cheery blaze, he suddenly faced round upon her, and said:

"Sister, we are about to trust you with a weighty secret. It concerns the King!"

"The King! Where is he?"

"He has been flying in disguise, this way and that, from the ardent pursuit of the Parliamentary soldiers. He has had many narrow escapes. A worthy miller and his sons have done good service by sheltering him; before that he was at White Ladies. To-night he is at Mosley with our good friend Mr. Whitegrave. To-morrow night he must come to Bentley!"

"To Bentley!—here?" cried Jane, clasping her hands.

"Ay, here to Bentley; and none must know it but you, fair sister, and I; and if you ask wherefore comes he here?—I answer you that it is that he may travel as your groom and servant when you ride forth to Abbotsleigh. To Bristol, by hook or by crook, he must be smuggled; and how to pass him through the Parliamentary lines is, indeed, a hard nut to crack. But see this pass—it makes provision for Mistress Jane Lane, her servants and friends, the latter being named as you see: our cousin Robert Lascelles, and Mr. Petre with his wife. But as for servants, there is no special mention as to them. Sister, you must ride pillion behind your King, and treat him as your servant!"

Jane's colour came and went, as well it might. She lacked not courage nor discretion; yet the magnitude of this great responsibility, so suddenly and strangely thrust upon her, seemed for a moment too great to contemplate.

"Alas, brother!" she cried, "and if by some folly I should betray my King to his foes!"

"Nay, think not of such a thing," said Lord Wilmot, speaking for the first time, "yet think of yourself, fair maiden. Should the thing become known, it may go something hard with you at the hands of the Governor of this unhappy realm."

The colour had come back to Jane's fair face. She looked fearlessly into the eyes of the speaker. "That is nought," she said quietly. "Could any ask a better fate than to lay down life in such a cause? If I may save the King, what matters all the rest?"

"That is the answer I looked to have from Jane," spoke the brother; and so the matter was settled.

It was agreed by all that the secret should be kept from the household. The sick father and old mother should not be burdened with the responsibility of the knowledge. Colonel Lane and Lord Wilmot were to ride to Mosley that same night when the late moon had risen, and upon the following evening they would return to Bentley, bringing in their train the new groom, William Jackson, who would be told off the following day to accompany his sister on her ride to Abbotsleigh.

It may be guessed with what feelings Jane watched for the return of the party upon the next evening, and how keenly she scrutinised the face and figure of the new servant riding behind her brother. He had a swarthy skin and very dark eyes, and a rough head of short hair that gave him something the look of either a Roundhead or a country bumpkin, and in his actions he seemed to be ungainly and loutish. Jane's eyes glistened as she realised that here was a Prince—a King as in her heart she called him—masquerading under the guise of a clown, and her heart beat high as she realised that she was to have the honour of assisting in the next stages of his difficult and perilous escape to the coast.

She had no speech with him that night; she heard her brother hand him over to the head servants with an injunction that he should be well cared for, as he was to ride with Mistress Jane upon the morrow. It was only on that morrow, when she descended to the courtyard dressed for the saddle, that she was brought face to face with her strange attendant. Her colour came and went with excitement as their eyes met, and for one instant she saw an answering gleam in his before they dropped, and he stood in decorous immobility at the horse's head.

It was a strong animal, as was needed to carry double, though Jane's light weight was no great burden. The mother herself descended to see her daughter depart, and to give her many last charges concerning her sick sister.

She gave a glance at the new serving man, in his sober suit of grey, and when Colonel Lane made him a sign to assist his mistress to mount, there was something so odd in his manner, an awkwardness partly assumed, partly the result of the strangeness of the office, that caused the old lady to laugh merrily, and say to her son in no very modulated tones:

"Faith, but my daughter has a goodly horseman to ride before her! Where didst pick up the rogue, my son?"

Jane was covered with confusion at hearing such words spoken; but in the bustle of the departure of the cavalcade, this was not observed, and when they were safely out at the gate, Charles spoke in a low and mirthful tone:

"Be not displeased, fair Mistress; such words as those are sweet to the ears of a fugitive. It is when men bow before me, and seek in secret to kiss my hand, that my heart sinks within me. For, however loyal and true they be, I would sooner they held me for the rogue I personate, than for their hunted King."

The party proceeded gaily on its way for a while. Lord Wilmot rode beside them and in advance, his hawk on his wrist, his dogs by his side, looking like a sportsman enjoying his favourite recreation. Mr. Lascelles generally rode with him, and Mr. Petre and his wife kept close together with their own servants. Jane and the King, being well mounted, sometimes drew ahead, though they were careful not to be far from their party, till at last the horse they were riding began to drag a little. He got behind the rest of the company, and at last seemed inclined to limp.

"Methinks he has lost a shoe," quoth Jane; and Charles, springing to the ground, found that this was indeed the case. By this time the rest of the party was considerably in advance; and Jane lighted off the horse and looked anxiously about her.

"We are not far from the village of Bromsgrove," she said, "and there is a farrier there who will shoe the nag. But I would one of the servants were here to take him."

"Here is the servant!" answered Charles, smiling, as he laid his hand on the bridle, "if you will show the way, sweet Mistress, we will soon have the horse at the forge door."

**"Well, now, I did hear as young Charles Stuart himself was taken,"
answered the smith.**

There was nothing else for it, though Jane shook with apprehension as they entered the village, and their presence before the forge attracted the usual small crowd of idlers.

But if the lady were anxious, Charles seemed sufficiently at his ease, as he held up the horse's foot for the smith to examine.

"What's the news?" asked the King of the man, as the task of shoeing was nearly accomplished.

"Why, I don't know as there has been any since the beating of those rascally Scots at Worcester," answered the other.

"Have they taken any of the English rogues that joined with the Scots?" asked Charles, with his habitual *sang froid*.

"Well, now, I did hear as young Charles Stuart himself was taken," answered the smith; "anyhow, they're so sharp on the look-out for him, that they're main sure he can never leave the country without falling into their hands."

"If they get that rogue into their hands," quoth Charles, "I reckon they'd best hang him forthwith; for he's been the cause of all the trouble, bringing the Scots into the country to fight, just as things were getting settled and comfortable again."

"Faith, and thou art right; and an honest knave to boot!" said the smith, as he finished his task. And Charles, after paying for the shoe, led the horse to the tree where his mistress stood waiting, smiling in her face as he observed the sudden pallor that had overspread it.

"Oh, my dear lord!" whispered Jane softly, as he swung her more deftly this time to her seat; but Charles only laughed as he mounted in front.

"Nay, Mistress, but if I get not my little jest out of all my troubles, I should belike go mad. Let us laugh and be merry while we may. Who knows what the morrow may bring forth?"

A little farther along the road they found the rest of the party awaiting them in some anxiety. Lord Wilmot had gone on in advance, not being one of those for whom Jane's pass was made out; but the others were waiting for them to come up, and were in much anxiety lest they had been detained by some evil hap.

They had now to ford the River Avon not far from Stratford, and proposed to stop for the night at the house of Mr. Tombs at Longmaston; but as they approached the ford they saw a most unwelcome sight. A troop of Parliamentary horse-soldiers had made a sort of bivouac on the river's bank, and were lying about by the ford, whilst their horses grazed and drank.

"We can never pass them!" cried Mr. Petre in great alarm; and forthwith turned round with his wife and servants, and sought to persuade the others to follow him, and find another route; but Charles whispered a word in Jane's ear, making no effort to follow the faint-hearted Petre; and Mr. Lascelles remained beside them.

"To fly is the greatest folly," spoke the King. "See, the fellows are eyeing us already. Let us wave farewells to our good Petre, as if he were riding a part of the way, and had turned back at the ford. But let us press on. You have your pass, Mistress Jane. If we want the whole troop after us all hue and cry—why then let us follow friend Petre!"

There was sound sense in Charles's words. As soon as the other members of the party showed that they were proceeding on their way, the soldiers ceased their significant handling of the horses' bridles and saddles, and only watched the oncoming riders with ordinary attention. Jane's heart was in her mouth as one of the men, whom she took to be an officer, rode up and examined the pass she held out towards him. But he looked only at her and the paper; he spared no glance for the stolid serving man in front, and the party was permitted to ride on unmolested and unquestioned.

Jane drew a long breath of relief as she dismounted in the courtyard after this first day's ride. There was still another night to be passed before they reached Abbotsleigh; and she did not yet know exactly whether she might have to accompany the party even farther, in her capacity of mistress to the serving man. But at least a halt of a few days was to be made at her sister's house; and she felt as though her responsibilities would then come in part to an end.

Charles seemed in a merry mood when they rode forth upon the morrow. Of course she never saw him when once they had called a halt for the night. He went to the servants' quarters, she to be entertained by the ladies of the house, her friends; and since the fewer who knew the secret the better it would be, she could not breathe a word of the matter lying so heavy on her heart.

But the King beguiled the way by low-toned tales for her amusement, though they seemed rather terrible to her too.

"I was bidden last night to wind up the jack," said Charles, with a twinkle in his eye; "and never a notion had I how the thing was done! We princes are taught a vast number of useless accomplishments; but how often have I wished these last weeks that I had been taught to cook viands or mend my clothes! I made such a bungle of it that the virago came at me with a rolling-pin in her hands. Odds fish! but what a rating I got! 'What countryman art thou, stupid-head, that thou canst not wind up a jack?' she cried; and I had to answer: 'I am a poor tenant's son of Colonel Lane of Staffordshire; and we seldom have roast meat; and when we do we don't make use of a jack. We put it in the oven.' Was that well answered, Mistress Jane?"

"Ah, my liege, I cannot bear that you should be thus served and rated! We should all be seeking your comfort on bended knee."

"Well, well, sweet Mistress, the day may come when the King will have his own again; but, meantime, let us enjoy a laugh over the fortunes of fallen royalty. Perhaps it comes not amiss for a prince to learn sometimes that, after all, he is but common clay!"

That night there was no friendly house to shelter Jane and her party, so they put up at the Crown Inn at Cirencester; and as there was always peril in such places of recognition, Charles affected to have an ague upon him, and retired promptly to bed.

Luckily no one in the inn or the town suspected or recognised the person of the King, and the next day's ride was without adventure. Just as it was growing dusk the party rode into the hospitable courtyard at Abbotsleigh, and Jane found herself being helped from her lofty pillion by her kindly host and relative.

"I would ask your good offices, dear sir," she said, "on behalf of this honest fellow, a servant of my brother's, who is suffering somewhat from the ague, that he may be better lodged and served than his comrades. My brother has a great affection for him, and gave him especially to me for this journey. I pray you see that he be well tended."

"It shall be done, fair sister," answered Mr. Norton at once; and summoning Pope, the butler, he put Charles—or William Jackson, as he was called—into his charge, telling him he was one of Colonel Lane's tenants and favourite servants, and must be treated with kindness, as he was suffering from ague.

Jane's time was naturally taken up with interviews with her sister, who had just given birth to a little child, who had not lived above an hour or two, so that the young mother was in sore trouble, and greatly pleased to have her sister's sympathy and companionship. This personal sorrow kept her thoughts busy with her own affairs, and she scarce spoke more than a few words about Jane's journey, whilst the grave face and rather preoccupied manner of her sister seemed explained by other causes.

It was not till the evening of the next day that Jane came upon the King, wandering in the shrubberies of the great garden. There was nobody near, and the place was so secluded that Jane did not hesitate to pause and speak with him. After all, even if anybody did see them, there was nothing very wonderful in her having a few words with one of her own servants.

"I trust, sire, that here, at least, you are subject to no ill words or hardships?"

"Nay, fair Mistress, I am but too well lodged and served. For that honest butler, Pope, who, it seems, was servant once to one of the gentlemen of my household, Jermyn by name, has recognised me, and will not be denied but to kiss my hand in private, and himself to wait upon me in my room. I tell him that a serving man has no need to be served, but he cannot see the sense of that. I truly think he is staunch to the core, else I would be uneasy; for there is a great price upon this head. Yet others have withstood the temptation to betray the secret, and methinks he will too."

"Oh, I would not fear for Pope," answered Jane eagerly, "he is a good and faithful servant. I am sorry—and yet I am glad that he should know; for now you will be served with the best that this house has to offer!"

"But we must have a care," laughed Charles, "there was a fellow sat beside me in the buttery this morning, who was giving such an excellent account of the recent battle that I took him for one of Cromwell's soldiers. But when I asked him he said no, he was in the King's regiment; and I thought at first he spoke of Colonel King, but he meant me all the while! So then I asked him what kind of man the King was? Whereat he replied, with a quick look into my face, that he wasn't anything like me, for all my swarthy skin; that he was half-a-head taller for one thing, and forthwith gave so accurate a description of my dress, and horse, and weapons, that I got frightened at the fellow's keen eyes, and got me away as soon as I could."

It was nervous work hearing tales like this, albeit Charles would laugh and make light of them. Too obvious a disguise would have provoked more suspicion than the one he was adopting, with soldiers and spies everywhere on the look-out for the fugitive Prince, whom so many already declared to be the King, and upon whose head so great a reward was placed.

"I marvel that each one who knows the secret doth not betray it, and make himself rich for life," quoth the young man many times, as he recounted his hairbreadth escapes. "What have we done that person after person, man and woman and gentle maiden"—and he bent his head before Jane with courtly grace—"should risk so much and lose so much in our poor service?"

"You are our King, sire," answered Jane simply; and that seemed to be answer enough.

Two days later Lord Wilmot came to her and asked speech. He had been hovering about them all the while, and lurking in the neighbourhood of Abbotsleigh watching and planning. Now he came to Jane, and spoke freely.

"Mistress," he said, "we still want your help for two more stages of the journey. Your pass will take us safely as far as Trent House in Gloucestershire, where dwells Colonel Wyndham, whom I have seen; and who will not only adventure life and estate in the King's service, but will gladly lose them both to save him from peril. Once at his house, where there are some excellent hiding-places, we shall be near enough the coast to make, I trust, some speedy arrangement for the transit abroad. But there are soldiers quartered in these parts, and we shall want your aid for the next stages. Will you give it to us, and be ready to start upon the morrow early?"

"Willingly, most willingly," answered Jane; "but bethink you, my lord, what can I say to the people here? My sister is very ill. She was taken last night with a fever, and now lies in a sorrowful state, and constantly desires my presence. There are her husband and several relatives to think of. What will they say if I incontinently depart? Will not such conduct excite the very suspicion we most desire to avoid?"

Lord Wilmot at once recognised the difficulty of her position, but his quick wit suggested the remedy.

"Mistress Jane," he said, "supposing that at supper-time a note should be brought to you purporting to come from your mother, saying that your father is taken worse, and that she earnestly desires your return, would that enable you to leave this house upon the morrow without comment?"

Jane nodded her head. It was a time when men were put to all sorts of strange expedients and stratagems. She had grown up in the thick of them; and knew how gladly all her family would join in the plot that had the King's welfare for its aim and object, though it was thought best to keep the matter as far as possible secret.

Her sister was not in peril of her life, and had other relatives with her. A summons from the aged father would weigh above all else; and when the soft-footed Pope brought her the letter as she sat at supper, and she read its contents half aloud, her flitting colour and fluttering breath seemed to bespeak just that amount of natural emotion a daughter was likely to feel.

"Bid William Jackson be ready to attend me on the morrow at daybreak," she said to Pope; and no one sought to stay or hinder.

So the brave young girl rode forth again with Charles in front as her servant. With calm courage she passed her little party through the lines of the Parliamentary soldiers whenever it was necessary; with ready and dexterous wit, she answered all questions put to her; and on the evening of the second day from leaving Abbotsleigh, she had the joy of seeing Charles taken into the house of Colonel Wyndham, where it was thought he would lie safely hid till a vessel could be chartered to take him over to France.

"Sweet Mistress, how can I thank you for this good service?" asked Charles, as she saw him on the following morning for a few brief moments, ere she started forth for home once more—her task so bravely accomplished.

"My reward is with me now, knowing your Majesty in present safety," she answered; "the rest I shall receive when I hear of your safe arrival in France."

"Nevertheless, sweet Mistress Jane," he said, speaking very earnestly, "if the happy day should come when I return as King to this realm, where I have so many brave and loyal friends, I will not forget those who have aided me in this time of storm and stress and threatened peril! Farewell; but something tells me that we shall meet again."

They did meet again. For the following year Jane was taken by her brother to Paris, and quite unexpectedly encountered Charles in some public place. He saw her instantly, and advancing, hat in hand, towards her, exclaimed:

"Welcome, my life!"

And since Charles II. has often been charged with ingratitude towards his friends, let it be said of him here that he showed a different spirit towards the Lanes upon his restoration to power. He settled upon Jane one thousand pounds for life, and half that amount upon her brother the Colonel; also to the girl he gave a beautiful gold watch, and a portrait of himself set round with pearls, which for generations (until, in fact, they were mysteriously stolen and never heard of again) were handed down as a precious family heirloom.

HELEN KOTTENNER

"To be a Queen, and a young Queen, and a widowed Queen in these stormy times, and in these stormy lands! Ah, Helen, Helen, that is indeed no light thing!"

"Indeed, madam, I know that it is not. I pray Heaven night and day for your Majesty, that strength and help may be given you!"

"Thanks, thanks, my faithful Helen. Sometimes I feel I have no one about me I can fully trust but thee. And oh, I have a load of care upon my head! I need a faithful and devoted servant, and where can I turn to find such an one?"

"Must that servant be a man, madam?" asked Helen. The sorrowful Queen turned her gaze upon the speaker, as though she understood the drift of the question.

"Ah, Helen, if we women were not such poor weak things!" she sighed, bowed down by the weight of her troubles. But, after all, woman as she was, the blood of kings ran in the veins of Elizabeth of Hungary, and after a long lingering sigh she lifted her head, and the light came into her eyes.

"Women are not always weak," spoke Helen, with a cautious glance in the direction of the Queen's maidens at their tapestry work away at the other end of the great hall. But they were laughing and chattering amongst themselves, as girls will do, whatever be the century or the surroundings; and then the eyes of the Queen and her lady met, and Elizabeth paused and hesitated.

Helen Kottenner was the eldest and most trusted of her attendants, and was devoted to her and to the little four-year-old daughter, the Princess Elizabeth, called after her mother. Although little more than a girl in years, Helen's life had been full of strange experiences and many sorrows; so that she seemed to the young Queen to be a tower of strength to her in her hour of perplexity and distress.

It was only a short while ago that her husband, King Albert, had died; and although the crown had been bestowed upon him in right of his Queen Elizabeth, yet so soon as she was left a widow, with only a little daughter, the haughty Magyars, or nobles of Hungary, repudiated the idea of being ruled over by a woman, and were casting about already to find some husband for her, whom they could make up their minds to recognise as King, in place of him who was dead.

"Helen," said the Queen, "thou dost know what the nobles are talking of. Hast thou heard more than they tell me?"

"I have heard, madam, that a powerful party is in favour of sending an embassy to King Wladislas of Poland, offering him the crown, together with the hand of their widowed Queen!"

The young widow started to her feet in uncontrollable emotion, and then as quickly sank back again.

"I have heard it too; but without my consent, without a word to me! They talk, and talk, and plot, and seek to settle questions, to dispose of the crown and a Queen's hand; and never so much as a word to her! 'Tis infamous!—'tis infamous!"

"That would doubtless come later, madam," said Helen gently; "at present they are scarce united among themselves."

"Then long may they remain so disunited!" cried the Queen, with energy. "It is time that I want, Helen,—time!—time! When the child that the good God is sending me is born, all may be different. I have prayed our Blessed Lady—ah, how I have prayed!—that she will send me a little son to reign in his father's stead. Verily I believe that she will hear my prayer. And shall my boy's birthright be given away before that happy day comes? Oh, the shame and injustice of it! I will not bear such a thing to be done. But how can it be stopped? Would it be enough were I to refuse, strenuously refuse, to have aught to say to such a marriage?"

Helen shook her head somewhat doubtfully.

"Madam, I fear, I greatly fear that it might not suffice. The wedding might, indeed, be postponed till your Majesty's pleasure. But if the Magyars once make up their mind, they will bring Wladislas hither and crown him King with St. Stephen's crown; and once so crowned nothing can change his right to rule, unless he grossly violate his coronation oath."

"I know it! I know it!" cried the young Queen, in keen distress; "if once that sacred circlet be placed upon his head, nothing can avail to change the thing that has been done!"

Queen and lady looked full into each other's eyes. They both knew that these words were the truth. In all the kingdom there was nothing so sacred as that sacred crown. Once let it press the brows of any crowned Prince, and his right was unchangeable and inalienable.

"You see, madam," continued Helen gently, "that the rule of an infant would be well-nigh as irksome to the proud Magyars as that of a woman. It may perchance be this very thing that is causing them to hasten to some decision. An infant Prince might be a hindrance. A party might gather—probably would gather—in his favour; and the land would be distracted by faction, and, it may be, become imperilled from outside adversaries such as Poland,

Bohemia, or even the wily and cruel Turk. Doubtless those who urge that the King of Poland be crowned King of this realm too, think they are doing a service to their country, and perhaps saving her from a bloody war."

"But are the rights of my child thus to be given away, ere we can claim them for him?" cried the Queen indignantly. "Oh, Helen, Helen, dost thou think this thing will be?"

"Indeed, madam, I fear it. All are not yet agreed; but every day there come over fresh adherents to the cause. I trow before long they will dispatch an embassy. But they will send first to know your Majesty's pleasure!"

"My pleasure!" repeated the young Queen bitterly. "How much do they think or care for that?"

"Indeed, madam, they are a wild and turbulent crew; and in very truth an infant King might have a task he would be little able to perform——"

"Helen, Helen, thou art not counselling me to let this thing be without protest?"

"Nay, madam, I would not dare to give such counsel. But I would remind you how the thing will look in the eyes of the fierce and restless Magyars."

The Queen sighed; her heart was full of bitterness and apprehension. A weaker woman might have given way to what appeared the inevitable; but Elizabeth was not a weak woman, and a mother will be brave for the rights of her children, where she might be willing to cede her own.

It was only a few days before the dreaded news was formally made known to her. Her nobles requested that she would give her hand in marriage to the King of Poland, and thus unite the two territories, and give them a King whom they would be ready to serve.

The young Queen's answer was slightly evasive. She promised to consider the matter carefully; but since she had been so recently made a widow, she begged that they would not press another husband upon her too speedily.

With this reply they had to be content; but it did not stop them from carrying on the negotiations with the neighbouring Prince on their own account. They began to arrange at once for an embassy; and the Queen heard words dropped from time to time that told her how much the matter was looked upon as an accomplished fact.

"Helen," she cried, in deep excitement, when she had one day dismissed her other ladies and was alone with her faithful friend, "Helen, you know what they are already talking of now?"

Helen shook her head in sorrowful acquiescence.

"Alas! madam, they are talking already of bringing him here, and of crowning him with St. Stephen's crown, and then of awaiting your pleasure to wed him——"

"Ay, ay, the cowards! They think to force the thing on me! They think that then I must needs do their pleasure! That, being Queen in my own right, as truly I am, I must needs wed with him they will crown as King to save my Royal station! Ah, how down-trodden and helpless are we poor women! Who will come to our aid? They talk of the days of chivalry! But where is true chivalry to be found?"

She paced up and down the room in her excitement; and then, suddenly stopping before Helen, she said in low, deliberate, but very cautious tones:

"Helen, thou hast said that they will crown him with St. Stephen's crown. But supposing that that crown could not be found—what then?"

Helen started and looked hastily round her. Her eyes dilated like those of the Queen, into which she was looking. The two young women stood opposite to one another, breathing hard, and gazing, as if fascinated, into each other's faces.

"How if the crown could not be found, Helen?" repeated the Queen, with bated breath.

"Oh, madam, how could such a thing be?"

Deep silence reigned in the room. The Queen gradually recovered her self-possession, and taking Helen's arm, walked back to the seat she had quitted; she was trembling a little, but it was not with fear.

"Helen, I have thought and thought of this thing till it has become strangely clear in my mind. If we could gain possession of this crown, and hold it in trust, till we can have it placed upon the head of the son whom our Blessed Lady will send me—oh, then, good Helen, all might yet be well."

"But, madam, how can the crown be got at? Do not the nobles guard it as the apple of the eye? Would it not be certain death if any were found seeking to gain possession of it, even in the Queen's name?"

"Alas, Helen, it would! Whosoever seeks to do this thing takes his life in his hand in so doing. And yet—and yet—God has watched over more perilous undertakings even than this, and has brought them to a happy end."

Helen looked into the Queen's eyes, and asked: "Madam, is it a task that a woman may perform? Can Helen Kottenner accomplish this thing for her Queen?"

The tears rushed to Elizabeth's eyes, as she cried:

"Oh, Helen, Helen, I verily believe that thou couldst do this thing—with one faithful knight to help thee, if only thou didst dare to adventure the peril thereof!"

Then the Queen rapidly unfolded her plan. The sacred crown was in the vaults of the castle of Vissegrad, where the nobles had jealously conveyed both it and the Queen upon her husband's death. The crown, with other Royal treasures, was locked in a great iron-bound chest in a vault beneath the castle, closely guarded by one or another of the leading nobles of the kingdom. To attempt to reach the vault now, when the castle was full of people, all more or less engaged in guarding the Queen's person, was a manifest impossibility, although there was an entrance to the vault from these very chambers, given over to her and her maidens. But the nobles wished the Queen to change her place of abode, and to remove her court to Presburg; and the thought had come to her that if the crown and other Royal jewels were left behind, as seemed probable, since no talk of moving them had reached her ears, then she might make excuse to send back Helen, as though for something left behind, to the comparatively deserted castle, and trust to her woman's wit and skill and address to find a way of entering the vault, and possessing herself of the coveted treasure.

For the Queen was possessed of a signet precisely like to the one with which the chest was sealed; and she had keys which, it was believed, might open some of the locks; and, if not, they could make provision against such difficulties as that. If once Helen could gain possession of the sacred crown, and carry it away from the power of the nobles, no King could be set upon the throne of Hungary, and they would be forced to await the Queen's pleasure. But it was a task before which even the bravest heart might quail. Those were days when human life was held of little count, and the fierce custodians of castle or vault would make short work of any intruder found engaged in such a task as the one proposed to Helen.

"They will kill you if they catch you, Helen," said the Queen, with a little catch in her voice; but Helen's mind was now made up. The bold blood of a soldier race ran in her veins. She was not to be turned from her purpose by the promptings of fear.

It was absolutely necessary, however, that Helen should have at least one assistant of the other sex, as the task of filing through locks and bars would be more than her strength was equal to. The Queen had sought to win one brave young noble to her service; but the first hint she dropped of the mission desired from him had so alarmed him that he had departed forthwith from the castle, leaving the Queen somewhat disturbed in mind, though she felt confident the young knight would not betray her.

Now, there was in the castle a young noble of Polish descent, who went by the name of Pan Vilga. He had always shown a great admiration for the beautiful Helen; and she believed that in him she would find one ready to do her behests, and to adventure even life itself where her safety was involved.

Cautiously she broke the matter to him, and was rewarded in the confidence she had felt. As soon as he understood the perilous nature of the task to which she had pledged herself, he took her hand, and carrying it to his lips vowed to her that he would do everything in his power to assist her in her dangerous mission; and told her that, although he was a subject of King Wladislas, yet he regarded it as nothing short of an outrage upon the Queen that her hand and her crown should be thus bestowed without her consent. If they could in any way hinder this conspiracy he would be ready to adventure life itself in the good cause.

"And more than this, sweet lady. I have in my service a foster-brother, of my own Christian name of Konrad, a fellow who will follow me anywhere—and will do my bidding, asking no question, and be as silent as the grave both then and afterwards. Indeed, he has so strange an impediment in his speech that I think only I can understand his mutterings. He is, moreover, a fellow of great size and strength, and was brought up to the trade of a smith, till he followed my fortunes as servant. Wherefore, the three of us may well contrive the thing together; and the Queen may trust us to the death!"

All was now arranged for the journey. The Queen with Helen and the bulk of the nobles, and the greater part of her ladies, removed themselves to the castle of Komorn, the little Princess accompanying them. But some few of the maids of honour were left behind to finish certain arrangements; and Helen was to return for them in the course of a few days, and bring them with her to the Queen.

When Helen returned to the lonely and now half-deserted castle, she travelled by sledge, for the snows still lay deep on the roads, and the Danube was frozen over. Her companions on the journey were an old woman and the two faithful Konrads, who had been told off to escort the remaining Queen's maidens to Komorn.

Meantime, the castle had been well-nigh deserted; and though it, together with the precious chest in the vault, were in charge of a sturdy seneschal, yet it so befell that on the day of their arrival this worthy had fallen ill, and, instead of occupying his usual sleeping-chamber that guarded the entrance to the vault, he had been taken by his servants to a more commodious chamber some distance away.

"Sure our Blessed Lady is watching over us!" breathed Helen, when this thing was known; for the great fear had been that when the conspirators entered the vault through the door from the Queen's apartments, the noise they must of necessity make would penetrate to the chamber of the seneschal, and bring him and his soldiers raging into the vault; and then, as they knew well, there would be no escape. Instant death might as likely as not be their fate.

The maidens who occupied the now desolate Royal apartments were overjoyed to see Helen, and to learn that they were to start forth upon the morrow. Helen arranged that she and the old woman should occupy the Queen's room that night, whilst the other maidens took the one adjoining. It seemed long to her impatience ere they had got their packings done; and their chatter sounded meaningless as it fell upon her strained and anxious ears. Pan Vilga came in and out to help and hasten matters, exchanging gay salutations with the merry girls, but striving always to hasten proceedings, and warning them to retire early, as they must be off betimes. Ever and anon he would give Helen a quick look of sympathy, and once he contrived to whisper as he passed:

"Have a care that we have candles enough and to spare!"

At last the girls had made their preparations and were ready to retire. The old woman had brought many tapers, as Helen had spoken of keeping a vigil in the adjoining chapel, and praying for the Queen's health and safety. This accounted to the old crone for the fact that her lady did not undress; but she had no mind to share the vigil, and was quickly snoring loudly in her bed in the corner.

With a beating heart Helen peered through the darkness into the chapel where Pan Vilga and his servant were awaiting her signal; and together they crept to the door of the vault, which the seneschal had carefully sealed up. But Helen was possessed of the Queen's signet, and they could remake or renew the seals in such a fashion as to defy detection; and soon the men plunged down into the vault, whilst Helen was left to keep guard above, and, if possible, give warning of any approach from without.

It was an eerie task that had been assigned to her. From the vault beneath she soon began to hear the sounds of file and hammer; and her heart beat fast and furiously as she listened, so that the echoes of the whole castle seemed to wake at last into awful life. In terror she raised herself up from her crouching position, and stepped within the gloomy chapel. What was that noise at the outer door? She thought she heard the tread of mailed feet and the sound of approaching voices. Flinging herself upon her knees before the shrine, Helen besought the protection of all the saints of the calendar; every moment she looked to see the door flung open to admit a band of soldiers, and was rehearsing by what strategic device she could keep them from penetrating farther. But the moments went by and they did not come; and at last she gathered courage to go forward and open the door herself, and peer forth into the darkness beyond.

The men plunged down into the vault.

All was silent as the grave; and Helen clasped her hands in an ecstasy of relief.

"It was a spirit!" she said, as she turned back; "surely it is true what we have read of the care they take of those who seek their aid. There be more that are with us than they that be against us. Now I will fear no more!"

And yet Helen had scarce gone back to her prayers, and to vow herself to a pious pilgrimage should this thing come to a safe issue, ere her nerves were all set tingling again by some sound from the room of the Queen's maidens, to the door of which she instantly rushed.

It was only a girl crying out in her sleep; but as Helen crossed to her side to soothe her, and caution her against waking the others, it seemed to her that the room was ringing with the sound of the muffled blows that were being struck in the vault below. So soon as she was assured that all were slumbering again, she could contain her anxiety no longer, but stole down into the vault herself, to find out what was passing there.

The great chest was open; but the little chest inside containing the sacred crown still defied their efforts to open it. They dared not carry it away as it stood; it was too heavy and cumbersome, and would certainly be recognised.

"We must burn the fastening away from the chest," said Konrad; "shut all the doors fast, Lady Helen, for it will smell. But 'tis the only thing to be done. And when we have the holy crown, where can we hide it?"

"I have thought of that," answered Helen, "I have a place for it when we have it."

Quickly ascending the steps once more, she shut all the doors behind her, and again made the round of all the apartments, to make sure that all was still and silent. Then, being satisfied on this score, she possessed herself of a very large crimson cushion from the chapel, carefully unripped a seam, and took out a considerable quantity of the stuffing which she burnt upon her fire in the stove. This, to be sure, made an unpleasant smell, but Helen was glad of it, for should any of the girls awake or the guards of the castle come to inquire what was being burnt she could point to the wool and hair in the stove, and tell some story of how she was burning up some old oddments of the Queen's. Then with her velvet cushion in her arms she stole down to the vault once more.

There lay the sacred crown that Helen had seen once upon the brow of the late King Albert! Pan Vilga and his servant were carefully removing all trace of their work, replacing filed chains and bars and broken padlocks by new ones brought for the purpose, and renewing all the seals with the Queen's own signet.

As for Helen, she rushed at the crown and fairly clasped it in her arms, crying out in her heart: "Ah, my Mistress, my dear, dear Mistress—you are safe for a time from the menaced peril!" Then, whilst the men completed their task, and set the vault in order, completely obliterating the traces of their work, Helen carefully placed the crown within the ample cushion, arranging the stuffing so as to keep it from injury, and finally sewing up the ripped seam.

What a journey that was upon the next day; when Helen with her precious cushion in the sledge behind her travelled back to her Royal Mistress at the castle of Komorn! A thousand times her heart was in her mouth; for every time the cushion was touched or moved she could scarce refrain from crying out; once crown and lady, knight and all were in deadly danger of perishing in the deep and treacherous Danube, which they had to cross upon the ice. For the spring was at hand, and the frost was yielding; and the ice cracked so ominously beneath their horses' feet, that the terrified driver lashed them into a gallop, and they saw a chasm yawning behind them as they fled.

But there was commotion and joy in the castle of Kormorn when Helen entered, carrying with her a big cushion that she declined to entrust to any servant. For a little son had been born that very day to the Queen; and she had said that when the Lady Helen returned she was to come instantly to see her.

Cushion in hand, brave Helen entered the Royal presence, and, going up to the bedside, saw the Queen with the tiny babe beside her. The light sprang into her eyes at the sight.

"I have brought my little King his crown," she said; and, sinking on her knees beside the bed, she told the whole tale to the Queen.

When a few weeks later the little King Wladislas was solemnly anointed and crowned by the Archbishop of Gran, it was Helen who held the babe in her arms, whilst the sacred crown of St. Stephen was placed upon his brow.

"What!" she cried, the indignant blood leaping to her cheek, "hast thou taken the Red Cross? Why, shame upon thee! Shame upon thee! Thou art not worthy the name thou dost bear!"

The young fellow stood before her twisting his bonnet between his hands in somewhat shamefaced fashion. From the likeness between them it was plain that they were brother and sister: but there was a courage and loftiness of purpose in the aspect of the girl which bespoke a higher nature than that of the stalwart lad, who looked half-afraid to face her.

"Others have done it before. They are all doing it," he argued. "They say 'tis the only way of safety now that the English King is so mighty in wrath, and will win by force what he cannot get by friendship. They say he will come himself, and carry away our young Queen to England, to wed her to his son; and that all who seek to withstand him will be slain."

Lillyard's lip curled; her eyes shot forth fire.

"England's Kings have tried ere this to conquer Bonny Scotland. Let them come again, and see the welcome they will get!"

"It is all very fine for thee to talk!" grumbled the lad; "thou art a woman. Thou dost sit at home at ease. It is us men who have to go forth and take all the hard blows. Thou knowest the fate that has befallen hundreds of us Border men at the hands of the English. Why should we suffer it? What care I who gets the best of this quarrel? We are well-nigh as much English as Scotch. What matters it on which side we fight? Thou needst not glower like that at me. Others say the same. It is better to take the Red Cross and serve with Sir Ralph Evers or Sir Brian Latoun, than to be slaughtered like sheep by their trained bands."

The girl was looking away from him over the smiling landscape. The expression of her face was one her brother could scarcely read aright. He cowered a little before it; and yet her voice was quiet enough when she spoke; quiet and almost dreamy.

"It is better to die a soldier's death on the field of battle, than to turn a traitor to one's home and country, and sell one's sword to an alien King!"

"Oh, ay, you talk—you talk!" answered Gregory in a tone of offence; "women can always talk. But if it came to fighting, then they would sing to a very different tune!"

The girl's eyes flashed; she turned their light full upon her brother, who moved uneasily beneath the gaze.

"Then let the men don women's attire and take the distaff and spindle in their hands!" she cried; "and let us women go forth and fight the foe! I trow we should make the better soldiers, if thou art a specimen of the lads of the Border!"

"Go to, for a sharp-tongued shrew!" cried Gregory angrily; "I am none worse than others. Duncan has taken the Red Cross too. Small peace would there have been at home had I refused it. And have a care how thou dost talk to him, Lillyard. He will have thee to the cucking-stool for a scold, an' thou treat him to such words as thou hast treated me!"

Lillyard's hands dropped to her sides, and her eyes dilated. She had not perhaps a very exalted opinion of her half-brother, Duncan; but at least she gave him credit for personal courage.

"Duncan has taken the Red Cross!" she repeated at last. "Art sure of that, Gregory?"

"I saw it pinned upon his arm myself," answered the big lad; "'twas he who called me up and bid me do the same. He told me how the English were mustering, and that there would be another great raid; and that he had no mind to have his house burned about his ears, and all his crops carried off, with the cattle and horses, and nothing left us save bare life, even if we escape with that. And I don't see but what he's in the right," added the youth defiantly, "for all thy black looks, Maid Lillyard."

"Duncan taken the Red Cross," breathed the girl softly, as she stood looking out straight before her with that inscrutable look of hers. "Then this place is no longer a home for me."

"What meanest thou?" cried Gregory angrily. "Thou dost talk like a silly wench, not like our wise Lillyard. What other home couldst thou find? And, as I tell thee, we shall be safe here now; for the English are not to harry the homestead of any of those who have taken the Red Cross."

She did not seem to hear him. She had turned back into the house and was putting together a few of her private belongings. Her brother watched her uneasily, shifting from foot to foot.

"Lillyard, be not so rash. Duncan will never forgive. He will never take thee back if thou dost go now."

"I shall not ask him," responded Lillyard quietly; and then, looking fixedly at Gregory, she said half sadly: "I would that thou wouldst come with me, and tear that badge from off thine arm. Better a thousand times death than dishonour—if that be the choice."

"Women cannot judge of these things," answered Gregory, with masculine arrogance of sex. Lillyard gave a little smile, and urged him no more.

The sun was setting over Ancram Moor as the girl stepped forth with her modest possessions in a bundle. She had no wish to encounter the half-brother, with whom she and Gregory had made a home ever since their father's death. He had been a more autocratic ruler at home than ever the father was. Lillyard did not greatly love him; but she had never before doubted his personal courage or his loyalty to Scotland's cause.

Those were evil days for the dwellers upon the Border; and it cannot be wondered at, if many in that region sought to trim their sails to the favouring breeze of the moment. There had been sufficient admixture of the two races here to lessen somewhat the passionate loyalty to country that ruled in more distant parts. When the Scotch ravaged the English borders, the inhabitants sometimes preferred to make terms with them than to fight, and to bribe them to retire; and when the English forces invaded Scotland, burning, plundering, and butchering through the devastated land, it was scarcely to be wondered at that some willingly temporised. If it were true that the little Queen was to marry the King of England's son, and unite the two countries in one, what need to cherish such strong hatred and angry feeling?

But the war was felt to be unjust and unprovoked, and much irritation was aroused. Henry VIII. of England had shown his intolerant and impatient temper in a fashion which brought about the defeat of his cherished plan. He angered the Scots by his demand to have the little Queen in his own keeping; and, by his persistence and autocratic conduct, he drove the adverse party into the arms of France, and caused a rupture in those very negotiations by which he had set such store.

Even then had he shown moderation and patience, he might still have won a diplomatic victory, when the proposed scheme had so much to recommend it; but the haughty monarch had never learned the meaning of that word, and in his ripening years was losing the self-control which in his younger days he had sometimes exercised over himself. Upon hearing the news of the negotiations with France, he had declared instant war, and had sent two bold knights to start a Border raid, whilst his ships should convey an army to their aid by way of the Frith of Forth.

All the Border country was in a tumult of alarm. Help was promised them from the Scottish army; but meantime this terrible raid had been made, in which above a thousand men had been either slain or made prisoners, nearly two hundred houses and towers destroyed, and such quantities of sheep and cattle slaughtered or driven away as to render the area of country completely desolate.

It was therefore perhaps no great wonder that those of the Border folk who did not feel very keenly with regard to this war, should gladly avail themselves of the offer made by the English commanders, and promise to befriend them and to fight on their side if their persons and goods might be saved from hurt. Those who made this concession were decorated with a Red Cross, which they undertook to wear in battle, to distinguish them, and which they were glad enough to have on at other times, as it was impossible to know at what moment a band of raiders might not appear, and how soon it might not be needful to display the badge of friendship.

But to the high spirit of Lillyard this kind of compromise was odious. As is sometimes the case in families, she seemed to have inherited everything that was distinctively and vehemently Scotch. The admixture of English blood seemed not to have touched her. To think of making such a compromise with the English was to her mind an act of black treachery.

Perhaps her feelings on this point had been unconsciously strengthened by her attachment to a young Highlander, whose mother had somewhat recently come to live in this Border country, where a little property had unexpectedly come to her.

Young Gordon was a Scotchman to the very marrow of his bones, and his mother was full of the legends and traditions of the Highland home they had quitted, to which Lillyard would sit and listen by the hour together. And so close a bond of sympathy had sprung up between the two, that when Gordon spoke openly of his love, and begged Lillyard to look upon herself as his promised bride, his mother was almost as eager as the son for her consent.

It was natural that Lillyard, in her trouble and dismay, should bend her steps towards that humble homestead, where the widow, Madge Gordon, had been settled by her son, ere he went forth to join one of those bands of soldiers that fought sometimes here, sometimes there, as occasion demanded, and helped to keep in seething life and activity those terrors and those enthusiasms of patriotism which were the life and soul of the struggle.

The old woman looked up with a smile as Lillyard entered her cottage; but she spoke no word, for something in the girl's face restrained her.

"Duncan and Gregory have ta'en the Red Cross," said Lillyard, in a low, hard tone.

"The deil fly away with all cowards who would sell their country to the usurper!" breathed the fierce old woman.

"So I have come to thee, mother," added Lillyard simply.

Madge rose and folded her in her arms.

"Thou hast come to thine own home, lassie," she said. "Alan will be braw and glad when he comes and finds thee here."

A quick flush mantled Lillyard's cheek. Her troth plight to Alan Gordon was a very recent thing. She could not think of it without a thrill. Would he come to the Border country in aid of the struggling Scotch, writhing beneath the savage raids of the English? Surely the leaders of the many bands of soldiers, regular and irregular, would fly to the aid of their brethren when they heard what things were being done! Ah, yes, she would see her Alan before long! And he would not chide her for seeking a home with his mother!

"I could not stay," said Lillyard, as the two women sat at their frugal supper together; "it was like a knife in my heart to see that traitor badge. I could not stay with those who had taken it. And to be told that were I a man I should do the same!—that it was easy for women who sat safe at home to talk of courage and devotion!—that were women called upon to face the foe like men, in battle array, they would be glad to save their skins by any chance that offered!" And Lillyard threw back her head and drew a deep breath of anger and scorn, whilst the eyes of the old woman flashed in the firelight.

"Said he so—the coward callant! Much does he know of the lot of the woman, left alone and unprotected in her cabin, whilst lawless hordes of brutal soldiers harry the land, and slay and outrage! Do we not say, 'Would Heaven I had been born a man, that I might go forth to the battle? Better a thousand times to die sword in hand upon the battle-field, than to be butchered in cold blood like the dumb brute beasts!'"

"Ah, yes, ah, yes!" cried Lillyard, "that is what my heart is always saying! Would that I might go and strike one blow for my country, though I laid down my life in the doing of it!"

"Other maids have felt like that, and have done the deed!" cried the old woman, firing up, as she was wont to do when that subject came to the front. And almost without prompting on the girl's part, she plunged into the legends and stories of which she had an endless supply on hand, telling how women and maidens, and even tender children, had done deeds of heroism and devotion, had fought beside their fathers, their brothers, their husbands, and had shamed into courage those who were growing faint-hearted.

Lillyard's eyes glowed brighter and ever more bright as she listened. She sprang to her feet at last, and paced the darkening cabin to and fro with hurried steps.

"What one has done, another may do. Oh, mother, mother, why may not I fight even as those of whom thou hast sung to-night?"

"Daughter, what wouldst thou?" asked Madge, with glistening eyes. She was excited, and uplifted by the cadence of her own words.

"Let me go forth and fight. They say that a battle must soon be fought, and that Ancram Moor is like enough to be the place where the hostile forces will meet. Alan will be there! I feel in all my being that he is coming—that he is near! He will fight, and why not I beside him? Let me but don the kilt and trappings of that young Norman whom thou didst lose, and I will show to those who scoff at woman's courage, what one girl can achieve! Let Gregory and Duncan fight against their brethren if they will; I will strike my blow for the honour of our name! Their treachery and cowardice shall be atoned by the valour of the sister. Maid Lillyard will uphold the honour of her father's name, which they have forgotten and smirched!"

The old woman kindled into enthusiasm as the words were spoken. She had been born and bred amid the clash of arms, the struggles of petty chieftains one with another, the perils of war from brother or from foeman. The blood of a wild race was in her veins, and neither time nor age had cooled it. She understood the mood which had come upon Lillyard, as few of her own kin or neighbours would have understood it. She rose to her feet, laid her hands upon the girl's shoulders, and, after gazing steadfastly into her eyes for several long seconds, led her into the inner room, and opened a great chest.

Next day Alan came; he rode in the three hundred horse under dauntless young Norman Leslie. Gallant and brave, did this band appear in the eyes of all beholders; and cheering was the news they brought, that Lord Buccleuch was on his way with all speed to join them; that other reinforcements had started from various points, and would all converge here; and that the astute Earl of Angus was narrowly watching the English, and was advising the Scotch leaders as to their best course of action in repelling this threatened attack; whilst that he himself would be with them before the day of battle.

It was splendid news for the loyal Borderers, and some who had taken the Red Cross in their hour of fear, were ready to tear it off now that they believed help was at hand. But others, like Duncan and Gregory, were too cautious to be easily persuaded. They feared to lose their comfortable homestead, and to suffer at the hands of the English. Moreover, it was known that the renegades who had taken the Cross and then flung it away, were the especial mark of English vengeance and cruelty.

Great was the joy of Alan Gordon to find Lillyard beneath his mother's roof; and eager was the interest with which he heard her tale. No love had ever been lost between him and the brothers of the maid he loved; and little recked he that, since they knew whither she had betaken herself, they had cast her off utterly.

"'Tis all in a piece with their coward treachery!" he cried. "But what matter, since thou art mine? and when the battle has been fought and won, we two will wed, sweet Lillyard, and thou shalt never lack a home."

She looked up into her lover's eyes, and smiled; but there was something in that smile which he did not fully understand.

Busy and stirring were the days that followed, and full of seething hopes and fears. The forces on both sides were mustering apace, and it was known that the threatened battle could not be long delayed. Both sides were eagerly anxious to come to blows.

The day arrived. No cloud dimmed the brightness of the sky. The two armies were drawn up in battle array; and Alan had but a moment in which to dash in and kiss his mother and his betrothed.

"A glorious victory will be ours!" he cried, "something in my heart tells me so! Thou wilt see somewhat of the fight, even from here, mother. Lillyard, beloved, one more kiss. We shall meet again with hearts full of gladness!"

She smiled a strange smile as she kissed him farewell, and watched the tall figure swinging away over the broken ground. The air seemed full of the blare of trumpets, the stamping of horses, the clangour of steel trappings. The girl's eyes kindled. She drew her breath in sharp, excited gasps.

"Now, mother," she said, wheeling round to where the old woman stood, her gaze resting so earnestly upon her that it might almost have scorched her by its fiery intensity.

"Thou hast no fear, daughter?"

"I know not the meaning of the word!" cried Lillyard. "My heart is yonder. Where my heart is, there would my arm be!"

"Then come, child, come. Thou art of the right stuff; and I will never hold thee back. Go, and may the God of battles be with thee, and give thee part in the glory of victory!"

A short time later there emerged from that cottage a goodly youth in the Gordon kilt, and with all the weapons that a Highland lad carries with him into the battle. The bonnet was set upon a mass of tawny floating curls, and the great grey eyes were full of fire and light.

She set herself in their ranks, and went charging down the hill.

Lillyard's great beauty was well known throughout the district. "Fair Maid Lillyard" had been the sobriquet ever since she had been a child. There was something almost dazzling in her aspect to-day, as she stood for a moment in the glory of the golden sunshine, and gazed across towards where the sounds of clashing swords and the booming of guns told her that the battle was raging; and then, with her light broadsword in her hand, she made a forward dash, and was soon in full sight of the fiercely fought fight.

The apparition of this fair girl, who was instantly recognised for her beauty and peculiarly lofty bearing, dressed as a soldier, and with a sword in her hand, evoked a yell of enthusiasm and joy from the whole of the Scotch ranks. It seemed to the men almost as though some angelic being had come down to their aid.

"Maid Lillyard! Maid Lillyard!" was the shout that went up; and when she set herself in their ranks, and went charging down the hill to meet the advance of the enemy, the fury of that charge was something so tremendous, that the ranks of the English were split into a score of scattered bodies, each flying back to the main body for safety, whilst the victorious Scotch pursued them with shouts almost to their own camp.

Who can remember or describe the fierce joy, the fearful peril, the wild exaltation of hand-to-hand fighting? Lillyard was in the thick of the most furious onslaughts, on whatever part of the field they took place. Attached to no company, under no authority, she seemed like a spirit of the battle, free, and with a charmed life, as she hurried hither and thither. All men saw her. A hundred voices testified to the prodigies of valour she performed; but it was only after she had seen the dead body of Alan Gordon lifted from beneath a pile of English corpses—men that he had slain—that that Berserker fury fell upon Lillyard, which has given her name to posterity, and caused the very name of the battle of Ancram Moor to be more generally known as the battle of Lillyard's Edge.

Was it her hand which slew the English leader, Evers, who perished on that field? Many declared it was so; but whether or no this was the case, there is no manner of doubt that Lillyard's strong right arm and dauntless heart carried her through the fierce fight, and that she inflicted her full share of death and wounds upon her country's foes.

As the tide of battle set in favour of the Scotch arms, numbers of those who had borne the Red Cross, and had fought in the English ranks, tore off their badges and went boldly over to the other side, seeing now greater safety there than in the ranks of the alien conqueror.

Of these time-servers were Duncan and Gregory. The latter had little of the soldier-nature in him, and had kept, as far as possible, out of the thick of the fight; but when he saw the Scotch arms victorious all over the field, he eagerly snatched off his badge, and made a dash for his countrymen. He was hotly pursued by half a dozen enraged English soldiers, but being fleet of foot, he might have escaped them had he not caught his foot in what was nothing more nor less than a heap of slain and wounded, and come heavily to the ground, yelling aloud in his terror.

Suddenly he was aware of a great tumult close about him. He raised his head and looked up. What strange vision was it that his eyes rested upon?

A young lad, as it seemed to him for a moment, had raised himself partially from the heap of dead and dying on which he lay. He seemed to be too terribly wounded to stand; and yet, with his swinging sword, he was keeping at bay the English soldiers who were in pursuit of Gregory; and there was something so strange and unearthly in his aspect that the men cried one to another:

"It is no human thing! It is some demon of the battle! I have heard that a spirit is abroad in the Scotch camp to-day. Let us leave it and be gone!"

They turned and fled, and the strange fighter, parting the mass of hair, partly clotted with blood, that hid its face, looked full into Gregory's eyes, whilst he shrank away, crying out in fear:

"It is Lillyard!—it is Lillyard!—or her wraith!"

She bent her clear, strange gaze upon him steadfastly.

"Not her wraith—yet, Gregory. Lillyard herself." The voice, though quite steady, was very weak. "It is not always the woman who fears the stress of the battle. Where wert thou when the fight was raging so fiercely?"

She looked him over from head to foot, and half-unconsciously glanced downwards at herself. The contrast was so marked that a glow of shame flamed in Gregory's face. He cried eagerly:

"I have pulled off my Red Cross, Lillyard. I will fight now beside thee. Thou shalt show me how to be brave!"

She gave him a long glance; a faint smile flickered over her face; then her eyes grew dim, and a ghastly pallor overspread her face.

"I shall fight no more," she said, in labouring gasps. "Lay me beside Alan. The battle-field was our marriage feast. Let our bridal bed be the quiet graveyard."

With that she fell prone upon the heap of corpses where he had found her, whence she had risen, though so mortally wounded, to beat off the pursuing foes who else would have slain her brother.

She and Alan Gordon were laid side by side, and every honour of war was paid to them.

MARGARET WILSON

It was ill work living in "the killing time"—as it was significantly called—for those whose consciences would not let them conform to the laws laid down by Charles II. and his advisers for the regulation of public worship in Scotland.

Religious toleration was no longer to be permitted. The Episcopal form of worship was to be made compulsory, and that amongst persons who hated and abhorred it, looked upon it as something emanating more or less directly from the Evil One, and who clung all the more closely to their own barer forms of worship and narrow purity of doctrine for the very opposition they had to encounter.

The Solemn League and Covenant had been formed for the protection of the Presbyterian form of worship, and Covenanters was the name given to those who continued to meet in the forbidden assemblies; and these were often held in the open air, in some wild and lonely spot, the men carrying weapons which were piled conveniently for instant use should an alarm be issued by the scouts set to watch, the women seated nearest to the preacher, and their horses picketed only a short distance off, so that flight should be quick and easy if there were danger of interruption from soldiers in the King's pay.

In those days it was no uncommon thing for houses and families to be strangely and pitifully split up and divided into hostile camps; but perhaps there were few instances so strange as that presented by the Wilson family, of Wigton.

Wilson was a prosperous farmer, a Presbyterian by tradition, though no theologian; but when the edicts went forth against the existing forms of worship, and attendance at the parish church was enjoined, both he and his wife made no trouble about conforming to the new regulations, though whether this conformity came from liberality of mind or from fear of consequences cannot now be determined.

But, to their great astonishment and dismay, their two little girls, Margaret and Agnes, at that time quite children, could not be induced to accompany their parents to the church. What they had heard against Episcopal forms in old days seemed to have sunk so deeply into their hearts and consciences that there was no way of eradicating it; and great fear fell upon the parents, for the thing became known somewhat far and wide, and began to excite comment and question.

"Where are the bairns?" asked the farmer, coming in one day, with a look of anxiety upon his face.

"Nay, I know not," answered his wife. "They did their tasks, and then they both slipped away. I have not seen them this two hours. Like enough they have gone across to see Margaret M'Lauchlan. They are for ever running in and out of her house, say and do what I will!"

"A pestilent woman! Covenanter to the backbone! She will bring herself and our bairns to ruin if something be not done! Why do you not keep them at home with you?"

"Why, husband, how can I be in three or four places at once? I give them their tasks, but they do them with a will, and are gone ere I have time to turn round."

"Ay, and are off to some Conventicle, I'll be bound. That woman M'Lauchlan is in the thick of all the Covenanters' secrets; and it's from her the bairns learn all those notions that will be their ruin one of these days. The Bible bids children obey their parents, but not a word will they hear from us! Or, rather, they listen, but will not heed."

"Alack!—and so said I to them but the other day! and Margaret turned upon me and answered: "Ay, mither, children are bidden to obey their parents in the Lord; but the Lord bids us not to sully our conscience by doing what is wrong, or bowing the knee to Baal.' They get taught by those who are good folks enough, but terrible stubborn, and wae's me, but I can say nought, and so they get the last word every time;" and the mother shook her head, for in her secret heart she was in far more sympathy with her bairns than was the father, who was seriously disturbed and anxious.

"They shall either learn to obey, or they must be sent away out of reach of that pestilent woman!" he cried, storming up and down. "If they stay here they will bring themselves to prison and death, and us into, I know not what trouble! I'll be bound they are off to some preaching now! I hear there is to be one somewhere hard by. But this shall be the last. If they will not promise to attend church with us they must be sent elsewhere. All the town begins to talk of it. Soon it will come to the magistrate's ears, and then——"

The mother clasped her hands, and the tears started to her eyes.

"They are but bairns; they are not near sixteen yet—not even Margaret. What could they do to them?"

"They will make them feel the hand of the law; ay, and us too, as thou wilt plainly see! They talk about sixteen; but have not babes and sucklings been slaughtered ere this by the ruthless soldiers?"

The mother wept, and the father stormed; but the hours passed on, and the girls did not return. It was almost dark ere they entered the house; and upon the fair face of the elder was a strange wrapt expression, that her mother had noted there many times of late, and which always filled her with a sense of awe.

She stood quietly beneath the storm of her father's anger; her deep blue eyes seeming to see away beyond him. Agnes, a slighter dark-eyed child, shrank away towards her mother, who could not repulse her; but Margaret was calm and serene.

"Dear father, thou dost not understand," she said very softly at last, when the storm had well-nigh spent itself; "perchance some day thine eyes will be opened to see even as we do. But——"

The sentence was not destined to be finished; a breathless messenger burst into the house, white-faced and wild-eyed. It was a tall lad, well known to the Wilsons, and his name was Archie Scott.

"The magistrate is coming—fly!—fly!" he cried. "He is coming to seize Margaret and Agnes. It has been told him how that they never come to church; and to-day one brought word that they and others have been seen at a forbidden gathering. The soldiers and officers are already started forth to make a raid on all suspected houses. The girls must fly!—must fly at once! I have come to take them to a place where others are hiding for the moment. They have been preparing for this. They will not be taken altogether unawares. But there is not a moment to lose!"

The mother had clasped Agnes in her arms, and her tears were streaming down. The farmer was storming up and down in a tempest of fear and anger—anger at the girls, at the law, at the barbarity of punishing mere children—at everything and everybody. Margaret alone was calm; her countenance had not changed.

"Let them come," she answered quietly, "men can only hurt our bodies. None can touch our true selves. Why should we be afraid? Why should we fly?"

But the mother rose and thrust the trembling Agnes into her sister's arms.

"Save her! save her!" she sobbed. "It is thine example that hath led her to this. To thee do I look to save her from the peril which now besets her. If thou hast no thought or care for thine own life, save that of thy sister!"

Margaret looked down at the little white tearful, and yet courageous, face of her sister and companion, and the dreamy look passed from her eyes, whilst her mouth grew resolute.

"Yes, yes," she cried, in a low voice, "they shall not touch Agnes! She shall be saved. Lead on Archie, lead on! We will follow you to the hiding place of which you spoke."

The youth was only too ready to obey; his own agitation was great. Although not himself of the same way of thinking as the Covenanters, he had the greatest reverence for their firmness and strong faith, and for Margaret he entertained feelings which, as yet, were scarcely understood by him, only it somehow seemed as though were he to lose her, life would be changed for him.

Margaret was but fourteen years of age at this time, and Archie was not twenty; but the girl had that within her and in her aspect, which made it impossible to regard her as a child. When stories were told of the virgin saints and martyrs of old, it was always Margaret's calm, sweet, young face that rose up before the eyes of the lad, and her resolution and courage in face of a threatened and fearful danger intensified this impression.

As he hurried the girls along towards the place which he knew would be a safe shelter for them and for others, and enable them to join with a party of fugitives whose arrangements were all made, he strove to change the purpose of Margaret, and to seek to win her promise to conform to the laws of the land.

But she shook her head, and the glow in her eyes made them shine like stars in the dusk.

"Nay, Archie, thou must not seek to turn me from the straight and narrow way, even though it be a thorny one to tread! I ask not of thee to follow it. If thou canst serve God and the King too, with a free heart and conscience, then thank God for it, and dwell in peace and safety! For myself I cannot. The Spirit hath shown me a more excellent way, and I needs must follow at all cost. What are the trials and troubles and sufferings of this present life when an eternity of glory lies beyond? 'To him that overcometh will I give——'"

She did not finish the sentence; her mind seemed to travel too swiftly for words. Archie looked at her; and Agnes raised her white, tear-stained face, and both felt that they were looking upon the face of an angel.

The King was dead! The news had reached the north; and for a brief moment the hand of the law was stayed. Persecution of Covenanters was temporarily abandoned till the mind of the new monarch should be known. There were those who shrewdly suspected that where Charles had chastised with whips, James would chastise with scorpions; but for the moment the country breathed again, and many hunted exiles and wanderers crept back to their former homes, to visit their friends and see how they fared, even if they did not mean to remain long.

Archie Scott was returning home from his work one evening, when he met an acquaintance of his, a man for whom he entertained a feeling of deep dislike and distrust, one Patrick Stuart, who seemed always remarkably well informed as to what was in the wind, and to trim his sails accordingly.

"Have ye seen them?" he asked of Archie, with a look of mystery on his sly face.

"Seen whom, man?" asked the other impatiently.

"Why, those two girls of the Wilsons, who went into hiding four years back— just escaping by the skin of their teeth! I saw the pair of them not an hour since, down there with old Margaret M'Lauchlan! I peeped in at the window, and saw them plain. A rare, fine girl Margaret has grown too—such hair— such eyes! But she needn't think that her beauty will save her, once the bloodhounds get on her track!" and an evil light sprang into the man's shifty eyes, whilst Archie felt his fingers tingling to be at his throat!

Patrick passed on, and the other looked after him; his heart was beating high with excitement and a strange foreboding. He almost followed the retreating figure, yet he knew not what to say. He had a premonition that Patrick meant ill in some way, but he had nothing on which to base his suspicions. And his heart felt suddenly hungry for Margaret. He turned his back on the vanishing figure, and strode rapidly away towards the lonely little house on the outskirts of the town where the old woman lived.

The girl met him with the same calm sweetness of aspect. She had a sister-like greeting for him; but he could scarcely stammer out the words of welcome and greeting that he had been rehearsing so eloquently all the while. There was something in her beauty, her purity of expression, her deep dreamy eyes and steadfast glance that stirred his heart to its depths, and yet left him tongue-tied before her.

She asked him if he thought their parents would receive them, and could do so without peril to themselves. Archie replied that when their flight four years ago had been discovered, the officers had forbidden the parents upon pain of death ever to shelter or hold any communication with their children again, and had, moreover, warned them that they must instantly lodge information with the authorities, should they ever discover their whereabouts.

"Poor mother!" said Margaret gently, when she heard these words. "How she must have suffered! Now I understand why we never had news from her! She was afraid of learning where we might be. Yet I would fain look upon her face again!"

"Have a care, Margaret—have a care!" cried Archie entreatingly, "the laws are yet unrepealed. There is nothing changed, and this breathing space may not last long."

"I will not run into needless peril," answered Margaret; "yet why should I so greatly fear? Is not God strong enough to protect His own, if it be His will?— but if He desire to prove our love by something endured for Him, shall we shrink back in the hour of temptation?"

When Archie came again the next evening, Margaret was not in the cottage, and Agnes's face wore a frightened look.

"Archie, I am glad thou hast come! I have been so unhappy. Patrick Stuart has been here. Tell me, is he one that we may safely trust? He spoke like one full of sympathy with us and our sufferings and wanderings; but at the last he pledged Margaret, and bid her drink to the new King's health. When she would not, there crept an evil and crafty look into his eyes. I have been so frightened since!"

Archie was frightened too, and asked where Margaret was.

"She has slipped out to take one look at mother and the old home, and, perchance, to get speech of mother too. Old Margaret was to go and whisper something to her, and perhaps—perhaps; but they would not let me go; and something seems to tell me that danger is near. Oh, I wish Margaret had not gone away! I am never frightened when I am with her; but alone I am."

Archie was frightened himself. He felt perfectly certain that Patrick had set a trap for the girls, and that already he might be on his way to warn the authorities.

"Agnes," he said, "I would you had never come back. I would that you would fly the place again. Ye are too well known here. Anywhere else would be safer. I will remain with you till Margaret gets back; I will tell her my fears. Then I would beg her to lose no time, but to fly this very night to some place of greater safety."

But, alas!—already it was too late. Soon their straining ears caught the sound of measured tramping. Agnes gave a faint cry, Archie sprang to the door, and an oath leapt to his lips.

"They have got Margaret, and the old woman too! God in heaven have mercy!—they are coming hither for thee, Agnes. Fly!—fly by yonder door into the coppice behind! I will detain them by any story I can invent. Fly ere it be too late!"

But the news of her sister's capture seemed suddenly to brace the nerves of the younger girl. She darted out of the open door and flung herself upon Margaret's neck—Margaret, who was being led along by the officers, her hands bound behind her, though upon her beautiful face there was an expression of almost ecstatic exaltation of spirit.

"Here is the third of them!" cried the men, as Agnes appeared; and, ignoring Archie's indignant reproaches of cowardice and cruelty, they bound her hands, and set her beside her sister, and drove them on towards the Gaol of Wigton, as men drive cattle into market.

"Margaret! Margaret!" cried Archie, in an agony; but she turned and gave him one of her deep spiritual glances.

"Pray for us, Archie, that our faith fail not; and remember that we are bidden not to fear those who can hurt the body alone, but only him who can destroy the soul. Fare you well!"

When next Archie saw again the fair face of Margaret Wilson, it was when, after a very harsh and cruel captivity, that had left traces upon her body, though none upon her courageous spirit, she was brought, together with Agnes and the old woman, M'Lauchlan, before the magistrates to answer to the charges laid against her and them.

They had refused attendance at church, it was alleged, had attended forbidden meetings, had been amongst the rebels at the battle of Bothwell Bridge; and the old woman had harboured fugitive Covenanters.

A faint smile played over Margaret's face as she heard some of the indictment. She had been twelve years old and Agnes eight at the time of the battle. They had been staying with relatives in the vicinity at that date; but to be accounted as rebels!

For the rest she had nothing to say. She received instruction from those who preached the pure word of God, and had followed the example of the Lord, who, when threatened in one place, had quitted it for another, and had addressed His followers in the open air or in secret assemblies, as His followers of all centuries had been forced at times to do.

But there was no mercy in the faces of the men who sat in judgment, and in whose hands were such terrible powers. The three women were pronounced guilty, and were sentenced to death. And this was the doom allotted to them:

"To be tied to stakes fixed within the floodmark in the water of Blednoch, near Wigton, where the sea flows at high water, there to be drowned."

Margaret heard these words with a strange smile upon her lips, and a great light came into her eyes. She stood for a moment as one who has a vision of some unspeakable glory, vouchsafed to no eyes but her own. In the dead hush of the court all glances were bent upon her, and suddenly a storm of sobbing arose from the women present.

Margaret started from her dream, and looked round at the faces, some of which had been familiar to her from childhood. Her lips moved, as though she would have spoken; but she was hurried away to the rigors of prison; whilst the whole town was thrown into a ferment of indignation and distress, though none dared to raise a protest.

No fear was in Margaret's heart as those bright days of May sped by; and she upheld the courage of her sister by her own tenderness and strength. But the poor old woman, alone and broken in spirit, was induced to promise that if her life were spared, she would abjure the principles of the Covenant and attend the parish church in future.

When Margaret was told this, and that, if she would join in a similar promise, her submission together with the strenuous efforts being made by her father and friends, might avail to save her life, her face took a grave and almost stern expression.

"Get thee behind me, Satan!" she exclaimed; and, clasping Agnes to her breast, she cried: "My sister and I will lay down our lives for the truth; but we will never, never consent to live by and for a lie!"

"Then your blood be upon your own heads!" cried the angry officer, as he banged the door behind him.

The morning of the appointed day arrived. The sisters were calm and strong in their resolution. Suddenly the door of their prison opened. Was it the men come to lead them to the stakes in the stream? Agnes gave a little cry of joy and amaze as she saw the white, worn face of her father.

"My child! my child!" he cried, clasping her in his arms. His emotion was so great that for a moment he could not speak. It was Archie Scott, with a face as white as death, who came and stood before Margaret.

"Agnes is saved," he said hoarsely; "she is not yet sixteen. She is to be released and set in her father's charge. And the Privy Council in Edinburgh, on receiving old Margaret's submission and the memorial sent by Wigton, promised a postponement of the sentence till the King's mind could be known. But the magistrates will not listen. They will hear nothing; they will go on their own way. Thou art to die to-day, Margaret; and I know not how to bear it!"

She laid her hand upon his arm. Her face was full of joy.

"Nay, if Agnes be spared, my prayers have indeed found their answer. For myself—Archie, Archie, do not look so—I have long thought that to depart and be with Christ is far better; where the wicked cease from troubling, and the weary are at rest."

There was joy and peace in the girl's face as she was led forth from her prison, and old Margaret, too, repenting her former weakness, held her head high, and spoke with courage and resolution to her friends who had assembled to see the mournful procession pass by. All Wigton had come forth to see the martyrs go to their death; and Archie Scott walked near to Margaret, and kept his eyes fixed upon her face, as though to seek to learn something of her spirit.

"Thou wilt be a brother to my sweet Agnes and comfort her," said Margaret to him once. "I trow she will be loyal and true to her faith, even though she may be forced to some outward compliance. The Lord will not judge her harshly!"

It seems sad that such noble and courageous souls as those that animated the martyrs of the Covenant should regard it as a possible offence against God to attend a service to His honour and glory, and by consecrated servants set aside for His service. Perhaps as Margaret Wilson stood in the midst of the waters, bound to her stake, watching the rise of the flood which must soon overwhelm her—perhaps something of the wider and grander aspects of the One Church—Holy and Catholic—with the Lord for her Head was vouchsafed in vision to her spirit. For, suddenly, as she saw the last struggles of the aged woman who was tied on somewhat lower ground, and knew that a few minutes more would see the end of her own young life, she first broke into words of psalm and holy writ, and then suddenly exclaimed:

"The King! the King! the poor misguided King! May God bless and pardon him and open his eyes!"

"She recants! she recants!" cried a multitude of voices from the bank—the voices of those who believed that in this prayer for the monarch Margaret was making a recantation of faith.

"Bring her out! bring her out!" shouted the crowd, in frenzy; and the magistrates, not daring to withstand this public clamour, gave orders for Margaret to be loosed and carried ashore.

"Will you retract your errors, foolish girl, and renounce the Covenant?" they asked when, astonished, but calm and steadfast as ever, she was brought to them.

"I will not!" she answered, with quiet steadfastness. "As I have lived so let me die! I have nothing to recant. I am Christ's—let me go to Him."

"Throw her into the water, for a pestilent Covenanter" cried the magistrates; and in another moment the deep swirling waters closed over the slight heroic frame of Margaret Wilson. Another Christian martyr had gone fearlessly to her death.

AGOSTINA OF ZARAGOZA

The beautiful young Countess Burita was the first to set the example of heroism and humanity.

Cowering behind their insufficient walls, and hearing the terrible roar and crash of artillery about them, seeing the French take up a firm position on the Torrero, from whence they could shell the devoted city of Zaragoza at their ease, what wonder that the Spaniards—the women and children at any rate—shrank in terror from the thought of a protracted siege, and cried aloud that nothing could save them?

But the old fighting spirit of the past was arousing and awakening in the souls of the men. The tyrannical temper of Napoleon, and his aggressive disposition of the Spanish crown to his own brother, had inflamed the ire of the Spaniards from the nobles to the peasants; and, though a long period of misgovernment had weakened the country, destroyed the vigour of the nation, and rendered the soldiers of little use in the open field, yet it had not killed the old stubborn fighting spirit within them, and when their passions were aroused, the flames had still the power to spring forth from the ashes of the past, and there were moments when all the old chivalry of former ages seemed to awake within them.

It was this spirit that animated the defenders of Zaragoza when Aragon revolted against the rule of the French, and they resolved at least to hold the ancient capital against the foe.

Hopeless the task seemed; for the defences were of the most meagre description; the only strong part of the wall being the ancient Roman portion, the high brick houses within having no shelter or means of defence from the shells and bombs that came screaming and rattling over them.

But there were heroic spirits within those frail walls, and one of the first to show an example of high-hearted bravery was the beautiful young Countess. Whilst her husband gave what aid he could to the military defenders of the city, she organised her band of women and girls for the work which was only a little less urgent.

She ordered them to get together from the houses those awnings which defended the rooms from the fierce heat of the sun, and under her skilful direction these were sewn into huge bags that were filled with sand and earth and used with great advantage to stay the effects of shot and shell continually bursting over them.

The houses actually built upon the walls were pulled down, and all the beams were employed in strengthening the defences in other parts, barricading exposed windows, and making covered ways along the streets where the townsfolk could walk in comparative safety, despite the rain of bullets dropping round them.

But these things were not done without terrible scenes in the streets, brave men falling at their posts, horrible explosions tearing up the ground and scattering destruction all around.

Small wonder was it, if at first the hearts of the women had failed them, and they had been ready to give way to a sense of despair. But quickly they rallied their courage, and the spirit of their ancestors entered into them. Although there were so few soldiers in the town—only between two and three hundred in the garrison—yet the townsmen offered their services and banded themselves together for the defence of their ancient city, and after the first panic had subsided, the women were eager to render every assistance that lay in their power, some even offering to serve in the ranks like men, if they could be taken on in that capacity.

There was, however, one way in which they could serve the men almost as well as by fighting beside them, and that was in bringing them food and water when they were mounted on the walls at their perilous posts.

This was rather a fearful task. The shells rushed screaming through the air from the height above, where the enemy's batteries were placed, and none knew where the deadly missile might explode. Bullets rained about the gallant defenders at their guns. It was like walking into the very mouth of hell, as many a woman shudderingly observed; and yet there were always volunteers for this perilous task. The noble Countess was the leader in every difficult enterprise, and she organised a devoted band who should carry on the work with order and system, avoiding needless exposure, but gallantly prosecuting the necessary and most perilous office.

Amongst the most ardent and devoted of this band of women and girls the Countess noted one very beautiful, strongly built, dark-eyed maiden, who seemed endowed with strength and courage beyond that of her compatriots.

Wherever the fire was fiercest and hottest, wherever the strife was direst and most deadly, there this girl was sure to be seen, waiting with her water-cans to make a dash towards the thirsty, smoke-begrimed soldiers, when a moment's respite allowed them to step back for the sorely needed drink. For the fierce heat of June was in the air, and the sunshine lay blinding upon the hot walls and ramparts, save where it was blotted out by the smoke wreaths from cannon and musket.

But there was one particular corner upon the old wall where the fight was often fiercely raging, and where this girl seemed oftenest to linger, and the Countess, observing her with more and more attention as the dire siege went forward, took the opportunity one day, when there was a little lull in the firing, to speak to her and ask her of herself.

"I am called Agostina," answered the girl, "and it is my father who serves yonder gun. He has the post of the greatest danger. I dare not tear myself away. Every day I fear to see him fall. Many have fallen at his side, but the blessed Mother of God and the holy saints have watched over him, and he has not as yet received so much as a scratch. Alas! if he should be taken, what will become of the little ones at home?" And over the girl's handsome, resolute face there swept an expression of pain and anguish that was sorrowful to see.

The Countess walked beside her to the spot where her father stood beside his gun, taking this moment of lull to clean it well, for often it became so hot that he was afraid it would burst. His dark, smoke-grimed face, handsome like Agostina's in spite of its black veil, brightened at her approach, and on seeing the lovely, high-born lady, he doffed his cap with the instinctive grace and courtesy that the humble Spaniard has never lost.

Agostina handed him the water-can, from which he took a deep, refreshing draught, sighing with satisfaction as he handed it back to the girl. The lady regarded the pair, and thought they looked more like husband and wife than father and daughter. He seemed not old enough for her father, though there was such a bond of affection and familiarity between them.

"Take it yonder to Ruy Gomez," said the man, pointing towards a fellow-gunner a little distance off. "He is parched with thirst, and has one of the hottest places on the wall."

Agostina moved forward towards the man—she knew the names of all the gunners in this corner of the fortifications—and the Countess remained and entered into conversation with the father.

"You have a good daughter, my brave fellow. I have watched her these many days amongst the rest. She seems to know not fear—not for herself; though she spoke but now as though she lived in daily and hourly fear for her father's life!"

"Ah, poor child, poor child! It would be a sad thing for her were I to be taken. You see there are the little ones at home; she is like a mother to them, and to her it would be like being left a widow were I to fall."

"You have other children too, then? Yet Agostina is always alone in her tasks."

"Ah, yes; the others are too little, too tender. You see it was so: I married almost as a boy, I was little more when Agostina was born, and my wife died in giving her life. She grew up my comrade and plaything. I soon ceased to regret she was not a boy. She was as brave, as hardy, as skilful at games and exercises, as free from fear, as bold to brave toil and fatigue. Ah, I should weary you, Señora, were I to try and tell you of Agostina's childhood and youth! We have been more like brother and sister, comrades, lovers, than father and daughter; and yet, with all that, no daughter was ever more dutiful and loving and obedient than my Agostina!"

The man's face had kindled into a great enthusiasm as he talked of his beautiful daughter; that she was the very apple of his eye none could doubt who heard him speak. The lady almost marvelled that he had taken to himself another wife, but in his own simple fashion he explained the matter.

"It was the year when that great sickness came. I was smitten down with it, and Agostina nursed me back to health. Indeed, I was never very ill; my life was not in danger, but she almost broke her heart in fear lest she might lose me; and when I was well she was taken, and lay for long at the very gates of death. And I, what could I do? A man is a helpless creature in such times; and many of the neighbours fled from us. But there was one who came to us in our troubles, a gentle creature who had lost father and mother in the sickness. She had always loved Agostina, and Agostina had loved her. She came and watched beside her day and night. She brought her back to health and strength. She was quite alone in the world; she had no one to look to; and so I married her, and Agostina was like a sister and a daughter in one."

"And is she living yet within the city?"

"Alas, no! She was taken to her rest last year; and at home are the three little ones, to whom Agostina is more mother than sister. A neighbour takes care of them now, for Agostina must do her duty with the brave daughters of the city. You, gentle lady, have taught them this. I thank the saints and our Blessed Lady that my Agostina has been one to answer to the call of duty. She has a heart of gold."

"I have seen it," answered the Countess; "a heart of gold and arms of steel. I have watched her often with wonder and envy. She has the strength of a strong man in that light frame of hers!"

"Has she not!" answered the proud father, his eyes shining; "and not only has she strength, but she has skill and dauntless courage. She can fire this gun as well as I can myself. She has stood at my side many times helping me to load and fire it. When I have been blinded by smoke and lack of sleep, she has crept up to me and whispered in the confusion and din, 'Let me take a turn for you, father, I can do it as well as you. Sit down a moment and breathe. I will serve the gun.' Ay, and she has done it, too—my brave little Agostina."

The man's pride in his daughter was almost as touching as her devotion to him. After that day the Countess watched Agostina with affectionate interest; and, indeed, others began to note her too; for in the many fearful casualties that befell the besieged, the explosion of the powder magazine, the firing of the convent, which had been turned into a hospital for sick and wounded, Agostina was ever foremost in the work of rescue, animating by her courage and example even the most faint-hearted, and performing miraculous feats of strength and courage and devotion.

In a city and at a time when all were heroines, Agostina began to be pointed out as the heroine of the siege; but she neither knew nor heeded. All she thought of was the safety of her father and the saving of her city. A passionate patriotism burned within her; she could face any personal peril if only the holy saints would grant them victory over their foes!

The gate near which her father served his gun was called the Portillo; and fearful was the fighting that raged round that spot one never-to-be-forgotten day of this memorable siege. The whole place seemed to shake and rock with the explosions of shells from the Torrero; fires were bursting out in many parts of the city. The sand-bags heaped up in defence of wall and building were igniting and dropping away. And around this special corner the fire was so fierce and furious that it seemed as though every living creature must be swept away, leaving the French a clear passage into the devoted town.

Indeed, so terrible was the bombardment here that the devoted band of women, ready with water-cans and fresh sand-bags to rush forward to aid their fathers and brothers, were for once driven back, and forced away by the smoke and heat and thick rain of bullets. Agostina stood her ground alone, peering into the smoke with anguished eyes; standing amid the leaden hail as though she bore a charmed life; wringing her hands together sometimes, when a cry or a groan seemed to bespeak the fact that another bullet had done its fatal work.

At last she could stand it no longer. With a cry like that of a wild creature in fury and distress, she leaped through the smoke and reek to the very wall itself; and what did her eyes see then? What sight was it that caused every drop of blood to ebb from her face, whilst the fire seemed to flash from her eyes and reflect back the sullen glow from the Torrero?

Every man amongst the besieged had fallen! Heaps of dead and dying lay at her feet. Her father—where was he? A cry of anguish broke from her as she stopped to look. From amid the heap at her feet a head was raised—a head and a hand—a hand holding a match.

"Agostina—fire—the gun."

It was his last word ere his head fell back in death. But the girl had heard, and every nerve in her body tingled in response to that dying appeal.

Through the lessening smoke wreaths she saw an appalling sight—she saw the rapid approach of the French towards the now undefended gate. It rested with Agostina alone whether or not they should win an entrance into the city.

With steady hand she adjusted the great gun that she had fired so often before. With perfect coolness and dexterity she applied her match. There was a crash, a roar, followed by the shrieks of wounded men, the oaths of their comrades. The French had believed the guns silenced; they had believed themselves secure of victory; and now their ranks were torn and mown by a well-aimed twenty-six-pounder. The officer in charge called a halt. The city was not as defenceless as they had thought.

Within the walls there was the sound of hurrying feet, as the Commander, with some troops, came hastening to the rescue. It had been told him how fearful was the peril here. Word had been brought that all the guns were silent now, and he knew but too well what that meant. Hastening to the spot in anxious fear, he had heard the booming roar of a city gun, had heard the cry of the advancing French; and now he pressed forward to the spot to find a girl seated upon the gun, which was still smoking, waving her arms above her head, and crying:

"Death or victory! Death or victory! Father, I accept your dying charge. I leave not your gun again till Zaragoza be saved! I claim it as my due!"

The next moment Agostina had sprung to her feet, for she was no longer alone with the dying and the dead. The Commander himself, Don José Palafox, a nobleman, who in this emergency had come forward and placed himself at the head of the troops of the garrison in the besieged city, was standing beside her, regarding her steadfastly; and, though perfectly fearless in the moment of danger, Agostina felt abashed before his fixed gaze, and dropped her eyes.

"Maiden," he asked gently, "whose hand was it fired that last shot, after the guns had long been silent?"

A wounded man half rose from the ground at their feet, and he pointed his finger at Agostina.

A wounded man half rose from the ground at their feet.

"It was she who did it, Señor; she is the daughter of one of those who lie dead beneath your feet. He had fallen. We had all fallen. Help did not come, but the foe was coming. We could hear the tramp of their approaching feet. Then Agostina was in our midst. Her father's last charge was given, 'fire the gun.' She obeyed. She checked the oncoming tide. She routed the advancing foe. Agostina did that."

But Agostina had not stayed to hear her praises sung; she was on her knees beside a mangled form. The tears were raining from her eyes. She was no longer the heroine of the gun. She was a daughter weeping for the loss of a loved and loving father.

"They loved each other so well—so well," murmured the wounded man, as his head sank back. "Poor Agostina!"

Don José would have said more to Agostina, but his kind heart told him that the moment was not yet come; and he merely ordered his men to lift up the body of the dead gunner, and to give it decent burial in any spot that Agostina should direct. It was some salve to her great grief that her father should lie in consecrated ground. So many heaps of slain had to be buried where they fell. The besieged had not time or strength to carry them away.

The following day Don José, making his rounds and instituting a more detailed survey of the wall which had been indeed terribly shaken and shattered by the firing of yesterday, was surprised to find Agostina hard at work cleaning the gun which had been her father's up till now, and to which, as yet, no fresh gunner had been appointed, for, indeed, the Commander was getting very short of men with skill enough to take charge of the guns. He stood for a few seconds watching her attentively; and when after loading the piece with the precision and skill which showed a thorough understanding of the task in hand, she raised her sad eyes, she coloured very slightly, and saluted exactly as a soldier would have done at sight of his commanding officer.

Don José returned the salute, and came up to the girl's side.

"I have been hearing of you, my brave child," he said. "What can I do for you in return for what you did yesterday for this city?"

"Señor," she replied, "I have but one boon to crave. Give me my father's place here at this gun. Let me serve it as he served it, so long as the siege lasts. He has taught me how. You shall not find me remiss. I think I am not unskilful. Yesterday, in the presence of the dead, I vowed a vow—I vowed not to leave my post here till the French should retreat from Zaragoza. Let me but keep that vow. Give me here the right to hold my father's place, the right to draw his pay, and that portion of food for the helpless babes at home that every soldier's family may claim. I ask nothing else!" She spoke very simply; there was no thought in her heart of playing the hero's part. She asked bread for the children, and the right to earn it for them. If deep down in her heart the fire of patriotism was burning fiercely, she never thought of posing as a heroine sacrificing herself for her country. No, hers was a simple nature. She loved her father with passionate devotion. She longed to accomplish the work which had been his. She yearned after the little helpless children, and felt she must earn for them the necessities of life. Provisions were beginning to run short. Rations were provided for the soldiers and their families; but the citizens were face to face with a scarcity that might become actual famine ere long. The little ones must not starve; such had been Agostina's leading thought. She would win for them their daily bread. She had been a mother to them for long; now she would be a father too.

Don José's face was gravely tender as he replied:

"My child, your petition is granted. No more noble or courageous custodian of that gun could I find within these walls. I appoint you its gunner, with double pay. When peace has been restored, and I can tell to the world the story of the Maid of Zaragoza, it will go hard if the nation do not provide a pension too for so brave a daughter of her soil!"

Agostina's cheek glowed; she bent her knee for a moment, and ere Don José quite knew what she was about to do, she had pressed her lips upon his hand.

"Our Blessed Lady guard and keep you, Señor," she said. "You have granted me my heart's desire!"

It was a strange heart's desire, in truth! To stand upon that battered wall in the teeth of the enemy's guns; to be a target for the shot and shell of those terrible batteries; to serve that smoking gun, and send its fierce answers forth into the hostile camp of the invaders. Others fell about and around Agostina, but no shot touched her. They came to say that she bore a charmed life; and it, at least, was plain that the thought of fear could never find a lodging place within her breast.

Then came a desperate day when it seemed indeed as though all were lost. A new battery was being built over against a convent, whose walls were weak already, and almost ready to fall. Strengthen them as they might, the garrison was helpless to effect any real improvement in their condition. They fell almost at the first shock when the new battery opened fire, and the French, rushing in through the breaches made, took possession of one quarter of the city, and sent a haughty summons to Don José to surrender.

The situation was tragic enough. They were now between two fires, and only a wide space like a boulevard separated the hostile camps. Don José had long been expecting succour from his brother, Don Francisco, who had sent word that he was marching to his relief with three thousand men and stores of food and ammunition. But there was no sign of his near approach as yet; and the city was in pitiful plight.

"Surrender! By capitulation alone can Zaragoza be saved."

Such was the haughty message from the French General Lefèbre, brought to Don José and his exhausted men after the fall of the quarter of the city called St. Engracia.

The Commander looked around upon the ring of gaunt men about him, and over at the shattered buildings of the town. What answer was it his duty to return? Was he justified in sacrificing all these brave lives? What did the people of Zaragoza think of it themselves? They had at least a right to be asked. It was they upon whom the brunt of these fearful days fell.

"What answer shall we return to General Lefèbre?" he asked, looking from one to the other; and the men themselves seemed scarce to know what answer to make.

Then a voice from the crowd shouted out the words:

"Let us ask the Maid of Zaragoza!"

Don José's face lighted at the suggestion. He turned in the direction of the speaker, and cried aloud:

"Go—ask the Maid of the Gun what answer we shall send back. By her word we will abide!"

A strange thrill of enthusiasm ran through the whole city as the messenger sped forth to the farther wall to ask of Agostina what the Commander should answer. Strange as was the choice of such an umpire, there was something fitting and dramatic about it that fired the Spaniards, and wrought a strange kind of exultation among them.

Soon a gathering murmur in the distance, which increased to a perfect roar as the crowd surged onwards, showed that the answer was being brought back, and that it had stirred to the depths the impulsive and excitable populace.

"War to the knife! War to the knife!" The words detached themselves at last from the general clangour, and the soldiers, flashing out their swords, took up the answer of the Maid of Zaragoza, and the welkin rang with the shout— "War to the knife!"

A few days after those four words had been sent by Don José to General Lefèbre, the longed-for help came; and the eyes of Agostina shone and glowed as she watched from her gun upon the wall the French soldiers in full retreat blocking the road to Pamplona. The siege of Zaragoza was at an end; and the Commander came himself and fastened a medal of honour upon the heroine's breast.

AGNES BEAUMONT

"Thou shalt never listen to the rogue again!"

"But, father——"

"Silence, girl! Have I not said it? Thou shalt never go to hear him preach again! He is a pestilent knave. He will bring all who hear him to trouble. Dost hear me, girl? Thou shalt not go!"

"Nay, but, sweet father!"

"Silence!" thundered the angry man. "I have spoken; let that be enough. Thou shalt have no more of this preaching dinned into thine ears, and neither will I. Thou shalt never hear Mr. Bunyan again. He has done harm enough already."

Agnes was absolutely aghast at this sudden outbreak, for which she was totally unprepared. She and her father had for some while been attending with great interest and profit the teachings and preachings of the notable Puritan, John Bunyan, whose wonderful personal experiences brought home to his hearers a sense of reality which was often lacking in other teachers.

Farmer Beaumont had, however, of late been strangely silent and morose, so that his daughter had been rather afraid to speak to him. She had noted that he had not mentioned the approaching preaching, which she was most anxious to attend; but she had no idea that any great change had come over him till he suddenly burst forth in this manner, as they were sitting together at supper, after his return from the neighbouring town, where he had spent the previous night.

Of course, Agnes was well aware that by many people this John Bunyan was regarded as a dangerous man, and that these inveighed against him as a preacher and teacher of strange new doctrines. Sometimes, she knew, it was dangerous to attend these meetings. She had heard it whispered before now that persons were often brought up before the authorities and fined or otherwise punished for offences of this sort, but it never occurred to her that her sturdy father would be frightened. She had no fear for herself. She believed she heard Heaven-sent gospel from this preacher, and she longed to hear him again.

It was plain to her that somebody had got hold of her father during his absence from home, and had worked upon the fears that were beginning to agitate him before. She knew that there was a lawyer there—a man she especially disliked and distrusted. Once he had been suitor for her hand; for Farmer Beaumont was reputed to be a warm man, and Agnes was likely to come into the bulk of his property and savings at his death. But the girl had repelled his advances with energy; having an intense dislike to the sly, fox-faced man of the quill, and he now repaid her dislike in kind, and she believed that on more than one occasion he had sought to poison her father's mind against her.

She suspected that this was the case now. It was plain that the old man was in a very angry mood.

After sitting awhile in glowering silence, he broke out again even more fiercely than before.

"I'll have a promise from thee, girl; thou shalt promise me here and now that thou wilt never go and hear one of his preachings more. Say the words and have done with it."

"Oh, father, do not ask me to make such a promise as that!"

"Ay, but I will. I'll have no disobedient daughter in my house. I've had a talk to Farry about it. Thou first will not have him for a husband at my bidding; now thou art taking up with this pestilent preacher Bunyan——"

"But, father, thou didst take me thyself to hear him, and said he was a godly man. It is Farry's evil tongue that hath wrought this change in thee. Prithee, pardon my boldness, but I dare not promise what is against my conscience!"

"It is against thy conscience to obey thy father, girl?" raved the angry farmer. "A pretty conscience in all sooth. I'll have that promise from thee to-night, or else I'll drive thee from my doors, and disown thee for my daughter!"

Agnes was in great distress, for she loved her father, and had always been an obedient daughter; but the stern tenets of the Puritan divines had penetrated deeply into her soul; and she was sorely afraid that by obeying her father she would be trifling with her soul's salvation. Most sincerely did she desire to do right; but it was so hard for her to know what was most right.

At last after much deliberation and some silent prayer Agnes brought herself to say, whilst her father had spent much of his energy in railing and threats:

"Dear father, I will promise you this, that so long as you live I will not go to one of these preachings without your consent; and I beg of you not to ask me more than that."

On hearing these words spoken whilst the tears ran down her cheeks, the father's rage suddenly abated. He kissed Agnes and told her that she was a good girl after all; and the storm in the house died down to a calm.

But poor Agnes was very unhappy. It seemed to her as though in obeying her father she had in some sort violated her conscience and betrayed her

Lord. When she consulted her married sister and brother-in-law on the subject (all ardent admirers of Mr. Bunyan), she found that they also took this view of the matter, and her trouble became very great.

It was now her chief aim and object to gain her father's consent to her attending the approaching meeting, where John Bunyan was to preach and afterwards to administer the Sacrament. It seemed to her equally impossible to remain away or to break her word to her father; and her only hope of real peace of mind lay in winning his consent to her going there.

During the last two days he had been much kinder to her; but still she was in great fear lest he was in the same mind with regard to Bunyan and the preaching. She got her sister to come over to the farm the evening before, and by talking and a certain amount of coaxing and argument, they at last won the old man's permission that Agnes should accompany her relatives to the meeting at Gamlinhay, they promising to get her taken and returned, as the farmer had no mind to assist her by sparing one of his own horses to carry her, and the distance was too far for her to walk.

It was a great joy to Agnes to win this permission; and she was more sure than ever that it was Lawyer Farry's jeering words and overbearing arguments that had caused her father so to turn against her and the preacher; for since he had been at home with her again, he had become quiet and reasonable.

But she thought it would be wise to be off and away early upon the morrow, lest he should in any wise change his mind; and so she rose with the sun, set about her morning tasks with great energy, and had taken her own breakfast and left everything in readiness for her father before she slipped into her riding dress, and made her way across the fields to her brother-in-law's house, without having caught a glimpse of the farmer. Indeed, she had left the house before he was astir.

Her sister received her kindly, and told her that they had arranged for her to ride behind Mr. Wilson, the minister of Hitchin, who would call on his way at the house. But time went on, and there was no sign of him, and poor Agnes's face grew pale with anxiety. Her brother had only one horse and would take his wife behind him. Agnes could not burden them; no horse could carry three riders. Strong as she was, she could not walk the whole distance in the time, since they had waited now so long. It seemed for a moment as though after all she must be left behind, when suddenly her sister, who had been gazing down the road, cried out eagerly:

"He is coming!—He is coming!—Surely, husband, that is Mr. Wilson on his nag?"

For a few minutes all thought this; but Agnes suddenly gave a little cry, and exclaimed:

Bunyan looked down at her with rather a grim smile upon his face.

"It is not Mr. Wilson—it is Mr. John Bunyan himself!"

"Then he shall carry you, Agnes!" cried her sister, "and you will have the pleasure of his godly conversation on the road."

The heart of Agnes was full of joy at the bare thought of such an honour; but when her brother ran out to the gate to make the request, they heard Mr. Bunyan's voice say quite roughly:

"No; I will not take her."

Sudden tears rushed to the eyes of Agnes; she hid behind her sister that he might not see her weep, and again she heard the tones of his voice—the voice she had come to love so well.

"If I do, her father will be grievously angry. I have heard how he has changed towards me. I will not set a man at variance with his children. Children are an heritage from the Lord."

At that Agnes ran forward, and told him what had happened, and how her father had consented that she should go to the preaching. Bunyan looked down at her with rather a grim smile upon his face.

"Ay, child; but did he say you might ride pillion behind the preacher?"

Agnes made no reply; but her sister pleaded for her, and in the end Bunyan consented to carry her, though he told her plainly:

"If I were you, maiden, I would go home to my old father, and seek to soften his heart by childlike obedience and submission, rather than urge him vehemently to gain mine own way."

They had not proceeded far on the road before they met a man on horseback riding in an opposite direction. To her dismay and annoyance Agnes saw that it was Lawyer Farry, and she felt certain he was on his way to her father's house. She knew well how he would stir up the old man against the preacher, and it could not be but that her father would be very angry to hear that she had been seen riding behind Mr. Bunyan to the preaching. Probably he would think this thing had been arranged beforehand, and no doubt Farry would do his best to encourage that idea.

Bunyan, however, not knowing the lawyer, paid no heed to the stranger, though he continued to give Agnes much good advice as to her relations with her father, advice that the girl promised faithfully to follow.

"For, indeed, I have always loved him dutifully; and till lately he has been a tender father to me. But he has been embittered against those things which I hold so needful for my soul's salvation, and I am torn in twain betwixt my duty to him and to God."

"Ay, ay, my child, thy path may be sometimes a difficult one; but remember that faith in Christ is enough for salvation, and thou wilt never imperil thy soul by abstaining from hearing some godly preaching, albeit such preaching may strengthen and sustain thee. God gave thee thy father and bade thee reverence and obey him. There is no doubt about that duty, so look to it in the future."

This gentle counsel set Agnes thinking deeply; and since it came from Mr. Bunyan himself, she could not but believe it good. Greatly as she delighted in the preaching and meeting which she had made so great a point of attending, she was possessed by a longing to be at home again, to ask her father's pardon if she had thought too little of his wishes, and to show him in the future a greater patience and affection than had been possible of late.

At the close of the meeting she was in some perplexity how to get home, since Mr. Bunyan was not going back that way; but at last she found a young woman who gave her a mount behind her on her horse, and in this way she reached her father's house, although it was now late, and her sister counselled her to come home with her for the night.

But Agnes thought her duty was to go home, as perhaps her father would be waiting for her. When she saw the house all dark and closed, her heart sank somewhat; but she would not be daunted. Going up she knocked at the door and then called aloud under the window of her father's room, asking him to throw her down the key, which he always took up to bed with him.

Suddenly a fierce voice came thundering from the lattice:

"Thou shalt never enter my house again. Thou art no daughter of mine. Where thou hast been all day thou mayest go at night."

"But, father, father, you did give me leave to go," she pleaded.

"Did I give thee leave to ride behind Mr. Bunyan? Go to him, thou disobedient girl; thou art no child of mine."

And so saying he banged to the lattice very fiercely, and Agnes was left standing without in the cold and damp.

For a moment she thought she would go to her sister's house, but then the memory of Bunyan's words came over her, and she resolved not to be driven away by her father's harshness, but to pass her night in the barn praying for him, and to seek on the morrow to soften him by her prayers and to tell him of the advice Mr. Bunyan had given her. She longed to be reconciled to him, and lead him back to the old paths by her filial gentleness. And as she made her way to the barn, she said in her heart:

"That is the work of wicked Farry. He has been with father again, poisoning his mind; but I will pray for him, and perchance on the morrow he will hear me, and let me come to him once more."

But upon the morrow the old man seemed more implacable than ever. He was rather startled at finding his daughter in the barn in her riding-dress; but he would not hear a word from her. He poured out his fury upon her in such ungoverned language that it was all the poor girl could do to keep from turning and fleeing from him. Yet, mindful of her resolve to bear all meekly, she continued to follow him about and plead to be taken in; till at last the old man in a fit of ungovernable fury ran at her with the pitch-fork that he had in his hand, and Agnes barely escaped receiving a serious injury.

"I will go to Prudence's house for a while, father," she said gently after this. "I trust by the morrow you will have forgiven me if I did wrong in riding with Mr. Bunyan. Indeed, he was loth to take me; but I was so anxious to go. Perhaps I was somewhat wrong to urge it so vehemently; but one day you will forgive, and let me be your daughter again."

Yet in spite of all the persuasions of the married daughter and son-in-law, and the dutiful gentleness of Agnes, it was not till the third day that the old man's fit of passionate fury spent itself, and he rather sullenly consented that Agnes should come home once more.

When first she began her accustomed duties about the house, he was very morose, and would scarcely speak to her; but gradually her gentleness and sweetness seemed to soften him, and upon the day following he appeared to have forgotten his ill-will, and they spent the evening peacefully together in cheerful conversation.

But the old man complained of being cold, which, indeed, was scarcely to be wondered at since the wind had changed and brought with it a fall of snow. Agnes gave him his supper somewhat earlier than usual, and he went to bed, she following his example only a little later.

Towards midnight she was awakened by the sound of dismal groaning from her father's room, and rushing to him discovered that he was in sore pain, and could scarcely draw his breath.

"I have been struck to the heart!" he gasped, "I am about to die. God be merciful to me, a sinner, and forgive me the sins I have committed towards you, my daughter!"

Agnes, in great alarm, flew about, kindling the fire, and making something hot for her father to drink, hoping thus to soothe his pain and restore him; but there was a grey, ashen look upon his face which frightened her terribly; and she was all alone with him in the house.

The terrible spasm lasted about half an hour, and then the old man fell back in a dying state. Agnes, so soon as she saw herself quite helpless to assist him, rushed forth to her sister's house, and make known her terrible plight. They all followed her back in great dismay; but only to witness the last struggle as the old man passed into eternity.

Agnes was crushed to the earth by this blow; but she was not suffered to mourn her dead in peace. The next day her brother-in-law came to her with a very disturbed face, and said that Lawyer Farry desired speech of her, and when Agnes would have refused to see him, she was told that it would not be wise to do so, as the matter on which he had come was of grave moment.

When she saw the lawyer's evil, shifty face, and the gleam of triumphant malevolence in his eyes she felt her heart sink for a moment; but then rallying her courage she met his gaze fearlessly, and asked him what his business was with her.

"I have come to offer you the only hope of escaping the punishment of your crime. There is one and only one way by which you can save yourself from the awful doom that awaits you."

"You are speaking in riddles to me, sir," said Agnes; "I pray you say plainly what you have come to say, and leave me."

His eyes looked more malevolent still as he came a step nearer.

"Girl," he said, in very low and terrible tones, "do you know that the doom of the parricide is death at the stake?"

Agnes recoiled in horror from the word parricide. The colour forsook her cheeks; she trembled as she stood. What awful thought had come into that man's evil mind?

"Yes, guilty woman, you may well tremble and quail, now that your guilty purpose is known. But listen yet. I am the only person who can bear testimony against you, and I will save you on one condition: Be my wife, and I will say nothing. The world will never know that Agnes Beaumont is a murderess—a parricide!"

Suddenly the girl's righteous wrath blazed up. She saw the man's motive in making this foul charge, this fearful threat. He knew that her father had left her a rich woman, that all he died possessed of was to be hers. To get her and her fortune into his power he was ready to perjure himself in the most frightful way; she saw the fell purpose in his eyes; but her spirit did not desert her. She stood for a moment in silent prayer, and then said:

"I will never marry you. God knows that I am innocent of the awful sin you lay at my door. I will trust to Him to save me from the malice of my persecutors."

It was in vain that the man by every argument and threat in his power sought to shake the steady courage of the girl, and to bend her to his will. In vain he painted for her the horrors of the fiery death of the parricide; in vain he sought to show her how impossible it would be to prove her innocence. She stood looking fearlessly into his evil face, and when he would have put out a hand to draw her nearer, she slipped out of his reach, and with a quiet and lofty mien walked to the door, turning round at the last to say:

"May God forgive you for the cruel deed you are about to do. Into His hands I entrust my cause."

Later in the day her sister came to her in deep agitation.

"Agnes, Agnes, why wouldest thou not submit to his will? He is such a crafty, cruel man. He will obtain thine undoing! Oh, sister, sister, dost know what he is about to swear before the coroner to-morrow?"

"That I poisoned my father—he has said as much," answered Agnes quietly; "but he can prove nothing that he says."

"Nay, but it is more than that. He has got such a story. He says that Mr. Bunyan did give thee the poison, and that he saw you twain riding together, and heard you speaking together of our father as he passed. He says that when he got here poor father told him that he was sure you meant him ill, and that you would find a way of getting rid of him, since you only promised obedience to his wishes so long as he lived. Oh, the story he has made of it! And then he points out how loth father was to take you back, and that he turned you away and said you were no daughter of his, and might go back to those you had come from. He learned so many things from us, ere ever we knew the hideous thing in his mind. Now he says his case is complete and that only by marrying him can you escape that awful death. Oh, Agnes, Agnes, wilt thou not do his bidding to save thyself from that fate?"

"Take a false vow of love and obedience to a man like that? Oh, sister, how could I? And what would life be with him afterwards?"

"But they say it will be death at the stake!" wept Prudence.

"And has not the Lord promised 'When thou passest through the fire I will be with thee'?" asked Agnes calmly. "I dare not be false to Him; and I know He will not be false to me. Be not afraid; this trial may be sent for some good purpose. But it cuts me to the heart that he should bring in Mr. Bunyan's name. That is a needless piece of wickedness and falsehood."

"It is all false together; but he vows that Mr. Bunyan wished to get possession of father's money by wedding with you, and that therefore he gave you the poison and bid you use it upon the first opportunity."

To the two inexperienced women, clinging together in their hour of affliction, it seemed to them as though the doom of Agnes had already well nigh gone forth. They knew how clever and unscrupulous Lawyer Farry was, and how successful he generally proved in carrying through the schemes to which he gave his mind. Already the neighbourhood was ringing with the story that Agnes had poisoned her father, and although many refused to believe in so monstrous a charge, yet it was very well known how violent the old man's rage had been against his daughter, and that he had died also immediately after Agnes had been taken back to his house. This was not evidence, but it raised doubts and suspicions in many minds.

The coroner and the jury had assembled, having first viewed the corpse, and Mr. Hatfield, the surgeon, testified emphatically that he regarded death as due to natural causes. The old man had long been suffering from some cardiac derangement, and the excitement into which he had recently thrown himself would be quite enough to account for the fatal seizure. Agnes Beaumont, he added, had given him free leave to make a post-mortem examination, but in his opinion the thing was not necessary.

Farry was then bidden to state what he knew and what grounds he had for asserting that his friend had been poisoned. At first he was very bold and confident in his manner, but he soon found that it was a very different matter intimidating young and ignorant women and dealing with a shrewd man of business. Under cross-examination his tale became confused, contradictory, absurd; his malice flashed out so unmistakably as to put all the jury on their guard, and when Agnes's sister stepped forward and asked to be permitted to say that Mr. Farry had promised to be silent if Agnes would consent to be his wife, a deep murmur of indignation ran through the room, and the man knew himself defeated and disgraced.

When Agnes was called, and came forward with her simple and unvarnished tale, it only needed a look into her calm, sweet face to know that she spoke the truth. She freely told of the difference she had had with her father, and how Mr. Bunyan had warned her not to urge her own desire too much, but to be dutiful and obedient. And her sister corroborating this statement, and adding all she had seen of Agnes's gentle submissiveness on her return, and another person giving testimony that John Bunyan had a wife living, and that the idea of his wanting Agnes's hand was nonsense, the whole of Farry's ingenious and malicious tale fell to the ground, and he stood like one who would never lift up his head again.

"But if there be any doubt," said Agnes, looking at the coroner, "Mr. Hatfield is here; he will make the needful examination."

"That is a question for the jury to decide," answered the coroner, with a smile. "Let them retire, and give us their verdict."

A few minutes was all these honest men required before announcing that death was due to natural causes; and then the coroner turned upon Farry and with a most scathing reproof dismissed him, warning him that he had brought himself perilously near a charge of perjury, had Agnes been a vindictive foe.

Then when the man had slunk out like a beaten hound, he took Agnes's hands in his, and said:

"You have been a courageous girl, my dear, in withstanding the artifices of that wicked man. Hardly another maid so young and unprotected but would have been intimidated into accepting his condition. What made you so brave to withstand him?"

"I do not think I was brave," answered Agnes; "but I knew I should be helped."

The old man smiled and patted her head.

"Perhaps that is the best kind of courage after all."

HANNAH HEWLING

The mother was stricken down with the load of her grief; it seemed to her more than she could bear. Her two sons—her only sons—young men of such promise, such beauty, such piety—lying in that foul prison of Newgate, of which many horrid tales were told; lying there waiting a trial, which all believed could only end in one way. It was well known how fierce was the wrath of the King against all who had taken any share in the late rebellion, and neither the youth of the offenders nor their virtuous lives would be likely to have any effect upon the sentence which they had brought upon themselves by their recent ill-advised act. The mother buried her face in her hands and groaned aloud.

Those were sad and anxious days in many homes, particularly in the West of England, where the Duke of Monmouth's rebellion had broken out, and had been quickly quenched in fire and bloodshed.

To Mrs. Hewling it seemed a terrible visitation of Providence that her two promising sons had been in any way mixed up in it.

"If I had only kept them with me here in England, they would have been safe!" she moaned.

It was not very long since Mrs. Hewling had been left a widow, in affluent circumstances indeed, but with a large family to bring up. She had two most promising sons, Benjamin and William, the first twenty-one and the second close upon nineteen years of age, and Benjamin's twin-sister Hannah was a beautiful girl of much promise, who, at this crisis of her mother's life, was acting as her chief support and helper. There were several little sisters, scarcely more than children; but the intermediate sons had died in infancy, and the chords of the mother's heart seemed to twine themselves about Benjamin and William in a fashion which made their present perilous situation a thing that could hardly be borne by her.

And the bitterest thought of all was that had she only kept the boys with her in London after their father's death, instead of letting them go to Holland, to see something of the world and complete their education, all this misery might have been spared.

Adverse as the citizens of London were to many of the methods and opinions of the King, still there was no desire at present to get rid of him by any violent revolution, or to place the crown upon another head. A few years later, and the whole nation rose in a bloodless revolt against the man who had broken his pledges and his coronation vow, and would have plunged England into a fierce struggle against the trammels of Popery. But at that time things were not ripe for such a drastic measure, nor was the Duke of

Monmouth such a sovereign as the nation could accept. But here and there where the Protestant spirit burnt more fiercely than elsewhere, or over in Holland, where the claim of the Duke had been more freely allowed, and where he was eagerly recruiting forces to take with him to England, his cause seemed a righteous cause, and inspired enthusiasm and devotion. Mrs. Hewling could not altogether wonder that her two sons, reared in all the most ardent Puritan and Protestant tenets of the day, should have been fired with a desire to join the expedition, and to strive to strike a blow for their faith upon England's shores.

And now, that ill-starred revolt having come to its tragic end, her boys were amongst those who, having first sought flight, had since then surrendered themselves to justice. It had been told her by friends that they were lying in Newgate prison, and would almost immediately be sent back whence they had come, to stand their trial at the Western Assizes, over which the fierce and notoriously cruel Judge Jeffreys was to preside.

So paralysed by horror was the poor mother, whose health had long been very frail, that she had been unable herself to leave the house and seek permission to visit her sons. And Hannah had persuaded her not to attempt a task so much beyond her powers.

"I will go first, mother," she said. "I will go with my good grandfather, who will gain me admission, and we will take money with us. Money will do much within Newgate, they say, to ameliorate the condition of the prisoners. Another day thou shalt go; but let me be the first."

So Hannah had gone under the safe-keeping of her grandfather, Mr. Kiffin, a citizen well known and greatly respected in the town, and the mother was awaiting their return in a fever of anxiety.

She was turning over in her bewildered brain a thousand schemes for the preservation of her boys. But the more she pondered, the more helpless did she become. True, she had many friends, and several possessed of wealth and influence in the city; but these were for the most part, from their strong Protestant and dissenting or Puritan leanings, so obnoxious to the Court party that intervention by them would do rather harm than good.

Her own father, Mr. Kiffin, was one of these He would have no fear in presenting a petition; yet if such a movement on his part were fore-ordained to failure, it would be better it should not be made. Others more likely to obtain a hearing would probably be afraid to intermeddle in such a matter. Those were the days in which it was none too safe to show sympathy towards the King's enemies, or towards those who had distinguished themselves by opposition to the Established Church. The penalty for showing kindness to dissenters was often extraordinarily severe; and what would it be to take a friendly interest in youths who had been concerned in treasonable rebellion?

With despair in her heart the mother sat waiting, pondering and weeping; longing unspeakably for the husband who was no more, and feeling the desolation of her widowhood as she had never felt it before.

Then the door opened quietly, and a tall figure glided in wrapped from head to foot in a long, dark cloak.

"Hannah!" cried the mother, "have you seen them?—have you seen my boys? Oh, give me news of them! My heart is hungry!"

The girl threw back the hood which was drawn over her head, and her face showed pale in the twilight. It was a very beautiful face, lighted by the enthusiasm of a great love—a love that conquers fear, and sinks all thought of self in devotion to the object at heart. It was such a face as we see sometimes on painted window, or in chiselled marble—a face full of lofty self-abnegation and simple heroism. The eyes shone like stars, and the mother, looking at her daughter, held out her arms, and cried:

"Ah, Hannah, Hannah, if any can save them it will be thou."

Hannah knelt at her mother's feet and spoke quietly and rapidly.

"I have seen them, mother. They were together, with many others. But my grandfather had them taken out and brought into a separate room, where we could talk. It was a dreadful place, that first,"—she shivered slightly as she spoke,—"but they will not go back to it. Grandfather is staying, and he will arrange all that. I saw them. Oh, mother, you need not fear for them! They have no fear for themselves. They are ready for the worst that may befall. Their only fear is lest they were wrong in taking up arms. When they did it, it seemed a right and holy thing. They have heard other things since coming to England, and are the less confident of that. But they have no other fear. If they have done amiss they are willing to die. They both say that. It is not death that can affright them. They have made their peace with God."

The mother's tears ran over, although there was something of joy in hearing such an assurance.

"But we must save them, daughter!—we must save them!"

"We will try," answered Hannah steadily, yet without the brightness of hope in her eyes. "We will leave no stone unturned. We will accomplish what can be accomplished. But——"

The last word was little more than a sigh. It was not meant to reach her mother's ears, yet it did: and Mrs. Hewling exclaimed:

"But what, daughter, but what? What hast thou heard more?"

"I have heard nought that we have not been told before; only, mother mine, when the grim walls of a prison are about one, and grim gaolers are talking with that cool certainty of things they have grown familiar with, the horrible reality seems to come over one like a flood; and the awful doom comes ever nearer and nearer. The boys have heard much—the implacable temper of the King; his bloodthirsty mood; his choice of the Judge who is to arraign them. In Newgate it is whispered that there will be such a slaughter in the West as has not been heard of in this land. I felt myself shaking all over at the things I heard there. Oh, I fear for my brothers, I fear, I fear!"

The mother clasped her in her arms, and they mingled their tears together. Hannah told in broken words of all that she had gleaned from her brothers, of what they had dared and done, how they looked, how they had stood the journey and the prison; and how they were soon to be sent down to the West Country, to be tried at those places where they had been seen in arms against the King.

"That is the worst of it!" cried the mother. "Had it been here in London town our friends and the influence of our party might have had weight. But over yonder—so far away! Ah, if I could but go there with them!"

"Mother, I will go!" said Hannah, speaking firmly and resolutely. "I have thought of it all the way home. I have plans of all sorts in my head. Grandfather will soon be here, and then he will tell you more, and we will talk it over together. But I must be there. I must go with them. I must—I must!"

"But, my child, my child, how can I spare thee? They say that the King is so incensed that even to show pity for the condemned—for the prisoners—is accounted as a crime. Suppose that hurt were to befall thee?"

"Mother," she answered gently, "God can protect me, and I think He will. But be that as it may, I cannot let my brothers go to what may be their death alone. I must be there to visit them in their prison, to lighten the rigours of captivity, to provide them with whatever may be permitted in the way of defence; to cheer and strengthen them (if so it must be) upon the very scaffold itself. Benjamin is as my second self. I could not be other than at his side. Oh, my brother—my brother!"

A rush of tears choked her voice; she sobbed upon her mother's breast; but the outbreak relieved the overcharged heart, and when her grandfather appeared she was the same calm, resolute maiden she had shown herself in the public streets, and in the dim retreats of the dreadful gaol.

Mr. Kiffin had made arrangements for the better lodging and treatment of his grandsons during their brief detention in Newgate; but he had heard that almost immediately they were to be sent west to be ready to stand their trial with others at the coming Assizes; and at the very name of these the mother's cheek paled.

"Yes, it is a terrible thought—the power that will be placed in the hands of one man—and he one noted for ferocity of temper and gross injustice to those who are brought before him. It is known too that the King has selected him for these very qualities to fill the dreadful office which will be his. Yet for our poor lads there may be this one chance: his cruelty is only rivalled by his greed of money; and we may appeal to his cupidity where we should appeal in vain to his clemency."

"Must we then offer him a bribe?" asked Mrs. Hewling, with a faint distaste in her tone, as though even with her sons' lives at stake, the thought of buying justice or mercy with gold had in it something repulsive to her better nature. Hannah's beautiful eyes were likewise turned upon her grandfather questioningly. It was an age when all sorts of things were bought and sold for hard cash, that never should have been so trafficked for; but in the stern Puritan tenets in which this family had been reared any sort of illicit bartering was strongly condemned.

"I did not mean exactly that; but yet we may perhaps move him through his love of money. You have both heard me speak of my old friend and fellow-citizen, with whom in past days I lived a long while, working with him as a brother might," and he named a name that was familiar to both mother and daughter.

"Well, strange as it may seem, the young barrister, now made a judge, this violent, bloodthirsty Jeffreys, is my old friend's kinsman, and, in fact, his next-of-kin. I had forgotten the fact, if indeed I ever knew it, till I had a letter from him a few days since reminding me of it, and asking if there was anything that he could do to aid us in our trouble. I have seen him, and he has promised to use every means in his power to gain the leniency of the Judge for our two dear lads. It is unluckily true that they have taken up arms against the King. It cannot but be proved against them, nor will they seek to deny it. By the law of the land they have merited death, and may even be condemned to suffer the full penalty. But as my friend informs me, out of the hundreds who will undergo sentence, not a few will escape the dread final penalty. Even the King in all his ferocity will not dare to slay by thousands, though he may by hundreds. Many will be condemned to death, who will afterwards be respited and undergo lighter sentences, or be let off with a heavy fine. In this matter the voice of the Judge will have weight; and my friend will use every argument to induce him to commute the death penalty (if passed upon Benjamin or William) into one that a heavy fine will cover."

Mother and daughter seemed to breathe more freely; and Hannah unfolded her plan of going herself to Lyme Regis and Taunton, the places to which her brothers were to be taken—she knew not exactly whither they were to be sent—that she might minister to them in every possible way, cheer and strengthen them in their hour of trial, and be there to forward any suit that might be made on their behalf.

"There will be peril in such a mission, granddaughter," said the old man. "Many a gentle-hearted woman has suffered grievously for doing less than thou dost propose to do."

"I shall suffer more by staying away," said Hannah simply. "I must go. Something within me bids me. I cannot hold back. Thou wilt be here to care for mother and the little ones. I must be with my brothers."

They did not try to hold her back. Her heart was set upon the sorrowful journey, and the mother, in her yearning over her boys, was ready to speed her upon her way. She had money, as much as she could use for every possible purpose, and letters to friends of their friends in the West Country, who would show her kindness and help her in her difficult task. Mr. Kiffin would have accompanied her, but that his daughter seemed to require him more, and he was something too infirm easily to endure the long, rough journey. But he sent two of his experienced servants with Hannah; and the journey was made easy to her in every possible way, albeit in her present mood she would almost have welcomed hardship and privation. What might not her brothers be suffering of both?

She found that they had been conveyed to Taunton, and lodged in the castle there. The building was densely crowded at this time; for the dread Judge was on his way, and the friends of the prisoners were in a terrible state of agitation and fear. Stories were flying from mouth to mouth of what the inhuman Judge had done and said at Winchester, and how he had condemned the aged and virtuous Lady Lisle to be burnt to death for no greater sin than that of harbouring some unhappy wretch, who had fallen beneath the King's ban. What hope was there for any here?

But through the influence of those who cared for her, Hannah obtained the grace of an interview with her brothers on the eve of their trial, and found them calm and resigned. It was keen joy to them to embrace their sister again, to give their last messages (as they thought they might be) to all the loved ones at home, and to know how much they were thought of and prayed for by many far and near. But they had no hope of mercy. They had heard of the implacable nature of the Judge, and were aware that their very wealth and importance, in one sense of the word, would be against them. Obscure persons might be respited, and those perhaps of noble blood; but not those whose fame came from their resolute adherence to precepts civil and religious that were abhorred of King James and his Court.

It was a fearful moment for Hannah when she was passed into that close and crowded Court upon the momentous day, and saw the red and bloated face of the Judge and his bloodshot eyes glaring at the prisoners, as a wolf glares at the victims he is about to spring upon and devour. What need to talk of that trial?—it was the veriest travesty of justice ever known. The prisoners were bidden if they desired mercy to plead guilty, and as soon as they had done so were sentenced to a traitor's doom in one solid mass. Respite would come later for some, that was partly understood; but whenever some special plea was put forward for an individual who had friend or counsel to speak for him, the fury of the Judge rose to a fearful pitch, and he roared down the voice of the defender, rolling his eyes and swearing with such hideous vehemence that soon none dared lift up a voice in his presence, and Hannah was supported half fainting from the Court, where she had heard both her brothers condemned to death.

But even then her courage did not desert her, and terrible as was the aspect of the Judge, and awful as were the things spoken of him, she resolved to place herself in his way as he came forth, and plead for the lives of her brothers, as the one last faint hope still remaining to her.

Alas! she might as well have sought mercy from the flinty rock, or the sea breaking in merciless fury. The bloated, evil face was turned upon her in savage fury. The Judge plucked his robe out of her detaining hand, and flung himself into his coach crying out:

The Judge plucked his robe out of her detaining hand.

"Madam, your brothers are a pair of pestilent rogues, who come from a pestilent nest of dissenters. I would I had the power to send you to the gallows with them! That is the only place for a cursed brood like yours!"

And as Hannah, fired by wrath and by her sisterly despair, would not even then be silenced, but continued her petition with her hands upon the window frame of his coach, he leaned out upon the other side and roared to his charioteer to cut at that pestilent woman with his whip; and the lash drew blood from Hannah's white fingers as she sank half fainting into the arms of her friends.

And yet that very evening, to her immense astonishment, she received a courteous summons to the presence of the Judge, and on presenting herself at his lodging in the castle, with the friend in whose care she was at that time living, she found Jeffreys in an extraordinarily different mood. He had, in fact, just made the discovery that the woman he had treated so brutally was one of the family specially recommended to him by his relative, who had said that the ultimate benefits he might expect from him would largely depend on what efforts he made to save the two Hewling brothers. If the Judge had not been so drunk overnight when this missive reached him, he might possibly have acted differently in Court that day; but now he assured Hannah that he would do all in his power to obtain a respite of the capital sentence for her brothers, though he implied that this might be an affair of money, and practically demanded three hundred pounds for his services, which Hannah in her bewilderment and by the advice of her friend was ready to pay.

But the days dragged on and no message came from the King. The gentle William, who had been sentenced to die at Lyme Regis almost immediately after his trial, met his doom upon the scaffold with unflinching fortitude, and all the grace his sister could obtain was that she might take possession of the unmutilated body, which was interred in consecrated ground, two hundred brave young maidens of the place incurring the possible displeasure of the King by walking in white robes at his funeral, and singing hymns over his grave.

But Hannah had no time for vain lamentations. The fire of despair was in her heart. Benjamin yet lived. He was not to die till the last day of the month. There was yet time to plead for him. She knew not whether Judge Jeffreys had been true to his promise or no; but at least she, his sister, would strain every nerve, would know no rest day or night till she had obtained his pardon, even though she should have to seek it from the King himself.

In vain her friends warned her of the uselessness and peril of her task; go she would, and as fast as horse could speed her. And with the last touching letter from her brother William in her pocket, and the scene of his death photographed upon her memory, she posted to London, to achieve what all men told her was impossible.

She scarcely paused to mingle her tears with her mother's. A fever was in her heart. Her grandfather had influence enough to obtain for her admission to the palace, and there she was met and kindly spoken to by a gentleman, whose name she knew not at the time, but who was no other than Lord Churchill, afterwards the great Duke of Marlborough.

Churchill regarded her with a look of exceeding compassion; Hannah presented indeed a touching picture in her girl's grief and sisterly devotion; and her unusual beauty had not been dimmed by all the troubles through which she had passed. Something of her story was known even at Whitehall, and known also was the character of the merciless man before whom her brothers had been tried, and the merciless monarch who had sent him forth to this work.

"Madam," said Lord Churchill, as the summons came for Hannah to be received by the King, and as he spoke he laid his hand upon the marble of the carved mantelpiece upon which he leaned, "my wishes for success go with you, and my most hearty sorrow for your distress; yet I dare not speak any word of hope to buoy up your sinking spirits; for this marble is not harder nor more susceptible of compassion than is the heart of the King."

Poor Hannah was destined to find it so. She was received with cold looks; her petition, so carefully worded and drawn up, was scarcely looked at before the King flung it down, and threw a curt heartless refusal at her.

She was hurried away by the attendants, who, though commiserating her grief and innocence, felt that she only ran a needless risk of drawing down the royal wrath upon herself.

"You are a brave lady," said Lord Churchill, himself bowing her out of the King's suite of apartments. "My heartiest sympathy goes with you. A man with so brave a sister will surely go bravely to his death. And there will come a time when that is all that the best of us can ask to do."

Churchill spoke the truth; the brave brother of a brave sister met his death with unshrinking fortitude, cheered to the last by the presence of Hannah, and by her sisterly love and care.

No thought of personal fatigue or personal peril sufficed to prevent her returning instantly to Taunton, and the last days of Benjamin's short life were rendered almost happy to him by his reunion with his twin sister, and by their constant intercourse.

Money could purchase this boon, though it could not purchase the prisoner's life.

He suffered upon the scaffold with so many others as little guilty as he of doing wrong, albeit something rash and ill-advised, and when Hannah had obtained with trouble and much cost the right to take his body and bury it, as in the case of William, she had only to return home to tell her mother the terrible and mournful tale.

"But thy courage sweetened death for them both, my child," said the mother. "In days to come that will be a thought that will bring to thee the comfort thou canst not feel yet."

"I never felt brave," Hannah would answer simply, when her friends praised her. "I only did what I had to do. I could not help myself."

MONA DRUMMOND

"You are a villain!" spoke the hot-tempered Irish maiden, with a glow in her eyes before which the evil-looking man before her quailed, although the scowl upon his face was an ugly thing to see. "You are a thief and a villain, and I will see the Governor myself and tell him what you have been doing. Oh, it is infamous!—infamous! My poor father!"

The girl put her hands before her eyes for a moment to hide the tears that rose to them. Mona had the tall, graceful figure, regular noble features, and great grey eyes of the typical Irish maiden. She was standing beneath the walls, and within the precincts of, Lifford gaol. Before her was a man of evil aspect, who wore the dress of a gaoler, and who swung a great bundle of keys in his hand. He had come forward confidently enough to meet the girl, smiling and almost cringing; but when she suddenly blazed forth at him in this impetuous fashion, he shrank and cowered before her as though he knew himself guilty of some dire offence.

"You have been taking our money all these years—money so hardly earned—so sorely spared; you have sworn that you spent it in providing better food and lodging for my dear father; and all the while you lied!—you lied! Black-hearted villain that you are! He has never been the better for it by one loaf of bread—by one flask of wine. You have stolen every coin. You have defrauded him and lied to us!"

The girl was shaken by the storm of her anger. The man stood before her tongue-tied and cowed.

He was not ashamed of his villainy; he was too hardened a wretch for that; but he was afraid lest the thing should become known to the Governor, who was a just and humane man, and who from time to time had been known to admit the prisoner's daughter to his presence at her earnest request.

"I am going to see the Governor about it," concluded the girl, with a scathing look. "He is a just man and merciful. He will at least know what to advise us for the future."

Fury and terror filled the man's face; he recoiled a little, and fingered his heavy keys as though he meditated a savage assault upon the girl, standing before him in this great solitary courtyard. What if he silenced her voice for ever? Who would be the wiser? He shot a quick glance round him, as if to assure himself that there were no eyes upon him, and Mona at the same moment gave a half-scared, half-defiant gaze around herself. Some instinct warned her of his fell purpose, and she knew she was no match for him; but to quail or cower would but bring down the meditated blow upon her head.

She stood with her clear gaze full upon his eyes, holding them, as men in the wilderness can sometimes hold a wild beast in thrall by the fixed stare of unwavering will.

She was not many paces from the little door by which she had entered. If she could gain that, she might be able to turn and fly. She made one backward step towards it; but even as she moved, she felt rather than saw that he was in the act of springing; and at that she darted backwards, tore open the door, and was through it before he could reach her. But she could not close it behind her to draw the bolt. He was too quick for that. She almost felt his hands at her throat, when suddenly she heard him utter a yell of terror; and turning saw him struggling in the grip of a tall and powerful young man, who must have been coming towards the door close under the wall, for she had not seen him as she darted out, and yet he had been there to catch her pursuer as he followed.

The terror of the man surprised Mona, as did also the fact that he made no resistance when once he saw into whose hands he had fallen. His arms dropped to his sides, and his jaw fell; he stood staring at the young athlete who had him in his grip as though bereft of sense.

"My father shall hear of this, sirrah!" spoke the youth with a final shake, as he let the wretch go; then he turned to Mona, and doffed his hat with a courtly air.

"He has not hurt you, fair maid, I trust!"

"Oh no, dear sir, I am not hurt. I thank you from my heart for this timely aid."

"And what do you in this gloomy place, if I may ask the question? What errand has brought so fair a flower within the portals of a prison?"

At that question Mona's eyes filled with sudden tears, and she turned away her head to hide them.

"Alas, dear sir! mine is a sorrowful errand, and I have not been able to accomplish it; for we have been basely tricked and cozened these many years by yonder miscreant, who is slinking now away like a whipped hound. I would fain see the good Governor, and tell my tale of woe to him. He was kind before, it may be he will find a way to help me now."

"I am his son," answered the young man eagerly. "I will take you to him speedily; and as we go you shall tell me your sad tale. Believe me, I will befriend you if I can. Have you some relative immured within the walls of this grim place?"

"Alas, sir, my father!" she answered with brimming eyes; "and he has been here so many long, weary years. I was but little more than a child when they took him away and brought him hither, and now I am within a year of twenty summers. My poor father!—my poor innocent father!"

"Of what crime does he stand accused?" asked the young man, with ready interest.

"Of no crime save that of holding the Presbyterian faith," she answered; "that is all the wrong he has done—believing it and teaching it; for he is a minister of the Word, and our church at Raphoe was his charge, and we were happy and he was beloved of all. But you must know how when the King was restored to his kingdom over the water after the death of the iron Cromwell, he or his ministers issued edicts in this land, as well as in England and Scotland, for the re-establishment of the Prelacy; and those who desire to worship after their own fashion, and not according to episcopal forms, are sorely beset and persecuted."

"I know, I know," answered her companion quickly and with sympathy. "And so your father was one of those who suffered for his faith?"

"Yes, there were four of them," answered Mona, her tongue unloosed by the friendliness of this stranger, "and Bishop Leslie had them all cast into prison at the same time. They lie in this grim jail; and God alone knows when they will be suffered to come forth. But we heard that the prisoners here were harshly treated, and had scarcely the necessaries of life supplied them. It was after hearing this that I went one day and craved speech of the Governor. I did first beg him to let me see my dear father; but that he might not permit. He said, however, that I might speak with the jailer who had charge of him, and obtain through him such things as we could make shift to purchase for him to lessen his privations and sufferings. The man promised faithfully, and every penny we can spare has been scraped and hoarded and given over to him; and we believed that father had such comforts as they could get for him; we believed that till a few days ago; and then—and then——" The girl's voice grew husky, the bright tears rolled down her cheeks. Her companion took the words out of her mouth.

"You heard in some roundabout fashion that your money had gone into the pockets of that wretch, and that your father had in no wise profited thereby."

"Yes, yes; that was it. One of our friends has obtained his liberty; they say there is hope that others will follow. We saw him. He came to us. He has now and then had a brief moment of speech with my dear father. Nothing has ever reached him from without. He has suffered all the rigours of his harsh captivity."

"And you did have the bravery to go to yon miscreant who has had the charge of your father, here in this prison, and who has appropriated the money, and tell him of his ill-deeds; and this it was that wakened his evil passions and ferocity? This it was that made him chase you forth, and seek to do you hurt!"

"I told him I would tell the Governor," panted Mona, with hot, indignant eyes; "and then I saw that he would fly at me; and so I sought to reach the door ere he had time. But he would have done me a mischief had it not been for your good help."

"Then come now to my father and tell him all the tale," cried the young man, whose name was Derrick Adair, "and we will see if some way cannot be found for mending matters for your good father. At least that rogue of a jailer shall receive his due reward—or punishment!"

Colonel Adair, the Governor, who had been kind to Mona before, listened very readily now to her tale, and was exceedingly displeased at what he heard as to the action of the warder. Of course he knew well the abuses that prevailed in all prisons at this epoch, and long afterwards; but though enable to institute any drastic measures of reform, he was able to punish individual transgressors when peculation had been proved against them; and he told Mona that he would see in future that her alms were rightly bestowed for the relief of the prisoner, adding that he hoped soon to see him set at liberty.

"I am perplexed to know why the Bishop speaks of releasing the other three ministers he sent hither—indeed, one was set free a short while since, as you know. But there is no mention of that grace being extended to your father; and yet his case was in no way different from that of others. Can you explain wherefore he is differently treated?"

A hot flush dyed Mona's cheek, and then the flash of anger awoke in her eyes. She spoke almost as if to herself.

"Oh, infamous, infamous! The coward! Did he indeed speak truth when he threatened? I did not believe he had such power."

"Of what do you speak, my child?" asked the Governor kindly. "Trust me and tell me all. You shall not regret your confidence."

"Oh, sir," cried Mona, struggling against her excitement and anger, "it is the doing of that wicked son of the Bishop. He professes to love me. He waylays me sometimes in my walks, and talks as he has no right to do. He is a great man's son. I am a poor minister's daughter. He declares he wishes to wed me; but I will not listen. He is a bad man. I fear him and I hate him. And it was but a little while back that he threatened me. He said that till I would give him the promise he asks, my father should never be released! I did not think as he spoke that he had power to contrive such a cruel thing. But here are others going forth, and my poor father kept still in ward. Oh, why are such cruel things suffered to be?"

"And what answer did you make him, my child?" asked the Colonel.

"The same that I have ever done, sir; that I have no love for him! Nay, I hate him and I fear him. I will never trust him; I will never be his wife. He knows his father would oppose such a marriage; it is always of elopement that he talks! But I will not hear! He is wicked, cruel! But my poor father; must he suffer too?"

"Nay; that he shall not. I myself will obtain justice!" cried Derrick, with sudden energy; and as Mona lifted her beautiful face, and gazed at him through her tears, he went on gently:

"It may indeed be that I can help thee, sweet maid; for when my visit here is ended, I return to Dublin, where I am finishing my course of study at Trinity College, and also acting in the capacity of private tutor to a great nobleman's son. This nobleman has much influence with the Government, and through interesting my pupil in your father's story, I doubt not I can bring this tale to the ears of those in power, and so effect his release. Therefore, weep no more, fair Mistress Mona; wait in patience for a few more weeks, and trust me not to forget your case, and to do all that one man may to right a wrong."

So Mona went home lightened of a sore burden; her heart full of thanksgiving. And when next the Bishop's son waylaid her, and promised to obtain her father's freedom if she would but consent to the proposed elopement with him, she answered him with steady scorn, looking so beautiful in her simple maidenly dignity and indignation, that the baffled man stood watching her with a look of mingled longing and anger.

"You obtain his liberty! It is you who are the present cause of his continued bondage! Why is he not released with the others? Oh, lie not to me! I know; I know. Wicked men do these things daily, and God does not smite at once; but the day will come, the day of vengeance, when the wicked will be overthrown, and the righteous will shine forth like stars in the firmament of heaven!"

He continued to gaze at her with an expression that would have terrified many girls; but Mona was not afraid. She felt that she had another champion now; and she feared no longer the machinations of this bad man.

She had seen Derrick Adair several times during the interval that had elapsed between her visit to the prison and the present interview with the Bishop's son. He had come to see her mother, and assure her that the prisoner had been taken to a more comfortable lodging, and had received better food and bedding than had been his heretofore. All the money sent by the careful family was now suffered to reach the prisoner himself, and his condition was greatly ameliorated thereby.

The dishonest jailer had been sent away, Derrick told them on his second visit; and he added he would like to make a clean sweep of many others; but even his father had not power for that.

Mona's heart was now relieved of the heaviest part of its burden. She was no longer afraid of the Bishop or his son; she was no longer torn in twain by the feeling that she might be standing between her father and his liberty, and that perhaps filial duty demanded the sacrifice from her of wedding a man she feared and hated. But she so distrusted the Bishop's son that she could never think of his proposal without a shudder; and now what joy it was to feel that their cause had been taken up by a stalwart champion, and that justice might be looked for without such a terrible sacrifice on her part!

Mona was a fearless girl, who had always led a free and hardy life. She had a very kind heart, and a skilful pair of hands, and wherever there was sickness in any of the cabins or cottages around, it was the custom to send for her, and she never failed to answer the summons. Often she was thus away from her home for a whole day, or for a night or two, and no anxiety would be aroused by her non-return from a sick-bed. When possible, she would send a message to this effect if she were detained; but no real trouble would be caused by her absence at night, should she have gone forth in response to a summons, and not returned.

One afternoon she received a message to ask her to come to a sick woman at some distance; and as she kissed her mother she told her not to be anxious if she did not come home till morning, as if she were detained late, it would be better to stay the night.

When, however, she arrived at the house, to her great surprise it was all shut up and empty. Could it be possible that the woman had died suddenly? she asked herself, and shook the door of the cabin. It yielded to her hand, and she went in; but there was no sick person on the bed; the place was neatly swept up and set in order, just as though the inmate had gone away for a visit.

A sudden odd sense of uneasiness came over Mona—a feeling of having been tricked. But who could have plotted to deceive her? The little boy who brought the message certainly delivered it in all good faith, and she had never questioned him as to who had bidden him bring it. But now there was but one thing to do; to get home as fast as possible, before it grew quite dark.

She turned to leave the cottage, when a shadow fell upon her from the open doorway, and with a shudder of horror she saw standing there the broad, squat figure of the wicked jailer, whose dismissal from the prison had been brought about through her instrumentality.

He gazed at her whitening face with an evil leer, and then made a wild-beast spring at her.

"My turn now, you hussy! My turn now! So you thought to ruin an honest man, and set at defiance a powerful one! But we will tame you between us, you little tiger cat! We will have our revenge!"

Even as he spoke the man with practised hands secured the girls slim wrists and clasped a pair of manacles upon them. He then bound them behind her back, and, after thrusting a gag into her mouth, he led her out of the house to a short distance, where in a ruined shed a horse was tied up. Lifting her upon its broad back, and springing up behind her himself, he set the creature at a steady gallop, and Mona felt herself being carried farther and farther away from home and friends, in the cruel grip of this evil man, who was plainly acting as the tool of the Bishops son.

It was a terrible thought, but Mona knew her only chance lay in keeping her courage and self-control. Whether anything could save her from her fate she did not know. But she closed her eyes in prayer, and entrusted her case to the God of all the earth, and having partially quieted herself by this, she opened her eyes and scanned the country through which they were passing with the keenest and most eager glances.

There was little to encourage her; all was bare and bleak and deserted. The man was evidently taking an unfrequented route. He desired no doubt to avoid encounters upon the road, although in the darkness no one was likely to note that he carried a prisoner before him, and Mona could give no sign and speak no word.

The light faded, the moon rose, and still they travelled on and on. Mona began to lose knowledge of the country through which she was passing. She fancied that they were on the main road for Dublin; but she could not be absolutely sure. It was like enough that she would be taken to a great city, where all trace of her would easily be lost. Sometimes as the long strange hours wore by, her heart almost fainted within her; but then again she told herself that to lose courage and hope would be to lose all. If she could but put her captor off his guard, perhaps things might yet go well. Some chance of escape might offer itself.

They could not travel all night without a halt. Man and beast must be fed. But as Mona saw in the distance a few twinkling lights, she pretended to be more heavily asleep than before (and for some time she had feigned drowsiness and broken slumber), and let herself rest heavily against the rider behind, who evidently had no great relish for the burden he did not dare to drop.

At last they reached the inn, and the man wrapped the girl up from head to foot in his great riding-cloak, taking care that her face should not be seen. Mona heard him mutter to himself:

"She is in a swoon; so much the better for me. I can take my ease after this weary ride; and if she comes to herself, she can neither speak nor use her hands. She must needs lie as I have placed her. I will just tie her feet to make all safe."

Then, lifting her in his arms, he cried to the host:

"I have got a sick daughter here I am taking to be cared for by my good mother. I will not bring her inside lest the distemper be catching. I will lay her comfortably on the straw in this barn, and let her rest there for an hour. She is in a sleep all the while. She will want nothing till I come out again."

So Mona was laid down on the straw in the empty barn, and the hint the man had dropped was quite enough to keep all other persons away from her. Under pretext of wrapping her up warmly her captor tied her feet together securely, and there she lay gagged and bound and helpless in the silence and the darkness. Yet she was hardly alone before she had struggled up into a sitting posture, and had flung off the heavy folds of the cloak.

Then very cautiously and carefully, and with some pain, she made the experiment she had been longing to do all the while—to try and twist her slim hand out of the manacle that encircled her wrist.

Mona, though a tall girl, was possessed of very delicate feet and hands, and her bones were small and flexible.

Had less been at stake she would have given up the task in despair; for the pain was severe, and she was altogether uncertain of success in the end, and feared that her hand was becoming swollen in the effort. But in spite of the pain, she persevered, and at last she drew forth her right hand free, and would have cried aloud but for the gag in her mouth.

To release the other hand when its fellow was free was an easier matter, and then she quickly unfastened the gag and drew a breath of deep relief as she flung it from her. It was hard still to be delayed by the knots that bound her feet; but they gave way at last to her strenuous efforts, and Mona stood up free and fetterless in the darkness of the barn.

"Thank God—thank God!" she cried in her heart; yet she knew her perils were not over yet. She must creep away from the inn and hide herself; but her persecutor would soon discover her flight and would pursue her. She dared not take the horse, as she feared to be seen if she approached the stable. All she ventured to do was to slip out of the barn through a broken portion of the wall, and looking well about her, and taking her direction from the friendly moon, she sped like a shadow along the road she had recently so painfully traversed.

She did not dare to leave it unless forced to do so. The treacherous bog-land lay about her, and she knew nothing of the safe tracks across, that were familiar in her own locality. The moon that gave her light would serve also to illumine her own figure for her pursuer when he should discover her escape. Swiftly as the girl raced onwards in the moonlight, she felt ever as though that strong horse and his wicked rider must soon be at her heels.

"Then will I plunge into the bog and hide me or perish there!" cried Mona, clenching her teeth; "but never, never, never shall he lay his hands upon me again. I fear not death—at least but little. I fear only to fall into the hands of wicked men!"

Suddenly upon the far horizon of her vision there loomed up a little black speck, and Mona's heart gave a throb of joy. It was surely some traveller approaching from the opposite direction! Upon his mercy she would cast herself, whoever he might be! No son of Erin would refuse to champion her in such an hour as this, and no traveller along these lonely roads ever went unarmed.

Yet even as her quick eyes beheld this traveller approaching in the one direction, her quick ears caught the sound of horse's hoofs galloping furiously behind her from the other.

Gathering all her energies together for a last effort, the girl sped forward like an arrow from a bow, her light figure clearly standing out in the bright moonlight. It seemed to her as though the traveller saw something of the pursuit; for instantly his horse sprang forward at a grand gallop. The fugitive fled onwards gasping, exhausted; and then in a moment she found herself upheld by a strong arm; she leaned almost helplessly against her preserver, and a familiar, agitated voice exclaimed in her ear:

"Mona!—Mona!—Sweetheart, what ails thee?"

"The jailer—the Bishop's son—they tricked me—they caught me!" panted the girl; "he carried me off; but I have escaped. He is coming after me now. Ah, do not let him have me! Kill me first; but never let me fall alive into his hands!"

"You give yourself to me, sweet Mona? Then I will hold thee against all the world!"

Derrick held her with his left arm, and levelled his pistol with his right.

"Dare to come one step nearer, and I fire."

"Dare to come one step nearer, and I fire. You know, fellow, whether or not I shall miss my mark!"

The two men stood looking at each other in deep silence for a few seconds, deadly rage and baffled hate on one face, on the other stern wrath and dauntless determination. At last the hireling with an oath turned his horse, and galloped back the way he had come. Revenge was sweet, and so was gold; but he cared not to purchase either at the price of life or limb.

"Thou art safe, sweetheart!" said Derrick, bending his head and touching her cheek with his lips. "Heaven be thanked that I was so hindered in my start for Dublin this day, that I had perforce to wait for moon-rise to sally forth. And now I will take thee home, dear love; and we will tell thy tale to my father, who will see thee safe guarded in the future."

Derrick Adair quickly procured the release of Mona's father, and married the daughter in the following year. Later on, after the rather tragic death of Bishop Leslie (caused doubtless by the conduct of his son, who was forced to fly the country after some notorious ill deed), the vacant office was bestowed upon Derrick, now a rising light in the Church, and he became Bishop of Raphoe, and his wife ruled in the old castle which was the home of its prelates.

Once a wretched-looking beggarman crawled to the gate as she was passing forth, and fell exhausted at her feet, asking alms.

She gazed at his face awhile, and he into hers; they knew each other, and the wretched man cowered against the stones, while the lady hastened indoors, to set servants or dogs upon him as the wretched man believed; for he was none other than the ex-jailer who had sought to do her so much ill. But quickly she returned with food and wine, and a handful of silver. She set the basket before him, and poured the money into his hands—stretched forth in supplication; and she gently made answer to his faltering words of prayer:

"Have no fear, my poor fellow. May God forgive you as I do. Eat and drink, and refresh yourself ere you go upon your way."

"And you will not punish me? You will not take your revenge!"

She looked gravely and sorrowfully at him as she answered:

"I think that God has punished you; that is His office, not ours; and for the rest—that is my revenge."

JESSY VARCOE

"There goes the witch's darter! Yonder goes the witch's maid! Heave a stone at the likes of her, lads! 'Tidden fitty as such spawn should live!"

Poor Jessy had grown up with taunts like these in her ears, till she had come to be too well used to them to pay much heed. Sometimes a stone would strike her; but she could throw as well as any lad along the coast, and she had proved as much upon the persons of her persecutors many a time and oft. On the whole the children and the lads and girls of Morwinstow had come to think it best to leave Jessy alone, especially since it had been whispered that she was learning the black art from her old grandmother, the Black Witch of the neighbourhood, and could overlook an enemy, or curse him and his goods and smite his crops with blasting and mildew.

So Jessy's life was perforce a lonely one. No kith or kin had she ever known save her old grandmother who lived in the hut upon the rolling downs land, not far from the margin of the cliffs. The old woman went out by night to gather herbs and simples, and these she brewed over the fire by day, muttering her strange incantations the while.

Although she was known as a Black Witch in her own neighbourhood, there were many persons who bought her wares, and found them excellent for sprains, rheumatics, and the like. But nobody visited in a friendly way at the lonely hut save certain wild and fierce-looking men, who always came at night, and were generally laden with packs of merchandise, which they hid away in some secret hiding-place beneath the floor of the cottage.

This much Jessy knew from peeping through the crevices in the floor of the upper room where she slept. She was never permitted to be present when these men came. She was sent to bed up the rickety ladder; and the ladder was invariably removed, so that she could not get down if she would, the bolt in the trapdoor by which she reached her attic being always drawn by the grandmother.

As the child grew to girlhood, she began to understand very well the nature of these visits from seafaring men. They brought smuggled goods to be concealed beneath the witch's hut, well knowing that nobody would willingly run the risk of being cursed or overlooked by the old woman. Moreover, Jessy had reason to believe that the cottage masked an entrance into a very large cave, which was probably a valuable hiding-place; for she always noted the extreme civility with which the rough men treated her grandmother, and how anxious they seemed to please her in the bargains that they made.

Nor was Jessy in any way disturbed by the knowledge of what was going on. Smuggling was a regular trade all along the coast, and she regarded it as a matter of course.

As the old grandmother grew more and more infirm, Jessy was of necessity taken more into her confidence, and soon found that her suspicions were quite correct. The old woman received the contraband goods from the smugglers, and hid them in the recesses of the great cave—the secrets of which were known only to herself; and though very occasionally the revenue officers came to the cottage and insisted upon examining the place most carefully, they never discovered the secret hiding-place. For the small cave was only the ante-chamber to a very much larger one behind, and the entrance to the latter was so cleverly masked that it was long before even Jessy could learn the trick of the sliding shale of rock, though she had been shown it many times by her grandmother.

Exciting scenes were often witnessed along the coast in those days; and bloody scenes were enacted between the smugglers and the "gaugers" or revenue officers, in which lives were often lost. One gauger, more resolute than some of his predecessors, after having killed many desperate smugglers himself, was dragged bodily into a boat that he was pursuing, whilst his head was chopped off on the gunwale and flung into the sea.

The *Black Prince* was a trim little vessel that did a great deal of illicit traffic all along the coast at that time, and was well known to every man, woman, and child in Morwinstow. Whorwell was the name of her captain. A daring fellow he was, and one of the most popular smugglers in those parts, free with his money, free with his contraband spirits, making friends with villagers, parson, and sexton alike, and even bribing old Tom Hockday, this latter functionary, to let him deposit his kegs and bales in the church till he could find a convenient opportunity of getting them away to old mother Varcoe's, or some other convenient hiding-place. The farmers would lend him their stout little horses to lade up with his goods from over the water; and the horses would be so shaved and soaped that they were slippery as eels, and being accustomed to follow some well-trained animals, would gallop away to the hiding-place, safe from any hostile clutches!

In scenes such as these Jessy had been reared, and although she herself was something of an outcast in the scattered community where she dwelt, her sympathies, such as they were, were for a time all with the smugglers, whom she regarded as friends; till something came to change the face of affairs for her.

It seemed to begin from one Sunday morning, when Jessy, for a wonder, went to the church, in spite of her natural timidity at facing the jeers of the boys and girls, and the suspicious looks of their parents. She often hung about the little windswept church whilst Sunday service was going on, feeling in her heart a vague yearning after intercourse with her own kind, and a longing for some knowledge of the mysteries of religion; but she seldom ventured inside the porch, and might not have done so to-day had it not been that there was a little lad, with curly hair and blue eyes, whose face she did not know, whom she encountered when not far from the building, and who began to talk with her in an unsuspicious and friendly fashion that went straight to her heart.

Before they had got to the church she had gathered that the boy was the son of one of the revenue officers lately come into the neighbourhood, and that he often went out in the cutters that pursued the smuggling boats, or hunted the coast for them. The fearless little fellow had had some adventures already, which he retailed to Jessy with great gusto; and remarked that he did not think the people of Morwinstow liked him or his father.

To this Jessy answered that they did not like her either, and this seemed a bond drawing the pair together; so that when they reached the church they passed in together, and sat side by side in a shadowy corner behind a big pillar.

But the service had not proceeded very far before there was a whisper and then a buzz at the porch door, and one by one folks slipped from their seats and stole out, till at last only Jessy, and Tim (as the boy told her he was called), and the parson, and clerk were left; and the parson shut up his book and whipped off his surplice, saying:

"Sure there is something amiss; and I must needs go and see!"

The churchyard overlooked the sea, and there sure enough was the *Black Prince* close under the land, and a revenue cutter in full chase, and so near that all held their breath to watch; and Tim seized hold of Jessy's hands, and cried:

"They'll get her!—they'll get her! Oh, why was not I there with them to-day?"

"Hush!" cried Jessy in sudden fear, "don't let the lads hear you talk so. They'd wring your neck, some of them, as soon as look at you! But look!—look! Whorwell is making for the Gull Rock! They'll never dare follow him there! There's not a man 'ud venture near that, save Whorwell himself; and they say the devil has given him a special chart, so as he can find his way through the rocks and shoals. There!—see, the cutter is sheering off. She daren't follow into that surf. The *Black Prince* will get off this time!" And Jessy's eyes lighted, for her sympathies were with the smugglers; and the congregation assembled on the cliff above gave vent to a lusty cheer.

"And now, my friends," said the parson mildly, "let us return and proceed with divine service."

He drove the flock back into the building, got into his surplice again, and went on exactly as though there had been no interruption: "Here beginneth the second lesson."

But though the hardy seaman Whorwell escaped the revenue cutter and got safe away, he did not live long after that, but was washed overboard on a dark night in a heavy storm; and his nephew and mate, one John Moffat, became commander in his stead.

Now Moffat was as daring a smuggler as Whorwell had been; but a man of a very different temper, fierce, morose, cruel, and of an implacable savageness towards any who had offended him. He had vowed vengeance against all King's officers with whom he should come into conflict. He had tasted once of prison discipline, and had had a narrow shave of the gallows. Since then his violent temper had become increasingly savage; and Rogers, the new officer, the father of Tim, found that he had a foe to deal with as daring as, and even more unscrupulous than, Whorwell had been.

Moreover, Jessy herself found cause to rue the day when Moffat had been left in command of the *Black Prince*. Her grandmother was now so infirm, that Jessy was obliged to receive the smugglers on their visits, and to show them to the hiding-places where the contraband goods were hidden. Before long Moffat began to make love to her in his fierce masterful way; whilst Jessy, who feared the fellow and dreaded his visits, shrank from him more and more each time she saw him.

She had grown to be a very beautiful girl, in a strange, wild fashion. Her hair was a tawny, golden colour, and it grew very abundantly, waving down below her waist when the wind caught it and loosened it from the heavy coils in which it was twisted up. Her eyes seemed to match it in colour, as did the thick brows and heavy lashes which veiled the fierce light that sometimes leapt into her glance when she was aroused to anger or hate.

The village folk, who liked either dark hair or flaxen locks, had no admiration for Jessy's tawny tresses. But little Tim Rogers told her that she was beautiful, and looked like a queen. The girl and little boy had become fast friends, drawn together by their own isolation and by kindred tastes.

Tim loved the sea and the rocks and the deep clefts and chasms of the coast; and Jessy knew every crevice and cranny as well as the sea-gulls themselves. They spent hours together, unseen by others, exploring strange spots, telling tales and legends, and growing in friendship every day.

As Jessy heard her boy-friend's stories of the hardships of the lives of the King's excise officers, and had the other side of the question unfolded to her—the need for taxes to be levied, to keep up England's power and greatness, to preserve her coasts from foreign invaders, to enable her to be a power amongst other nations with greater territories—she began to understand that the smugglers were really defrauding the King of his rightful dues; and whatever might be said in favour of the landing of an occasional keg of spirits or bale of silk without paying duty, the regular nefarious traffic of such a vessel as the *Black Prince* could not be regarded as anything but a wrong done against the King and the nation.

It was the easier for Jessy to assimilate this new teaching because of her hatred towards Moffat, which was growing with every visit he paid. Her grandmother was now almost in her dotage, and was no real protection to the girl; and she sometimes almost feared that Moffat would carry her off to his vessel by force, so wild were his outbreaks of so-called love-making, and his gusts of rage when she repelled him, and would have none of his courtship.

Jessy's one weapon of defence was in the superstition of the man and his subordinates. They believed that the girl had inherited, or had acquired from her grandmother, some occult powers, and that she had the power to do them some injury by her fiery glance, or by word or spell. This knowledge had come accidentally to Jessy, from something she had overheard the men saying one to the other; but she had found that it was true, and that they really had some superstitious fear of her when she flung herself away from Moffat, and stood regarding them with her fiery glances of fear and desperation. Afterwards Jessy made some study of her part, and got her grandmother to teach her some spells and some curses; and although still in no small fear of Moffat's evident intention of making her his wife, she felt not quite so unprotected as before.

Soon, however, she was to find, as other women have found before her, that the surest way to turn a man's love to hate is to flout him, and refuse his courtship. When Jessy, driven one day to bay, flatly refused to marry Moffat, and added that she hated him worse than she hated any one but the devil himself, and didn't see as there was much to choose between them!—then the man's passion flamed forth, and the girl might have been killed, had not the old woman, suddenly aroused and alarmed, begun to curse so lustily that the seamen were filled with terror, and dragged their leader off with them, he shouting out all sorts of threats against Jessy, and vowing to be revenged upon her before he had done.

It seemed as though disappointed love had filled the man's heart with passions fiercer than their wont. It was but a few days later that Tim told the girl how his father had heard that the *Black Prince* was coming in soon with a contraband cargo, and that he was going to keep a very sharp look out for her.

"I wish your father would kill Moffat, and have done with him," cried Jessy, with sudden vehemence.

"Why, then, Jessy, you must be on our side?" cried Tim joyfully. "I never quite liked to ask you before; because, of course, all the folk you know are with the smugglers——"

"But they don't care for me, and I don't care for them—not a snap!" cried Jessy; "and as for Moffat, I'll never be quite happy so long as he's above ground. But my granny she cursed him properly the other day. Maybe that'll bring him bad luck and you good!"

"Then is it true as your grandmother is a witch, Jessy?"

"I dunno; that's what folk say. She don't do nobody no harm as I can see; nor good neither, save with her herb potions, and them I make as well as she. But she's got a few queer books, and things she calls charms. She tells me about them sometimes, and she teaches me spells and curses and things; but I'd be half afraid to use them. Suppose they came true; how would one feel?"

"If it were a curse against Moffat and his crew, and it came true, I don't think I should feel very bad," answered Tim. "They're a wild, bad lot, my father and his men say. The sooner they are got rid of, the better for some of us!"

"Yes, indeed!" answered Jessy with a sigh; "but they are bad ones to tackle, and no mistake."

It was a few days after this, and Jessy was alone in the cave just as the sunset light was beginning to turn the water red. A load lay upon her heart; she knew not why. She felt as though something terrible were going to happen, but she could not guess what it could be.

Suddenly from over the water there came the sounds of voices,—angry, passionate, triumphant voices,—voices that she knew.

She ran out of her shelter; and then what did she see? The well-known sails and masts of the *Black Prince* almost close in shore, not being pursued by, but in hot pursuit of the revenue cutter, that had been watching for her, and had suddenly darted out to seize the prey.

Now it was a most unusual thing in those days for a smuggling vessel to turn aggressor. They were always built for speed, with a view of getting clear away from the King's boats and officers. The *Black Prince* had always escaped by speed or seamanship hitherto; but to-day it seemed as though the fierce demon of hatred that possessed Moffat had dominated every other feeling.

It was he, not the revenue cutter, that was in pursuit; and even as Jessy gained the cave's mouth she saw the terrible work of butchery begin.

Moffat was the first to spring into the cutter and slash with furious rage at the man Rogers, whose head was laid open by a ghastly blow. Other daring smugglers had followed, and the water was dyed red with something beside the sunset glow.

To her horror Jessy saw that Tim was in the boat.

"Swim for your life!" she cried; "you can do nothing there. Jessy is here. Jessy will help you!"

The boy heard; the men did not. They were otherwise engrossed. The boy, powerless to help either father or friends, obeyed the call that had reached him, and as he dropped silently over the gunwale of the boat and struck out, Jessy plunged into the sea from her rock, and swam bravely out to meet him, uncertain whether or no he might have received some wound.

And it was well she did; for, though unwounded, the boy had had a severe blow upon the arm, and was only able to swim a short distance without feeling the numbness and powerlessness come again upon him. But Jessy was beside him; she could swim like a fish, and even weighted by her clothes, could give her shoulder to Tim, to support his useless arm, whilst she made her way with swift, strong strokes towards one of the darkest and narrowest crevices between the frowning cliffs, where she thought she and he might be safe from pursuit.

No direct rays of light came into this narrow cave, and there was a ledge of rock upon which she hoisted Tim, and where she scambled herself when he was safe, both gasping and exhausted; but, as they hoped, safe.

"Jessy, you have saved me! How brave you are!" cried Tim. But Jessy suddenly laid a hand upon his mouth.

"Hist! be quiet!" she whispered; "they are coming after us! I hear their voices—and the plash of oars!"

It was too true. Moffat's wicked eyes had seen the golden head of Jessy; and he had missed the boy from the bottom of the boat, where he had been knocked over.

"They are in here!" cried a cruel voice; "I saw them go myself. We have them here like rats in a trap."

"Tim, have you a knife?" asked Jessy between shut teeth.

"The first man that touches him I'll kill!" cried Jessy.

The boy was trembling; but he did not give way. He pulled a little dirk from his belt.

"Yes; but I must defend you, Jessy; not you me. You have risked your life already. You must not do more. It is me they want—not you."

But the injured arm had no power to strike a blow. Jessy tenderly took the dirk from between the numbed fingers.

"Say your prayers, Tim, if you can remember any," said Jessy, between long breaths, "for we shan't easily get out of this alive."

"There they are—see them? The witch-wench and the boy? Ah, ha, my fine maid, you'll sing a more civil tune to-day I warrant. Give us over the boy, and maybe we'll let you off easy!"

"The first man that touches him I'll kill!" cried Jessy.

"Curse her for a witch," cried one of the men, recoiling before the fierce aspect of the girl; but Moffat was filled with the lust of blood and of fury, and with a yell of menace, he pushed up the boat against the narrow shelf on which the pair were cowering.

"Hand over the boy."

A yell of pain interrupted him. Jessy, seeing better than she could be seen, had seized the moment and driven her dagger clean through the arm of the man who was seeking to clutch at the shelf.

Just for a few minutes the girl held her ground against the six furious men below, who, losing all sense of humanity at last, lifted their cutlasses and struck her blow upon blow; some of which missed their aim, for Jessy was nimble as a wild cat, but some of which fell upon her flesh, and at last brought her blinded with blood to her knees.

A stifled gasp close at hand told her of another deed of cruel cowardice. She turned to see Moffat wiping his cutlass, and little Tim lying stark and dead at her very feet.

At that sight a strange phrensy fell upon Jessy. Forgetting her wounds and her weakness, inspired as it seemed by some spirit other than her own, she rose to her feet, her eyes blazing in her head, and, with a loud and sonorous voice, she spoke the words of a terrible curse. She cursed the vessel whose crew had done this deed of infamy and shame; she cursed the men who had been the instruments of a bad man's rage; above all, she cursed the master himself, turning her gaze upon Moffat with such fearful effect, that he slipped back into the boat, and his men pulled away in the direst terror they had ever experienced.

Next morning Jessy Varcoe was found by some fishermen, seated on a ledge of rock just above high watermark, with the corpse of little Tim, whose life she had sought to save at risk of her own, folded in her arms.

She begged them not to wake him; she called him her baby, her darling. When they laid him to rest in the churchyard, she would spend long days sitting beside the mound, gazing over the sea for the sails of the *Black Prince*.

But from that day forward the *Black Prince* was never seen or heard of again. Perhaps the crew, fearing to return to a place where they had done such evil work, changed its name and rig, and took up life elsewhere. Perhaps she foundered in a gale, or fell a prey to some enemy's ship. But no news of her ever reached Morwinstow again.

Somehow the story of Jessy's curse got abroad, and her reputation as a witch was made for ever; but she hardly knew it herself. From that day she never fully regained her faculties; and at last poor Jessy's life was ended through a fall down the cliffs from the heights above, near to the grave of the little boy, and from whence she had kept a ceaseless watch for the return of the *Black Prince*; terrified alike at the thought of its return with the dreaded Moffat, or of its destruction in response to her curse.

The children will look fearfully down this chasm, and whisper that Jessy leapt down it to expiate the curse; but whether or not this was so, will hardly now be known, for her mind was never the same from the dreadful day when she risked her life to save that of the boy, and saw him slain at her feet.

URSULA PENDRILL

The Captain's face was so grave, that instinctively the passengers exchanged anxious glances. He had given out that he had something to say to them, and they had assembled in the large saloon in full force.

When he came amongst them the look on his face was different from anything they had seen before. The cheery expression was replaced by one of clouded anxiety; and the infection of it spread quickly amongst the group in the saloon.

It was not a very large number of passengers that this steamer carried. This was before the day of pleasure trips to and from India. Those who went to that land or returned from it, only did so when necessity compelled them. The voyage was not the speedy matter it has now become, and there were far more hindrances and hardships than since the days of the Suez Canal. Still there was a fair gathering to hear what the Captain wanted of them, and it was plain that the matter in his mind was a grave one.

"Oh, Captain, is there danger?" asked a lady, cowering upon one of the fixed seats, and holding a little boy clasped in her arms.

The keen blue eyes of the Captain turned upon her for a moment, and glanced away to the circle of strained eyes fixed upon him; he seemed to understand what it was that all these people were thinking, and hastened to reassure them.

"Danger? Nonsense! What put that into your head? The ship is right enough—nothing wrong there. It is quite a different matter from anything you are thinking of."

There was a distinct look of relief in the faces turned towards him, and yet the expression of care upon the Captain's did not sensibly lighten.

"I have in the first place one unwelcome piece of information to give you," he said, "although I do not think that any of you need apprehend personal danger or inconvenience. Perhaps some of you remember the delicate-looking lady who was brought on board by her husband at Bombay, and whom you have none of you seen since?"

"Young Mrs. Varden?" queried a passenger who had just known the name of the lady before starting. "I asked the stewardess about her once, and heard that she was prostrated by sea-sickness. Some people never get over it all the voyage."

"Exactly; and that is what, until a couple of days back, we believed about her. She was always ill and ailing, quite unfit to sit up or leave her berth; but though the doctor saw her every day, he suspected nothing till a couple of days back,—when the stewardess, who was taking care of her, and luckily looked after nobody else, the ship not being very full, was taken with a sudden attack like convulsions, and died within two hours. That aroused his suspicions. He made a careful examination of Mrs. Varden's condition, and his suspicions were strongly aroused. On the following morning there would have been no room for doubt in any case. The small-pox erruption was out all over her. To-day she is almost black with it."

There was a shudder of horror through the assembled passengers. The thought that the ship was infected by that terrible disease was fearful indeed. The Captain spoke on doing his best to reassure them.

"Fortunately the lady has been kept very carefully isolated. She was so delicate when her husband brought her on board, that everything was done to ensure perfect quiet for her. She has occupied one of a little nest of cabins, all the rest of which were empty. The husband bespoke the sole attendance of one of the two stewardesses, and as my ship's doctor is a cautious man, and was rather anxious about Mrs. Varden's condition, he has used every precaution himself; though he suspected as little as the patient or her husband, that she carried in her the seeds of so dire a disease. I can assure you with good conscience that I do not believe any of you have run any greater risk of contracting the disease, than you might do by walking the street of any Oriental city."

Passengers on shipboard come to trust their captains in a way which is creditable to that calling. Captain Donaldson's words carried weight, and a sigh as of relief passed through the group gathered to hear him. But one gentleman put the question that was rising in each mind.

"And what is to be done now?"

The grave, anxious look returned to the Captain's face. His eyes instinctively scanned those turned towards him.

"There is only one thing I can possibly do, compatible with my duty to my ship and its company and passengers," he said; "Mrs. Varden must be put ashore at dawn to-morrow morning."

"Where?—How? Is it possible to do it?"

Quite a little hubbub of questions arose; and the Captain made shift to answer them all.

"It will have to be done," he said; "I know the place where it must be done. We shall touch in, and send a boat ashore. I have had to leave a sick sailor there before this. There is an old leper-house standing near to the margin of the sea. For a long time now it has been used in the fashion in which I purpose to use it. Fever-stricken sailors are left behind, and there are certain conditions they have to observe before they can be picked up again if they recover. But when a sailor is so left, some messmate remains with him to care for him, and submits to the loneliness and danger and discomfort, out of compassion for a comrade's need. The thing is not so difficult when it is one of one's own men who is the victim of disease."

He paused, and glances were exchanged by the bystanders; and one tall, rather rough-looking Irishman, who had come from Australia, and whose loud voice and hearty ways had made him something of a power on board, exclaimed eagerly:

"But look here, Captain, there is somebody there to look after the sick surely! You don't mean they are just dumped down in an empty leper-house, and left to live or die as they can? There is somebody there to look after them, and give them food and medicine and all that? Why, one wouldn't treat a dog so—to throw him ashore and leave him to his fate!"

"It is like this," answered the Captain gravely: "There is no trouble about food and water and a supply of such simple drugs as may be ordered beforehand. I can make certain arrangements as to that; and the food and fresh water and so forth will all be duly left each day at the leper-house by an Arab, who will be told off for the service. But as for getting help in nursing, that is simply impossible. I know what I am saying. Money would not purchase it; and it would be such service, even if attainable, as I think an English lady would sooner die than receive. No; this brings me to the question which I have to put to her fellow-passengers. Is there any lady on board willing to face the awful peril of taking the malignant disease, the awful loneliness of the leper-house upon the sandy shore, with only Arabs near, the awful doom of dying alone there, or of seeing her companion and patient die, and of being in that case quite alone during the necessary period of quarantine which must elapse before she can be taken off in another ship? Whatever man can do for making these conditions bearable, I will do. But none know better than I do the terrible nature of such a task as the one I ask from one of you. Nay, I do not dare to ask it! I feel that it is more than flesh and blood can stand; but yet the thought of putting ashore, alone and unconscious, that poor young wife, just to die, without the presence of a human creature near her—that seems an equal impossibility. Ladies, I do not ask an answer yet. I would not take an offer were it given. It must not be an act of impulsive generosity, should one of your number be able to face the terrible thought of such a sacrifice. It must only be undertaken after much careful and deliberate thought."

The Captain with that turned on his heel and went his way, leaving the passengers gazing mutely one at the other with pale faces and anxious eye. Just before he reached the companion, he turned round to say:

"Before putting the case to you, ladies, I have individually interviewed every woman in the steerage company, to see if it would be possible to procure the services of one of them as nurse. But all of them have husbands and children. I have failed entirely there, and I may not spare my one stewardess, even would she go, which I greatly doubt, knowing the fate of her companion only a few hours ago."

Amongst the passengers who had listened to this pitiful and terrible tale was one young girl, travelling from India quite alone. Her name was Ursula Pendrill. She had stood rather apart during the Captain's speech, and now, slipping away from the excited hubbub of talk that arose on all sides, she fled to her cabin almost as though some grisly phantom were at her heels, and, sinking down upon her knees on the floor, buried her head in her hands and rocked herself to and fro in a sort of agony.

"Must I do it? Must I do it? O my God help me to see my way!" were the words that fell brokenly from her lips. "How can I? How can any one? But oh that poor, poor creature—that awful death for her; for death it must be without any to care for her! O God help me!—help me! There is nobody else—only me—to do it. All the rest have children, friends, husbands, brothers. I am quite alone. O God help me! Help me!"

The broken words were merged in sobs, as the tears gushed forth, bringing a measure of ease to the overcharged heart. Ursula sat crouched up on the floor of her little cabin, with her face buried in her hands, and her loosened hair falling around her, but the sense of storm and strife was merging in one of a strange and settled peace. Down in the depths of her spiritual being it seemed to her as though a hand had been laid upon her, and as though a voice had spoken in her ear:

"Inasmuch as ye have done it unto one of the least of these My brethren, ye have done it unto Me."

Ursula Pendrill was a girl of good family who had been left a year or two ago an orphan, and with very narrow means. She was, however, a girl of high spirit and brave heart, and instead of asking a home with any of her kinsfolk, she preferred to supplement her small resources by working in various ways herself.

The field of woman's work in those days was much narrower than it has since become; but Ursula knew a lady who had been a nurse under Miss Nightingale in the Crimean War, and had since then given much of her time to the service of the sick. She was then in charge of a hospital, and welcomed

Ursula on a long visit, where she learned considerable skill in nursing, and made herself acquainted with the right treatment of most ailments.

After that she had often nursed private patients in their own houses, and had travelled a good deal with invalids going to Madeira and other places in search of health. So that she was no timid, helpless girl, but a rather experienced and resourceful woman, who would not easily be frightened or nonplussed in ordinary cases of sickness, or in the ordinary circumstances of travel. But there was nothing ordinary in the charge which she felt had been laid upon her to-day!

Yet no one expected this thing of her. Probably she would be the last person the Captain would think of for such a service. Ursula was young, and she looked younger than her years. She had not talked about herself to her fellow-passengers. She had not told how she had been taken to India by a delicate lady to look after her and her fragile children. She had not supposed that anybody would be interested in her private affairs. She was surmised to be one of those growing-up girls sent home from the perils of the hot season to their friends in England. Nobody would expect a young thing like herself to volunteer for such a deadly and terrible service.

But the more Ursula thought of it, the more resolved she was to make this sacrifice. It seemed to her that she had received a message from on high; that she had been shown it was for her to take up the cross and carry it, and that if she did so in fearless faith and obedience, she would receive help and blessing and strength for the task.

At dusk she left her cabin and went on deck, and asked where she could find the Captain. The officer she addressed looked at her keenly for a moment, and then pointed to where the Captain was standing alone, save for the presence of the big Irish-Australian with whom he was often in company.

Ursula slowly approached, and the two men stopped talking and looked at her. The Captain stepped forward.

"Did you wish to speak to me, Miss Pendrill?"

"Just for a minute, please," answered Ursula, with a beating heart, but with outward self-possession. "I came to say that I will go ashore to-morrow with Mrs. Varden, and take care of her."

"You, child?" ejaculated the Captain incredulously.

"I am not a child," answered Ursula steadily, "I am older than I look, and I know a great deal about nursing. Once I lived in a hospital for a year. I have often taken care of sick people since. I understand about fevers, though I was only once with a small-pox case, and that only for a little while, as she was taken away when the symptoms declared themselves. But I have been vaccinated quite recently. I have never taken anything from a patient yet. I am not afraid. I will go with poor Mrs. Varden—if there is nobody more suitable and more efficient."

The Captain paced once or twice up and down the space between the rails, and came back to where Ursula was standing.

"There is nobody else at all. I have had the husbands one after the other—or the relations and friends. Nobody can bear to face the awful task—or be spared to do it——"

"Yes, I understand. Other people have ties—so many to cling to them—to miss them, so many depending on them. If it were so with me perhaps I could not offer. But it is not. I have no very near relations. I have no parents or brothers and sisters. If anything happened there would be a few to be sorry; but nobody would feel life to be shadowed. I am the sort of person who can do this thing."

"You are the sort of person from whom the world's saints and heroines are made!" cried Captain Donaldson, with a most unwonted outbreak of emotion. "My dear young lady, I do not know how to accept the sacrifice, nor yet how to decline it. God will bless and reward you, I truly believe; for He only can reward such a deed as the one you are about to do."

"I do not want any reward," answered Ursula simply; "I only want to do what is right. Suppose it were somebody very dear to me, it would be no sacrifice; and Mrs. Varden is very near and dear to somebody—to her poor young husband. I saw him as he went off the vessel."

"Poor fellow—yes. I fear——" but the Captain pulled up short, and kept the fear to himself. Ursula moved away towards her own cabin.

"I have a few preparations to make; but I shall be ready to-morrow when you send for me. I think I shall not come up any more till then."

She disappeared in the gathering gloom, and the Captain stood looking after her, till a hand was laid upon his arm, and the deep voice of his Australian passenger said in his ear:

"Is that girl going ashore with Mrs. Varden?"

"Yes; she has volunteered, she has all the qualifications for the task; but I don't know now how to let her,—that lonely leper-house,—that awful fear before her eyes. Mrs. Varden will not live the week out. But I dare not keep her on board. My duty to my passengers and to the company prevents it. But those two frail young creatures—set down alone——"

"Look here, Captain, you may make your mind easy there. They won't be alone. I shall get off there too. I shall see them through!"

"You, Mr. Kelly? Why, man, what do you mean? There is no accommodation in the Arab settlement—nothing but the squalid place, and the leper-house beyond. You cannot be in there——"

"No; I shall pitch my tent just beyond, but within sight and sound. Jehoshaphat, man! Do you think I have never roughed it in a tent before this? Do you think I can't speak the primitive language, common to all races, enough to get those dirty Arabs to do all I want of them? Do you think British gold will ever fail to work the will of its master in any quarter of the globe? You go and make all your palaver with the heathen Chinee, or blackguard Arab, or whatever he may be. I'll pitch my tent, and I'll be there as long as any British woman is, and I'll see the thing through. As a nurse I'm no good, even if a rough fellow could volunteer for the task where a lady is in the case. But I'll be hanged, Captain, if Brian Kelly will stand by and see that brave young girl and that poor dying wife left alone in a place like that without a countryman near them. I've nobody specially waiting me in the old country. They've done without me all these years; they can do without me a few weeks longer. I'll see this bit of business through. If those poor creatures die there, I'll stop and give them such Christian burial as is possible; if they live through it, I'll be there to bring them home—one or both. Confound it all, Captain, d'ye think I'd ever know another night's sleep in my bed if I looked on at a bit of heroic devotion like that—and walked on with me hands in me pockets!"

The Captain put out his horny hand and wrung that of his Irish passenger. He had liked Kelly from the first; now he felt a new and warmer feeling towards him.

"Heaven bless you!" he said rather hoarsely; "you've rolled a ton's burden from my heart to-day."

Before sunrise next morning, but while the sky was beginning to lighten in that wonderful way one sees in desert countries, a tap came at Ursula's cabin door. She was quite ready: dressed in her cool, linen garb, with her white apron concealed by the folds of the long cloak. The things she wanted to take with her were ready in a modest valise. The rest were to go on to England under the care of the Captain.

Her face was quite calm and serene as she came up on deck; a few gentlemen passengers were about to see her off and wish her well. The Captain made his way towards her and took her hand.

"Mrs. Varden has been carried to the boat already. We are ready for you. Mr. Brian Kelly is going ashore too. He is, in fact, there already with my steward, bargaining about a tent in which he means to live for a time within hail of the leper-house. So you will have a friend at hand in case of need. He, like you, is one of the lonely ones of the earth, who can do these things. I am very thankful not to leave you quite alone with your patient! There yonder you see your future home—or prison. You will be quite safe there,—you would have been safe even without Kelly,—but I am thankful he remains too. I shall leave word at the nearest station what has happened. You will have friends looking after you, in a sense, whom you will never see. But Mr. Kelly will be at your beck and call. Now we must be going."

It was all like a dream to Ursula: the confused sound of voices, the earnest pressure of farewell hand-clasps, the words of praise and blessing lavished upon her; then the sight of the swathed white figure in the bottom of the boat that looked almost like a corpse in its graveclothes, the vivid golden glow over sea and land, the stretches of yellow sand, the white domes of the Arab settlement, and the square stone walls of the place to which she was bound.

She only seemed to awaken to the realities of life when the Captain held her hands in a last farewell, and just stooped and touched her forehead with his lips.

"I have a little girl at home—about your age!" he said huskily, as if in explanation. "Pray God she may be as brave a girl as you—though may she never be so sorely tried!"

Then he was gone,—they were all gone,—and Ursula was left alone in this strange, silent place, with that sad sight before her eyes—poor Mrs. Varden, stricken down with that most terrible malady, and in its most malignant and deadly form.

The patient was quite unconscious, and lay upon the narrow bed which Ursula found already neatly made up, muttering in the delirium that knew no lucid intervals. She was not violent—had never been violent, the doctor told her—and there was little enough to be done for her. But the thirst was constant, and Ursula seldom left her side for long. Although there was something so terrible in the poor young wife's disfigured face, yet it seemed to Ursula that she was the one link between her and the unknown. She did not shrink from her. She was as tender as though it had been her mother or sister. She shrank from no task that would bring relief or ease. She knew what to do and she did it unflinchingly.

And then as the day went by and the shadows of evening began to steal over her, she went to the door, to look at the sea and the sands, and see whether it was a dream what the Captain had said of that big Mr. Kelly staying behind too.

No, it was no dream: there was the stalwart figure pacing to and fro; there was the tent, picturesque and cheerful, with its fire close beside it, and a couple of turbaned Arabs cooking something over the red glow.

"Miss Pendrill, I have been hoping you would come out for a mouthful of fresh air. And how goes your patient?"

"Very, very ill; but always in a stupor. I can leave her for a few minutes sometimes——"

"Ah, good; then we will have supper together out here on the sand; it will eat better to you than in there, and——"

"Oh, but, Mr. Kelly, I am infectious——"

"Stuff and nonsense!—as though I cared for that! We are in the same boat as to that, for I helped to carry her ashore. But we needn't be more doleful than circumstances make us. I am peckish, if you are not. Do let us have supper here together!"

That was the first of many such meals, taken just in those moments when Ursula could leave her patient, and run out into the fresh air. It seemed as though those Arabs must be cooking all day long, for there was always some appetising dish ready; and oh, the blessed relief of those odd minutes spent with one who could give word for word, and whose eyes shone with friendly sympathy and kindly concern! Ursula said in her heart every day as it went by, that but for this she must have died or gone mad.

The Captain had been right in his prognostication. Mrs. Varden sank gradually, and by the end of the week passed away in her sleep; and it was Ursula and Mr. Kelly who bore her to her narrow grave upon those spreading sands; and it was he who filled up the grave that he had dug, and, bringing out a well-worn Prayer-book from his pocket, read over that lonely resting-place those words of hope and promise that have been the consolation of Christian mourners for all time.

Ursula did not take the fell disease. She was unnerved and unstrung for a time; but the quiet days went by one by one, and the consciousness of that watchful presence without kept her from any of those fears and tremors which must otherwise have made this period of waiting an agony to her.

They met every day. They took their meals together, and walked up and down beside the margin of the sea in company. They had to wait till the time of quarantine had gone by; but at last there came the blessed day when a steamer stopped and dropped its boat to fetch them; and the two exiles from humanity looked one at the other, and then at the great vessel awaiting them, and they knew that their time of trial was over.

The passengers on that vessel were disposed to make much of them, and laud the girl's heroism to the skies; but she shrank from praise, and kept herself quietly aloof from the little world of the ship, till at last the day came when they steamed slowly into the beautiful harbour at Southampton, and dropped anchor there.

Ursula's few possessions were quickly gathered together; she stepped alone into the bustle of the great world, where welcomes were being bandied about on every side, and every passenger seemed to have some loving friend or relative to greet him.

Not quite every one. A tall figure pushed its way towards Ursula. A strong hand possessed itself of her bag.

"I'll put you into your train," said Mr. Kelly; and she gave a little sigh of relief.

He stood at the window holding her little fingers in his big hand. He looked straight into her eyes.

"I'm glad you've got some people to go to—even if they are only cousins. I hope they'll appreciate what they have got. I'm off to Ireland. I must see the Ould Counthry first of all. But I shall be back in England before very long. When I come back, may I come and see you?"

She looked him full in the eyes. Her colour rose.

"I have never tried to thank you all this time——" she began.

His big voice cut her short.

"The train is just off. I want my answer. May I come and see you by-and-by?"

There was a dew on her eyelashes, and her lips quivered; but the smile won the day as it beamed out over her face. The soft voice was quite steady, except for a little glad catch in it, as she answered:

"Yes."

THE END.

Milton Keynes UK
Ingram Content Group UK Ltd.
UKHW040838141024
449705UK00006B/352